Canada's National Defence

VOLUME I
DEFENCE POLICY

Canada's National Defence

VOLUME I
DEFENCE POLICY

Edited by
Douglas L. Bland

School of Policy Studies
Queen's University, Kingston, Ontario

Canadian Cataloguing in Publication Data

Main entry under title:

Canada's national defence

Includes bibliographical references.
Contents: v. 1. Defence policy.
ISBN 0-88911-790-X(v. 1.: bound) ISBN 0-88911-792-6(v.1.:pbk.)

1. Canada – Military policy – Sources. I. Bland, Douglas L.
II. Queen's University (Kingston, Ont.). School of Policy Studies.
UA600.C345 1997   355'.033571   C97-932637-0

Contents

Preface

The volumes in the *Canada's National Defence* series present an annotated collection of government statements on defence policy and internal studies and reports prepared by senior military officers, defence officials, and consultants to governments and ministers during the period from about 1945 to 1997. Together they trace the history of the ideas that give Canada's defence policy and defence organizations their unique character. Many of the ideas in these papers have been advanced at one time and then rejected only to reappear perhaps in another context. This turbulence illustrates the ever-present tension in the defence establishment caused in part by the competing concepts inherent in any long-standing and complex institution.

These papers were assembled mainly for two reasons. First, because students, scholars, and even officers and officials find it increasingly difficult to locate complete copies of the documents that have guided Canadian defence policy and organization since 1945. Second, while the documents are useful when read alone, their significance is most evident when they are drawn together. For instance, Paul Hellyer's *White Paper on Defence 1964* is important even today, but it cannot be fully appreciated without careful reference to the so-called Glassco Commission report of 1961. It is hoped that easier access to the documents will encourage a wider consideration of their import and, therefore, a more comprehensive understanding of the history of Canadian defence policy.

Every effort has been taken to preserve the format, style, and wording used in the original papers. Therefore, where anomalies and errors occurred in the original text, they too have been preserved.

Each paper in these two volumes has been put in context by a brief description of the issues and, in some cases, the main participants involved in its preparation. I have also made some comments concerning the fate of the documents and their place in Canadian defence history. These remarks are mine and readers should consider them in that light. Finally, in most cases, I have provided a selected bibliography for the papers and the period in which they were produced.

These papers represent a history of ideas and it is these ideas that we should keep in our sights as we read them. They also represent, in important respects, Canada's way of war. In other words, they present a history of how Canadians, and especially those Canadians who direct and lead the defence establishment, think about the aims, organizations, and resource requirements for Canada's national defence. If there is an enduring Canadian strategy for national defence, it is expressed in these basic papers.

Douglas Bland
Queen's University
Kingston

Acknowledgements

In the *White Paper on Defence 1994* David Collenette, Minister of National Defence, announced that a chair in defence management studies would be established at a Canadian university. In June 1996, Mr. Collenette awarded the chair to Queen's University following an independent review of proposals from several universities in Canada.

Thanks to Mr. Collenette's initiative, the Defence Management Studies Program opened as part of the School of Policy Studies at Queen's University in 1996. This new program is intended to fill a gap in the study of defence matters in Canada and to engage the interest and support of scholars, members of the Canadian Armed Forces, public servants, and members of the defence industry in the examination and teaching of the management of national defence.

The successful launching of the Defence Management Studies Program at Queen's University was made possible also because of the continuous support of officers and officials who administer the Defence Forum program in the Department of National Defence. I especially note the contributions made by Marc Whittingham and Mae Johnson.

I wish to credit the many people in the Department of National Defence, particularly in the Directorate of History, who over the years have assisted me in assembling this collection of documents and studies. Without their selfless efforts many of these papers might have been lost or destroyed.

These volumes were assembled with the aid of several individuals at Queen's University including Lois Jordan, assistant to the Chair, and Mark Howes and Valerie Jarus of the School of Policy Studies publications unit. Hazel Fotheringham edited the introductory chapters and Moira Jackson proofread the reproduced documents. I owe special thanks to Dr. Keith Banting, Director of the School of Policy Studies at Queen's University, who not only supported this project, but was instrumental in organizing the proposal that brought the Chair to Queen's University.

Douglas Bland
Queen's University

Introduction:
White Papers on Defence

Canadian governments have not issued many policy statements on national defence since 1945. Most of those they have presented to Parliament, especially after the early 1950s, have been simple pronouncements of the status quo. Occasionally, however, ministers have attempted to take defence policy in new, and sometimes, radical directions. The special policy papers issued on these occasions are included in this volume of *Canada's National Defence*.

The first white paper, although it is not referred to as such, in this series is Brooke Claxton's *Canada's Defence 1947*. It is obviously important not only because it frames the beginning of the period under review, but also because the strategic context in which it was written is unique. Claxton and his prime minister, Mackenzie King, had two principal objectives in mind when they presented the paper to Parliament: retrenchment of the defence budget and the orderly demobilization of the armed forces to near prewar status. That is not to say, however, that Claxton wished to dismiss defence policy from the national agenda, but rather that he wished to create an efficient defence force for the much more orderly and perhaps gentler world anticipated by most informed persons after 1947. Claxton, one of Canada's "active ministers of national defence," was a reformer who took the defence establishment, sometimes against its wishes, towards a more nationalized, unified, professional, and more technical future than it had ever experienced. While the strategic rational behind the 1947 statement on defence did not survive the first icy blasts of the Cold War, the organizational and administrative concepts at the heart of the document persist to this day.

Paul Hellyer's *White Paper on Defence: 1964* is obviously important if only because it expressed the reason and the vision for Canada's unique single service. But it is significant also because Hellyer carried forward many concepts Claxton had introduced, such as unification of the armed forces. Hellyer's strategic objectives, centred on a truly Canadian strategy, are usually overlooked and this is a major weakness in most analysis of the Hellyer period. Therefore, Hellyer's white paper is an essential part of this collection because of its significance for present defence organization and because it presents perhaps the first example of Canadian strategic reasoning from a national interests perspective.

The third paper in this volume is Donald Macdonald's *Defence in the 70s.* Although Macdonald held the defence portfolio for less than two years, he directed the Liberal party's attempt to take defence policy and the defence establishment away from its cold-war, NATO orientation and into a type of Canadian neo-isolationism paradigm. Macdonald, supported by Prime Minister Pierre Trudeau, like Hellyer, attempted to find a Canadian-interests defence policy and to use it to reorder defence policy and the defence establishment. Some contend that, in fact, neither Macdonald nor Trudeau really changed Canada's NATO-oriented defence policy other than by crudely reducing defence capabilities. That may be so, but the same thing cannot be said concerning the internal control and direction of defence policy and defence administration. It is in these respects, therefore, that the Macdonald white paper is fundamentally important.

No statement on defence policy of any real significance was issued by any government between 1971 and 1987. Then in 1987 Minister of National Defence Perrin Beatty, presented to Parliament a grand white paper, *Challenge and Commitment: A Defence Policy for Canadians.* The policy of the Mulroney government seemed tailor-made for the Cold War of the previous era, but it soon ran aground on the shoals of strategic change and domestic fiscal realities. Many commentators would say that the 1987 statement never was the policy of the government because it was so soon overtaken by the ending of the Cold War. Nevertheless, the paper is included in this volume because it is the clearest statement of what the defence establishment thought were Canada's defence requirements at the time. Moreover, it is the product of a very unusual (though short-lived) policy consensus between political, military, and public service leaders.

The final policy document in this volume is *Defence 1994,* prepared by Minister of National Defence David Collenette. It represents the first comprehensive reaction of Canadian defence planners to the end of the Cold War. Moreover, unlike Beatty's 1987 white paper, it was constructed typically in an atmosphere of tension and competition between service-oriented interest groups, outside interest groups, ministers, and soldiers. The times seemed to demand a fundamental reshaping of defence policy and the reordering of long-standing defence priorities.

In interesting ways Collenette's white paper addresses many of the issues that Brooke Claxton faced in 1947: what to do in the absence of obvious military threats, how to get the most from the defence budget, and how to ensure that the defence establishment responds appropriately to the direction of the government. While one could easily argue that these are perpetual problems for ministers, they became especially poignant for Collenette in 1994 as they had for Claxton in 1947 because the strategic situation had changed radically.

There are several ways to approach these papers and to draw lessons from them, but it is important to see them as declarations of intent made in the midst of ongoing policy and administration. Ministers rarely begin the policy process with a blank piece of paper before them. Canada's defence ministers are always confronted with the facts of defence policy — certain senior leaders, capabilities, commitments, organizations, and processes — which are difficult, if not impossible, to change in the short-term. Moreover, Canada's defence policy has always been greatly influenced by allies and their plans and this fact of life has shaped (some might say contorted) ministers' options. The real divide between declared policy and actual policy is easy to see when one compares ministers' declarations with the result years later.

Each white paper and every defence policy, generally, has had to contend with the attitudes and opinions of senior military and public service leaders who have, not surprisingly, their own views on policy. Ministers who challenged these views usually have had to force their way forward opposed by soldiers and officials. In such circumstances, the minister's policy preferences may be "a sometime thing" seldom retaining their original shape and intent once the minister departs. The history of policies declared in white papers, therefore, provides a glimpse at the realities of civil-military relations in Canada. The question is: Whose policy survives and why?

In a more mechanical sense, white papers are always about certain aspects of policy. What roles and tasks; how much is enough; who decides who gets what; what capabilities for what kind of future conflict; and how can the policy be "sold" to Canadians? These questions flow through all the papers presented here.

What is less obvious is that, although the context changes and the political rhetoric varies, the actual policy that has directed Canadian defence policy is very nearly always the same. Is this because there is a natural defence policy for Canada or is it because the establishment, wed to its own views, takes policy back to the status quo soon after ministers have had their policy fling? The question is important and, therefore, observers should not let the obvious statements about roles, resources, and capabilities overshadow the more important issue of public administration, "who decides who gets what." The papers in this volume provide examples of what political leaders think about Canada's defence. The outcomes, however, might reflect more what military and public service leaders think about Canada's defence and their places in it. Who then decides for Canada?

Introduction to Canada's Defence 1947

Brooke Claxton served as the minister of defence in the Liberal Government from 1946 to 1954. Although it is said that he was a reluctant defence minister, he presided over the Department of National Defence and directed the three services of Canada's armed forces with vigour and imagination. Claxton expected "bitter and biased opposition"* to everything he did, but he was the quintessential "active minister" and during his term in office the civil control of the armed forces and the department was never in doubt.

Prime Minister Mackenzie King selected Claxton for the defence portfolio because he had specific defence objectives in mind for Canada after the Second World War and he needed a strong minister to carry them through. King was determined to demobilize the nation and to reintegrate members of the services into the civilian community without dislocating the country or sparking a recession as had happened after the First World War. Moreover, the prime minister wanted Claxton to greatly reduce defence expenditures, almost to prewar levels.

---

*As quoted in David Bercuson, *True Patriot: The Life of Brooke Claxton 1898-1960* (Toronto: University of Toronto Press, 1993), p. 153

Claxton's task was complicated by the processes of national defence shaped by six years of war. In particular, he faced a corps of young but senior officers who had grown accustomed to commanding large forces and being centre stage. They were also for the most part conditioned to accept an allied and, in some cases, a British view of the world rather than a Canadian view. The new defence minister, therefore, had first to establish his authority over his subordinates and then to convince them to join in dismantling the institutions they had so carefully constructed.

The Canadian defence establishment before the war was small and almost insignificant. Not only were the services limited in capabilities, but the department of defence was a minor government agency managing a small budget. However, within a few months after the beginning of the war the armed services had increased beyond all prewar expectations and were deployed around the world. The department grew rapidly, then split into three service-oriented departments under three ministers and deputy ministers. Naturally, these departments developed their own institutional and bureaucratic interests and procedures. While these differences could be tolerated during the war, Claxton had to find a way in 1946 to reduce the complexity and cost of his portfolio without upsetting completely the future management of national defence.

Although the prime minister and the defence minister were determined to greatly reduce the armed forces and defence expenditures, they were not about to return to prewar laissez-faire ideas. Most Canadians were convinced that the Second World War had started because no nation stood firmly against Mussolini and Hitler in the 1930s. Canadian elites, at least, also believed that Canada had won a place on the international stage and that Canada would have to contribute to international security decisions to keep this new position. Moreover, Canadian leaders had enthusiastically supported the founding of the United Nations as an institution to prevent aggression from leading to general war, and Canadian diplomats and politicians generally were committed to supporting the UN and to taking as prominent a role in international affairs as circumstances allowed. For all these reasons, Canadians understood that some armed forces would be needed in the future, "but not too many."

Claxton's challenge, therefore, was to reduce the size of the armed forces and the department and reduce and control defence expenditures while maintaining some modern capabilities for contingencies. The defence statement, *Canada's Defence*, was his answer.

The 1947 white paper on defence (although it was not called that) begins with a review of Canada's wartime accomplishments. The minister noted the important contribution Canadians had made to the war effort at sea, on land, in the air, and at home. Claxton then set out the three roles for the armed services of the future.

Canada's defence forces may be required:
(1) to defend Canada against aggression;
(2) to assist the civil power in maintaining law and order within the country;
(3) to carry out any undertakings which by our own voluntary act we may assume in co-operation with friendly nations or under any effective plan of collective action under the United Nations.

The first two missions were the obvious and irreducible responsibility of government. The third mission implied that Canada's defence was linked to international security and especially to the defence policies of the United States. This North American relationship matured during the war mainly as a result of the wartime cooperation between Canada and the United States and the agreement reached by Mackenzie King and President Roosevelt at Ogdensburg in 1940. Defending North America in cooperation with the United States would eventually become Canada's second most important defence objective and it held that place in all subsequent defence policy statements. These two missions, defending Canada and North America, reflect the "defence imperatives" in Canadian defence policy.

However, the third defence requirement was a broad statement of intent. There is no compelling reason drawn from an appreciation of

Canada's security situation that requires Canada to send armed forces overseas. Yet the Liberal government in 1947 — and every government since then — chose to include an international dimension in Canada's defence policy. The wording in Claxton's third mission is important. It reflects both a determination that Canadians will decide where and when its armed forces would be employed and a willingness to deploy them outside Canada, if necessary. These ideas provide room for "strategic choice" in Canadian defence policy, then and now.

Thus the 1947 defence policy explicitly rejects any lingering idea that Canada might follow automatically some form of British imperial defence or the policies of any other external authority. On the other hand, the statement rejects isolationism and shows a willingness to join with others to preserve world peace. Here there is a clear reference to the fledgling UN and the idea of collective security. The notions captured in this third mission would also become steady sentinels of Canadian defence white papers, although with the advent of the North Atlantic Alliance in 1949 the choice of "working with others" would specifically include NATO as well as the UN.

Claxton introduced other ideas that would survive even into the 1994 white paper. For instance, he was a strong advocate of unification. Like most ministers, Claxton viewed defence policy as a single problem and not as three (or more) problems divisible on service lines. He pushed service integration as far as he could but not as far as he would have liked. Claxton did succeed in unifying the defence department by collapsing the naval and air ministries into a more general department forming a new Department of National Defence. Thus he eliminated two deputy ministers and created one central civil service staff. He also brought the separate military staffs together, albeit imperfectly, into a kind of military council under his close direction. Claxton reinforced this effort by appointing in 1951 a chairman of the Chief of Staffs Committee to try to develop a military consensus on the main issues of the day. Finally, Claxton rewrote the National Defence Act and used it as the basis for instituting common laws and regulations governing the armed forces and the code of service discipline.

Brooke Claxton recognized that advances in weapons and delivery vehicles during the Second World War were changing the shape "of world events and the changing centres of power [thereby putting] Canada in a more important strategical position than she has ever been in before." But these same changes had made Canada more vulnerable than ever before. He also understood that these changes were only the beginning of a technological race that included "a new world of supersonic talk and saucers flying in formation." These were not frivolous concerns and Claxton worked hard to improve the Defence Research Board as an essential part of national defence plans and policy. He was particularly aware of the need (made obvious during the war) to integrate the work of military officers with civil servants and scientists, and that is one reason why he founded the National Defence College in 1951.

The defence minister paid particular tribute to the reserve forces and stated that he intended to strengthen and improve their situation. Indeed, Claxton declared that "the importance of the reserve has been shown in two wars and we should now take them for what they are — probably the most important part of the armed forces of Canada." He would "wipe out" the differences between the active and the reserve forces and create a harmonized force.

Many of the main timbers of Claxton's defence policy of 1947 remain firmly in place in 1997. Certainly the description of the requirements of the armed forces have not changed significantly, although the order of the strategic choices circle each other from time to time. Now that the Cold War is over, the strategic choices have become much less specific, but one can see Claxton's imprint on David Collenette's white paper of 1994. The idea of unification of the armed forces and of the defence establishment generally continued to develop after Claxton left the portfolio and was ultimately expressed by Paul Hellyer in 1964 and by Donald Macdonald in 1970.

Some things Claxton could not correct or solve. For example, his desire to find an efficient way to manage defence policy was never fully satisfied. The armed forces, but especially the army, remain divided into two main elements, a modern-style professional force and a militia with its conceptual roots in Canada's colonial history. Worse, the underlying animosity that Claxton hoped to wipe out remains stubbornly in place. Finally, Claxton was faithful to his prime minister's direction to keep the armed forces at levels just strong enough to meet the commitments the government had accepted, and that policy, too, has survived throughout succeeding years. As a result of this parsimony and the uneven understanding between politicians and soldiers of what exactly "commitments" mean, Claxton might also have been the father of the "commitment-capabilities gap" that seems to plague Canadian defence policies.

Some might suggest that because the strategic situation and the armed services changed radically between 1947 and 1952, mainly because of the war in Korea and the deployment of forces to NATO, the 1947 statement on defence is not important. But such assessments miss the essential point. The armed forces and the Department of National Defence were able to cope with these new demands precisely because of the reforms Claxton made between 1947 and 1950. Certainly the large increases in the defence budget in 1950 and 1951 were instrumental in the expansion of Canada's defence capabilities, but it was the central organization that allowed the expansion and deployments to go forward reasonably (if not perfectly) well. In the years following the crisis of 1950-1952, Claxton's efforts to build a viable permanent force, provided not only with modern weapons but also with good terms of service and family support, allowed Canada to field competent forces more or less continuously in Europe and in some UN posts. Moreover, the country did this without undue strain on the national purse and without resorting to conscription as General Guy Simonds, for one, declared was necessary.

Would the Canadian Forces have been able to meet the demands of war if the Cold War had turned hot in the mid-1950s or early 1960s, the two periods when this seemed possible? The answer depends on many factors, not least of which is the speed of such a deterioration into intercontinental nuclear conflict. But the aim of defence policy in this period was to deter a war between the superpowers and from this perspective the policy succeeded.

Selected Bibliography

David Bercuson. *True Patriot: The Life of Brooke Claxton 1898-1960.* Toronto: University of Toronto Press, 1993.

Douglas Bland. *The Administration of Defence Policy in Canada, 1947 to 1985.* Kingston: R.P. Frye Co., 1987.

James Eayrs. *In Defence of Canada*, 4 vols. Toronto: University of Toronto Press, 1972.

Joseph Jockel. *No Boundaries Upstairs: Canada, the United States and the Origins of North American Air Defence, 1945-1958.* Vancouver: University of British Columbia Press, 1987.

Guy Simonds. "Where We've Gone Wrong on Defence." *Maclean's.* 23 June 1956, pp. 28-68.

NATIONAL ARCHIVES OF CANADA

Brooke Claxton. *Memoirs.*

DEPARTMENT OF NATIONAL DEFENCE: DIRECTORATE OF HISTORY

Defence Committee Minutes, 14 October 1947.

The Woods/Gordon Report, 14 December 1948, File 79/670.

Memorandum, Claxton to the Chiefs of Staff Committee and the Deputy Minister, 31 January 1949, File 79/670.

CANADA'S DEFENCE

Information on
CANADA'S DEFENCE ACHIEVEMENTS
AND ORGANIZATION

Issued under authority of
HON. BROOKE CLAXTON, M.P.
Minister of National Defence

Reproduced in The Department of National Defence

Canada's Defence

New weapons forged in The Second Great War and revolutionary changes in the comparable strengths of many nations make the defence of Canada a matter of major national policy and of direct concern to every individual Canadian. The object of Canadian policy is to do all that we can to prevent the outbreak of another world war, or, failing that, to ensure that we and our potential allies are in a position to win it, and win it quickly, if and when it does start.

The following paper is intended to provide information about the wartime achievements of Canada and her defence needs and objectives, as well as to outline organizational changes that are underway. The first part is largely taken from a statement by the Honourable Brooke Claxton, Minister of National Defence, in presenting the Department's Estimates to the House of Commons on July 9, 1947.

PART I

Minister's Statement on the Estimates

On June 17, 1947, P.C. 2372 was adopted providing that the members of the armed forces shall cease to be on active service as at September 30, 1947. At that time the formal change from a war to a peace footing for the armed services will be related to the inauguration of a campaign to obtain recruits for the active and reserve forces. In the meantime, however, now that our wartime forces have in fact ended the work to which they had set their hands, it will, I believe, be the wish of honourable members that a brief summary of the facts and figures of their accomplishments should be set down in Hansard as a permanent record of a magnificent achievement.

Canada's war record, in reminding us of the nature of modern war, will inspire and strengthen us to work with other nations to create the conditions for enduring peace. Canada's part in two wars will lead us, until progress is made in ensuring peace through collective action, to establish our own forces on a post-war basis which will be related to the defence needs of the country as these may change from time to time. Our policy must be informed by wartime experience, just as it is inspired by war-time achievement.

In the statement which follows, after reviewing the achievements in war, I propose to set out what I take to be the defence needs of Canada, to indicate some of the matters which must receive the most immediate attention and to describe long-term objectives with regard to the Department of National Defence and the armed forces.

THE WAR

The war of liberation started on September 1, 1939. Germany's brutal attack on Poland was followed by the so-called "phony war", when Germany was growing in strength to make the sweep through Denmark, Norway, the Netherlands, Belgium and France. From the fall of France in June 1940, until Russia was brought into the war a year later, Britain and the countries of the Commonwealth stood almost alone. The will to be free was for a time the main armour that stood against the evil thrust to make Germany supreme and everyone else slaves. Canadian territory was not attacked but from the outset we recognized that this was a fight in which our vital interests were involved, and, by act of our own government on the all but unanimous support of our own Parliament, we entered the war on September 10,1939. Our contribution mounted steadily.

The Royal Canadian Navy

At sea, our main job was to keep the bridge of ships open to Britain. The submarine menace was a major threat.

From the start our young and growing Navy carried its share of the work of escort, and by the later stages of the war, the R.C.N. was undertaking the major portion of the close escort of Canada-US-Great Britain trade convoys to the United Kingdom. Our ships took an active part in the Aleutian Islands and Mediterranean campaigns and participated in the conquest of Japan. 10,000 officers and men in 109 ships of the Royal Canadian Navy took part in the European landings from D-Day onward. At the start of the war our Navy had 1,769 full-time officers and men. Before its end, 100,000 men had passed through its ranks and we had a total of 780 ships.

The Army

The First Division left Canada in December 1939, and was joined by the Second Division in 1940. These two divisions were among the few bodies of trained troops ready to withstand a German assault on Britain; some of them at Dieppe paved the way for future landings. The first Canadian Infantry Division landed at Sicily in July 1943 and was followed soon by the Fifth Canadian Armoured Division and other units. These comprised the First Canadian Corps which fought up the whole long length of Italy until withdrawn to join the First Canadian Army in North-West Europe early in 1945.

The Third Canadian Infantry Division landed on D-Day, June 6, 1944, followed by the Second Canadian Infantry Division and the Fourth Canadian Armoured Division. In July 1944, the Second Canadian Corps and the First British Corps were grouped in the First Canadian Army, which carried a tough assignment on the left flank in the fighting in Normandy and up the channel ports through Holland, and Germany beyond the Rhine. Forming part of the Canadian Army at one time or another were all but two of the British divisions, as well as a number of American divisions, a Polish armoured division, and Belgian, Netherlands, and Czech brigades. The first Canadian Army was an effective international force and its components got on well together under the leadership of our own General H. D. G. Crerar, C.H. Early in 1945 more than half a million men of half a dozen countries formed the Canadian Army which stretched over 250 miles of front and was at this time probably the largest single army formation on the western front. From the beaches, through Caen and Falaise up by the channel ports, over the Scheldt, the Maas and Rhine, the Canadians lived up to the reputation they had gained in the First Great War.

During the war our peacetime permanent force of 4,492 officers and men was multiplied more than a hundred and sixty times. Before the war was over 709,007 personnel had served in the Canadian Army, in addition to 21,618 members of the Canadian Women's Army Corps.

R.C.A.F.

The British Commonwealth Air Training Plan from its start in December 1939 was a spectacular undertaking. In a short time we had nearly 200 training schools across Canada. By the time the plan was finished it had trained 42,110 young flyers from the United Kingdom (including 5,293 Royal Air Force and Fleet Air Arm pilots trained in Canada at R.A.F. schools prior to July 1942 when these schools became part of B.C.A.T.P.), 9,606 from Australia, and 7,002 from New Zealand. Of the total of 131,553 air crew trained under the plan, the great majority were Canadians — altogether 72,835 Canadian air crew were trained and it is believed that Canada had the highest per capita number of air crew of any nation fighting in the war.

The first Canadian flyers to reach the other side were members of Auxiliary Squadrons. These were soon followed by a steady flow of pilots, navigators, air gunners, radar operators and the all-important ground crew. At the outbreak of war there were 2,948 officers and men in the R.C.A.F. During the war a total of 249,624 Canadians served in the Royal Canadian Air Force in addition to another 4,000 who served with the Royal Air Force. They fought and flew on every front.

Record in Figures
Canadians came to play their part — to offer their lives, from the farms, the woods, the mines, the city streets, the workshops and the schools. Here is a summary of their numbers and of the losses suffered.

Served During the War

	Men	Women	Total
Navy	99,479	7,043	106,522
Army	709,007*	21,618	730,625
Air Force	232,594	17,030	249,624
Totals	1,041,080	45,691	1,086,771

*Includes 3,633 women members of the Royal Canadian Army Medical Corps.

Casualties

	Killed	Wounded	Total
Navy	1,981	319	2,300
Army	22,964	51,410	74,374
Air Force	17,047	1,416	18,463
Totals	41,992	53,145	95,137

A summary of all awards from the commencement of the War in September 1939 to March 31, 1947, follows

	Navy	Army	Air Force	Total
British Awards	1,677	11,932	8,735	22,344
Foreign Awards	54	1,475	213	1,742
Totals	1,731	13,407	8,948	24,086

SUPPLIES

Canada made notable contributions to the war in the supply of munitions, food and financial assistance to the allied cause. Canada produced finished munitions of war to a total of about $10 billions. Although 25 per cent of our farmers joined the armed forces or worked in munitions, the farmers of Canada produced more then 40 per cent more food than in 1939, and, by making our surpluses available to Britain and other countries, prevented starvation succeeding where the enemy had failed.

The total cost of the war to Canada, and its immediate aftermath, to March 31, 1947, is estimated at $20.25 billions. Of this $6.43 billions was spent in mutual aid or other financial assistance to our allies.

At the peak of war production 1,166,000 men and women worked directly in the production of munitions and, with the 1,086,771 in the armed forces, made a total of more than two and a quarter million Canadians who served either in the fighting forces or in the direct production of munitions.

DEMOBILIZATION

These figures give the measure of the problem of demobilization, rehabilitation, and reconversion. At the peak, which may be taken to be V-E Day, May 8, 1945, there were 349,159 Canadians in England and Europe, including R.C.N. who moved under their own steam. Before they had all been brought home, there were 37,016 wives and 14,630 children, making a total repatriation job for about 400,000 persons. In addition to this total some 10,000 dependents, wives and children had been brought to Canada prior to V-E Day. Repatriation was proceeded with more expeditiously, more smoothly and with less discomfort than anyone could have hoped for and is now complete. At present, there are some 400 members of the armed forces in the United Kingdom and Europe, doing work in connection with graves and records, including our military mission to Berlin and liaison staff in the United Kingdom. That work will have to continue for some time. There are some 1,000 dependents who have long ago been offered transportation which for one reason or another they have so far been unable to take advantage of but who still want to come to Canada.

The repatriation and demobilization of the armed forces ranked first in priority and the way this was organized and pressed through to completion by both my immediate predecessors earned the gratitude of the hundreds of thousands concerned and of their families, indeed of all Canadians.

From time to time tributes have been paid to the ministers and deputies, to the generals and privates, to the workers and the farmers who did their utmost in our war effort. Canada's national effort in the war was a great national partnership.

We have tried to ensure for our sailors, soldiers, and airmen that they should not be any worse off because they had served. Consequently Parliament authorized the introduction of what is regarded everywhere as the most comprehensive and generous plan of rehabilitation in effect in any country. That work and the work of hospitalization and treatment will go on.

WAR STORES

The liquidation of surplus war stores proceeded alongside the demobilization of men. At the close of the war in September 1945, we had in Canada more than a billion and a half dollars worth of military equipment and munitions. At one time or another there had been some 6,000 different military establishments, all of which had to be examined to decide which should be kept and which should be disposed of.

We have kept the munitions necessary to equip the Canadian active and reserve forces on a scale never before known. We have also quantities of stores for mobilization reserves. But more than a billion dollars worth was declared surplus, and the operation of putting all this material in condition for distribution, storage or disposal made the Canadian armed forces and War Assets Corporation the greatest warehousing and merchandising concerns in the history of the country.

CIVILIAN PERSONNEL

When men were demobilized from the armed forces, a number of civilians had to be taken on to carry through the work of demobilization and liquidation, with the result that in December 1946 the civilian personnel with a total of 33,000 increased again almost to the wartime peak. As the work of warehousing and disposal was being pressed forward, we were able to reduce the number of civilian personnel and at March 31, 1947, the figure was 20,131, or a reduction of 13,131, representing 37 per cent in four months.

Further reductions will result from time to time and every possible care will be taken to see that these reductions are effected with the least possible hardship to individuals. The small amount of disturbance or complaint in consequence of reductions already made reflects the capacity of our national economy to absorb these people and also shows the good sense of the Canadian people in recognizing that there is no justification for keeping personnel on strength any longer than they are needed.

Civilians in the department total 19,783. Of these 9,249 are civil servants, or do work similar to that done by civil servants; the remainder are prevailing rate employees engaged in the dockyards at Halifax and Esquimalt, in the construction or conversion of married quarters, in the handling of stores, in various duties, like watchmen, caretakers, firefighters and so on. Our plan is to have as much of this type of work done by civilians as possible, so as to have as many as we can of our armed forces engaged on planning, training and operations.

DEFENCE NEEDS

This brings me to a consideration of the defence needs of Canada, the organization of our defence forces and the progress made to date.

Taking up first the question of the defence needs of Canada, Canada's defence forces may be required:

(1) to defend Canada against aggression;
(2) to assist the civil power in maintaining law and order within the country;
(3) to carry out any undertakings which by our own voluntary act we may assume in co-operation with friendly nations or under any effective plan of collective action under the United Nations.

Obviously our needs must be considered in the light of circumstances as they change from time to time. The actors bearing on this are numerous. Among them, the following are particularly important:

(1) the geographical positions of Canada;
(2) the capacity of any possible aggressor to make an attack;
(3) the disposition of friendly nations;
(4) what may be called "the international climate".

Developments in warlike materials, particularly new weapons, have an important bearing on the whole position. As the war neared its end, four new weapons had been introduced or were in process of development. These were the atomic bomb, jet-propelled planes, long range rockets and higher speed submarines.

Sufficient quantities of any one of three of these four new weapons would probably have been sufficient to win the war for the side which had them first. These new weapons, and the chemical and bacteriological agents now known, are so much more devastating than anything previously used that of themselves they may make major changes in the nature of war, should war come again to scourge the earth.

These new powerful weapons reinforce the powerful appeal of those who work to make war impossible. What we have seen of destruction and devastation in the First and Second Great Wars would be small in character or extent compared with the appalling destructiveness of any further large-scale war. For this reason our first line of defence and the object of all our policy must be to work with other nations to prevent war.

This is just as true today in Canada as it is in every other country. Distance and space still combine to give us great natural advantages for which we cannot be too grateful, but distance and space have been drastically reduced and are still shrinking; and the shaping of world events and the changing centres of power have put Canada in a more important strategical position than she has ever been in before.

Let us set down here that we believe that it is possible for nations to live in peace — perhaps the fate of humanity depends on this belief becoming an eternal fact. We also believe that in the United Nations there is the beginning of an organization which may be developed progressively into a great instrument for peaceful co-operation. But progress in peace depends on the way in which powers, and particularly the great powers, work with each other. While the proceedings of the Assembly of the United Nations in December 1946 gave some ground for encouragement, it is still too early for this or any nation to rest on its arms with the assurance that there will be no aggression.

As the first aim of our foreign policy is peace, so the first aim of our defence policy is defence against aggression.

DEFENCE EXPENDITURES

Having set out what I take to be the defence needs of Canada, it is quite evident that the need for defence forces at any given time must be considered with regard to the portion of the national budget which we are prepared to spend for that purpose. The business of government involves balancing of means and ends. No government department would be worth its salt if it was ever satisfied with the functions it was exercising. No defence force will ever be completely satisfied.

Leaving budgetary considerations aside, it may be doubted if more than the sum sought of $240,000,000 could be wisely spent in Canada on defence during the current fiscal year. While much progress has been made no one appreciates more than myself that there is still a lot of work to be done in reorganization before we can provide a proper organizational and administrative basis for the defence forces that we may have in the future.

This sum of $240,000,000 represents about 12 per cent of our national budget. It compares with $35 millions spent in 1938-39 or the low figure of $14 millions for 1932-33. For the year ending March 31, 1947 the appropriations voted for the three departments totaled $486,849,141 and the expenditures for the year totaled $383,325,686. The amount underspent is partly accounted for by the very much more rapid rate at which our forces were repatriated and demobilized than anticipated. The estimates for 1946-47 were prepared on the assumption that the strength of the three services would total throughout the year 98,360, whereas halfway through the year, by October 1st, the actual strength had been reduced by demobilization to 55,132. Another reason contributing to the difference between appropriations and expenditures was the postponement of defence purchasing and construction in favour of civilian purchasing and construction.

The work of repatriation and demobilization is to all intents and purposes complete. The work of overhauling and liquidating stores is rather more then 75 per cent complete. We still have, however, large numbers of civilians and service personnel engaged in this work and some of them will be engaged in this for a year or more longer.

CONVERSION

In addition, we have a very large number of civilian and service personnel engaged in making necessary conversions in camps and air stations so as to fit in with the post-war plan.

MARRIED QUARTERS

The biggest construction job being undertaken is to provide married quarters for married personnel. This is the most urgent single need in all three services. We have personnel at work to convert into married quarters every available convertible hutment. Our target is to create more than a thousand new dwelling units in Canada this year; but whether or not it can be done depends on the availability of materials and labour. For officers and men with active service we have removed the limitations on what used to be called the married establishment so that anyone in the services who saw active service and is married is entitled to the relevant allowances. So also are officers of 25 years of age and men of 23 after they have completed their initial training. Because a large proportion of the officers and men in the armed forces saw service overseas, many of them from the start of the war to the close, and there was no restriction on marriage in their case, an unusually large proportion, probably 65 per cent, are married.

To illustrate the kind of life led in the new army let us look at Shilo Camp in Manitoba which was among the establishments I was able to visit during the Easter recess of Parliament. In June the military hospital provided assistance at the birth of four children. Under the Regimental Institute committees of officers and men and their wives run on a co-operative basis, modern well-equipped butcher and grocery shops, a garage, a hairdresser's, a shoemaker's, wet and dry canteens, a moving picture theatre, swimming pool, all kinds of recreations, concerts and dances, as well as a nursery school. In addition to the usual facilities, the Army provides a library and a two-room elementary school where sixty children are taught by Army-hired instructors. This and similar arrangements elsewhere for the education of the children of our men in the armed forces in isolated communities are being geared into the provincial school system;

Educational opportunities are being provided for officers and men in addition to the camps and trades schools. This all goes to show the changed nature of Canada's post-war armed forces. We aim to create conditions which will attract the best of our young men and enable them to live useful lives as respected citizens of the community.

DEFENCE PRIORITIES

As in other countries, this is still a year of reorganization. Without excluding other objects of activity, I might mention particularly five matters which have a very high priority in all our activities today:

(1) Organization
(2) Training of officers
(3) Reserve training
(4) Research
(5) Industrial organization.

Since my appointment in December I have taken advantage of every possible opportunity to visit units of the Navy, Army and Air Force in many parts of Canada. The total strength of the active forces today is 32,610. They represent a fine body of fit and highly qualified Canadians, well worthy of continuing the record made for them in the First Great War and which so many of them helped to make in the Second Great War.

CO-OPERATION

I have taken advantage of every possible opportunity to meet representatives of Reserve Associations, and co-operating organizations like the Navy League of Canada and the Air Cadet League, as well as representatives of industry and experts from other countries. All these have extended the most helpful co-operation.

In this new world of supersonic talk and saucers flying in formation, it is important that there should be a wide measure of informed and interested support of adequate defence measures by people who have a sense of responsibility and who are willing to accept responsibility. We can never express too warmly the appreciation this country owes to the officers, N.C.O.s and men and their civilian friends who by their voluntary support maintained our reserve forces through the difficult period of the years between the wars. We should be most grateful to them and to their successors who are carrying on now and to all those who have been of such great assistance in the work of national importance.

DEFENCE OBJECTS

In closing this statement, I enumerate the long-term objects of the department and services:

(1) Progressively closer co-ordination of the armed services and unification of the Department so as to form a single defence force in which the three armed services work together as a team.
(2) Joint intelligence and planning groups to review defence appreciations and plans.
(3) Clothing, food, quarters, pay, pensions and working conditions suitable for young Canadians of high physical and education standards.
(4) Means to provide the active and reserve forces of the three services with adequate numbers of highly qualified officers.

(5) Development of reserve forces of an age and with educational and physical standards and training approximating those of the active forces and who will in time be capable of entering speedily on active service at sea, on land or in the air.

(6) Provision for reserve forces of the most modern training methods, administration and training officers, and adequate equipment.

(7) Maintaining adequate reserves of equipment and weapons.

(8) Close integration of the armed forces, the defence purchasing agency, government arsenals and civilian industry, looking towards standardization and industrial organization to permit of the speedy and complete utilization of our industrial resources.

(9) Co-operation between the armed forces, the Defence Research Board and private industry regarding defence research so that we keep up to date with regard to the design and planning of weapons.

(10) Support for Canadian Arsenals Limited and a limited number of Canadian industries to maintain and increase skills in the design and manufacture of munitions and aircraft.

(11) Organization of government departments and civilian agencies so as to enable us to put a plan for civil defence into immediate effect.

(12) Government leadership to obtain civilian support of the armed forces.

(13) Armed forces to form an integral part of the life of the community.

(14) Co-operation with the countries of the British Commonwealth, the United States and other like-minded countries in working out common standards, planning and training.

These objectives will not be achieved at once but we are working towards them. I hope we shall have the support of all parties and members of Parliament, of members of the active and reserve armed forces, of industry, indeed of the whole community of Canada. The measures to be taken for the defence of our country are matters of individual interest as well as national responsibility.

PART II

Defence Organization

In the following part of this Paper, matters mentioned in the foregoing statement of the Minister of National Defence are further developed.

BETWEEN THE WARS

Towards the end of the First Great War the mood of war weariness carried the note "this must not happen again." Such planning as there was of post-war defence forces was hardly put on paper when the depression immediately following the war caused large cuts in defence estimates. In 1932-33 defence expenditure fell to 14.1 millions. At that time the R.C.A.F., which had been struggling to live up to the fine record won during the war by Canadian flyers, was reduced to a total personnel of 694 officers and men.

The story is told in defence expenditures during these years.

1919-20	335,525,512	1933-34	19,563,192
1920-21	31,052,562	1934-35	22,286,732
1921-22	24,164,263	1935-36	27,368,163
1922-23	18,577,504	1936-37	26,669,941
1923-24	14,183,045	1937-38	32,760,306
1924-25	13,320,037	1938-39	34,432,839
1925-26	14,229,038	1935-40	125,679,888
1926-27	14,975,234	1940-41	647,922,940
1927-28	17,661,015	1941-42	1,011,451,064
1928-29	19,786,342	1942-43	1,865,622,615
1929-30	21,979,245	1943-44	2,629,094,792
1930-31	23,730,388	1944-45	2,938,377,688
1931-32	18,361,670	1945-46	1,715,731,491
1932-33	14,123,742	1946-47	383,325,686 (not final)

ORGANIZATION DURING THE WAR

Until 1939 matters relating to defence were dealt with in one department and were the business of a single minister, In 1940 two additional ministers were appointed and two additional departments were created to deal with the Navy and the Air Force. To effect co-ordination, the Defence Council was created, with the Minister of National Defence as chairman and the other two ministers, the three Chiefs of Staff and the three Deputy Ministers as members, the Defence Secretary being secretary. The Defence Council met usually once a week. In addition there was the Chiefs of Staff Committee and numerous inter-service committees.

In Canada's war effort the roles of the Navy, Army and Air Force differed from each other fundamentally. Although recruited from every part of the country, the Navy operated in two oceans, principally in the North Atlantic where it carried on a large part of the dangerous and essential work of convoy. The Royal Canadian Navy worked in close co-operation with both the British and United States Navies. Because of the nature of escort work with ships of every allied flag represented, it cannot be said that the Canadian Navy, engaged in the work of convoy, acted as an operational unit, although the Canadian Commander-in -Chief, North West Atlantic, was responsible for co-ordinating all convoy escort in this vital area.

In Canada the R.C.A.F. was organized in five commands largely for administrative and training rather than operational purposes. A major task of the R.C.A.F. was to provide training facilities under the British Commonwealth Air Training plan for men from the United Kingdom, Australia and New Zealand, as well as Canada. Once qualified, the new air fighters were rushed overseas and to save time were largely fitted into existing R.A.F. training and fighting formations. Canadians sometimes were with Canadian squadrons or a Canadian bomber group, but more often were with R.A.F. squadrons. Overseas, the R.C.A.F. did not work as an operational unit.

In the Army, however, the situation was different. The two first divisions overseas were followed by three other divisions and by numerous ancillary units and troops of every kind. Canadian soldiers operated as an army in England, as a corps in Italy and as the First Canadian Army in western Europe, other allied troops forming part of a Canadian formation.

In Canada the Army was dealt with for training and administrative purposes through the eleven military districts. With the formation of three additional divisions in Canada, Atlantic and Pacific Commands for possible operational purposes were superimposed on the district organizations.

PLANNING FOR POST-WAR ORGANIZATION

Germany's surrender on May 8, 1945 started the process of repatriation and demobilization. Before this, preparations were well under way for the organization of the Pacific forces, 150,808 men and women of the Navy, Army and Air Force having volunteered by July 1945. Further organization of the Pacific forces was stopped on September 2, 1945 following the surrender of Japan.

Simultaneously with the work of repatriating and demobilizing the three-quarters of a million men and women who were in the armed forces at V-E Day, the work was commenced of putting the organization of the Defence Department and the services on a post-war basis in accordance with plans which had been in preparation for some time.

In the Army, as a transitional measure, five commands were superimposed on the existing districts with the intention that the districts would disappear when the requisite legislation was enacted. In the Air Force, the number of commands was reduced to four. Steps were taken to put the pay and allowances of officers and men in all three services on an identical basis. The Militia Pension Act relative to all three services was substantially amended so as to put the pensions of officers and men in the services on much the same basis as that of civil servants under the Superannuation Act. A number of inter-service committees were set up to co-ordinate the three services.

MINISTER OF NATIONAL DEFENCE

In order to bring about the maximum possible degree of co-ordination and to eliminate duplication of functions in the Navy, Army and Air Force, it was decided to have one Minister of National Defence responsible for all three services.

Under the Department of National Defence Act the Minister is charged with responsibility for all matters relating to defence. Under his authority, military command is exercised by those having a commission from the King.

The objects of unification included:

(1)   The adoption of a unified defence program to meet agreed strategic needs;
(2)   A single defence budget under which funds and resources would be allocated in accordance with the program;
(3)   The elimination of duplicatory and even competing services;
(4)   Consistent and equitable personnel policies;
(5)   Greater emphasis on defence research and closer co-ordination with other government departments and with industry.

In the United Kingdom and Australia, the same need of co-ordinating the three services was felt as in Canada. In the United Kingdom, the means so far adopted has been to appoint a fourth Minister with over-riding and co-ordinating authority (see U.K. White Paper, Command 6923, presented to Parliament in October 1946). In Australia, the wartime arrangement of a Minister for Defence controlling co-ordination of the defence services and general defence policy is being retained. In both countries the three services and corresponding departments are left under their separate Ministers.

In the United States the National Security Act of 1947 was enacted on July 25, 1947, to provide for a Secretary of National Defence with Departments of the Army, Navy and Air Force under three secretaries not having cabinet rank (see communication to Congress from the President of February 26, 1947).

In Canada we have endeavoured to meet the necessity for co-ordination by the appointment of a single minister and the creation of a single department.

On December 12, 1946, Honourable Brooke Claxton was appointed as a single Minister of National Defence. At that time Honourable Colin Gibson, who had been Minister of National Defence for Air, was appointed Secretary of State, and Honourable D. C . Abbott, who had been Minister of National Defence and Minister of National Defence for Naval Services, was appointed Minister of Finance.

DEFENCE COUNCIL

The Defence Council's wartime function of co-ordinating the work of the three departments is no longer necessary with the creation of a single department. The Defence Council was reconstituted by P.C. 887 on March 13, 1947 and consists of the Minister who is chairman, the Parliamentary Assistant, the Deputy Minister, the Associate Deputy Ministers, the three Chiefs of Staff and the Chairman of the Defence Research Board. The chairman of the Personnel Members Committee, the chairman of the Principal Supply Officers Committee or other officers attend as required; the Defence Secretary acts as its secretary. The function of this committee is to advise the Minister with regard to administrative matters. It is the place where administrative matters of importance affecting the department as a whole or of inter-service concern are raised and discussed as a preliminary to their being disposed of by the Minister or under his authority.

DEFENCE COMMITTEE OF THE CABINET

During the war, in Canada as in the United Kingdom, Australia and other countries, the need for quick action, close co-ordination and complete security produced changes in cabinet organization. In the United Kingdom the War Cabinet replaced the ordinary cabinet. In Canada the War Committee of the Cabinet made decisions on the matters with which it dealt, but it continued to operate alongside and within the framework of the cabinet as a whole, which continued to exercise its functions throughout the war.

The War Committee of the Cabinet was first appointed on December 5, 1939 and consisted then of six members including the Prime Minister, the government leader in the Senate, the Ministers of Justice, Finance, National Defence and Mines and Resources. When it last met in the spring of 1945 it consisted of the Prime Minister, and the Ministers of National Defence, National Defence for Air, National Defence for Naval Services, Munitions and Supply, Justice, Mines and Resources, Finance and Transport.

This committee was succeeded in October, 1945 by the Defence Committee which now consists of the Prime Minister, who acts as chairman, the Minister of National Defence (vice-chairman), the Secretary of State for External Affairs, the Minister of Finance and the Minister of Fisheries. The Defence Committee is attended by the three Chiefs of Staff and the Chairman of the Defence Research Board. Other cabinet ministers, officials or officers attend as required. The terms of reference of the Defence Committee of the Cabinet are to consider defence questions and to report to the Cabinet upon major matters of policy relating to the maintenance and employment of the three services. The Defence Committee also deals with matters referred to it by the Cabinet or Treasury Board or business which may be put before it by the Minister or the Chiefs of Staff Committee. On questions of major policy it makes a report to the cabinet for its action. On less important matters it gives directions which are carried out by the authority of the Minister. While its main function is to deal with matters of defence planning, it may deal with matters of defence administration which involve major questions of policy or concern other departments.

It may be noted that the Defence Committee of the Cabinet of the United Kingdom was set up in February 1947 and consists of the Prime Minister who acts as chairman, the Minister of Defence, who replaces the Prime Minister as chairman, the Foreign Secretary, the three service ministers, the Minister of Supply, the Minister of Labour and the Lord President of the Council who has extensive functions with regard to research.

CIVIL ADMINISTRATION

The administration of the Department of National Defence is under the direction of the Deputy Minister as its permanent head responsible to the Minister. There are two associate deputy ministers; one deals particularly with finance and supply, the other has to do with personnel and pay questions. Under them matters are further sub-divided with three assistant deputy ministers respectively responsible for civil administration of properties, stores and equipment, and personnel.

Instead of three departments and three sets of civilians providing certain services for the Navy, Army and Air Force, the aim is now to have a single civilian service. As far as possible, clerical and similar functions at headquarters at Ottawa and elsewhere are performed by civilians so as to:

(1) achieve greater economy;
(2) perform common functions for all three services for example, security guards at headquarters; and
(3) permit the highest possible proportion of the men in our armed forces to be actually engaged on military work.

SINGLE DEFENCE HEADQUARTERS

As a first step in amalgamating the three departments and co-ordinating the three services, a single National Defence Headquarters has been established. The Navy, Army and Air Force have been organized so that all their activities are channeled in three main divisions:

(1) planning, intelligence, training and operations, corresponding to the General Staff or G branch of the Army;
(2) personnel and pay, corresponding to the Adjutant General's or "A" branch in the Army; and
(3) supply and equipment corresponding to the branches of the Quartermaster-General and Master General of the Ordnance in the Army, which have been combined.

The officers and staffs of the Navy, Army and Air Force dealing with these three sets of matters are headed up in three inter-service committees:

The Chiefs of Staff Committee,
The Personnel Members Committee, and
The Principal Supply Officers Committee.

This arrangement of functions extends to physical location. National Defence Headquarters at Ottawa is now contained in a single group of three buildings all on Cartier Square. The first of these, the old Naval Building (now A building) contains the Minister, Deputy Ministers, Chiefs of Staff, and all the personnel directly related to policy-making, planning, intelligence, training and operations, as well as the Chairman of the Defence Research Board.

In the old Air Force Building (now "B" building) on Lisgar Street are the people dealing with personnel and pay matters.

In the old Army annex on Cartier Square (now "C" building) are the personnel dealing with supply and equipment matters for all three services.

In this way the officers and departmental officials having to do with the same matters in each of the services now work alongside each other in the same buildings. The three buildings are adjacent and connected by passageways.

CHIEFS OF STAFF COMMITTEE

Planning and training, as well as the overall supervision of each service, is carried out by the Chief of Staff of each service and by the Chairman of the Defence Research Board. These four constitute the Chiefs of Staff Committee, which meets regularly to discuss matters of common interest and major importance. The Under Secretary of State for External Affairs and the Secretary to the Cabinet attend when matters of general interest are under consideration. Periodically, the Chiefs of Staff Committee gives the Defence Committee and Minister a joint report appreciating the military situation.

In the United Kingdom, the United States and Australia, there are similar Chiefs of Staff Committees, though in these countries the official in charge of research is not a member of the Chiefs of Staff Committee as he is in Canada.

PERSONNEL MEMBERS COMMITTEE

Corresponding to the Chiefs of Staff Committee as regards matters of personnel, medical services, pay, pensions and the like, is the Personnel Members Committee, consisting of the Member for Personnel for the Navy, the Adjutant General of the Army, the Air Member for Personnel of the Air Force and a representative of Defence Research. Insofar as it does not interfere with the efficiency of the service, the aim is to ensure that personnel in the Navy, Army and Air Force are governed by the same regulations, receive the same pay, pensions, allowances and rations and wear the same clothing except for the distinctive uniform of their service.

PRINCIPAL SUPPLY OFFICERS' COMMITTEE

The Principal Supply Officers' Committee was recently created to complete the pattern of top level joint service committees. This committee deals with matters of supply and equipment in the same way as the Personnel Members Committee deals with personnel and pay.

In both the Personnel Members Committee and the Principal Supply Officers' Committee the chairmanship rotates among the services. The appropriate associate deputy minister attends meetings.

THE PROBLEM OF COMBINED FUNCTIONS

In order to avoid duplication and ensure the greatest possible amount of co-ordination of the three services, an Inter-service Combined Functions Committee was set up some time ago and more than thirty different activities of the armed services have been subjected to an intense examination.

In the result, fourteen of these have been amalgamated so that where there was a separate group of people engaged in doing the same thing in each of the three services, what is now necessary is done by one service for all three.

Where it is desirable to have a single agency perform an activity which is common to all services, difficult administrative problems arise which have not yet been satisfactorily solved in any country. These problems include such questions as:

Will the activity be carried on by the Navy, Army or Air Force for the other two services and if so by which; or will it be carried on by a central or "neutral" service?

In the latter event, will it report to one of the inter-service committees such as the Principal Supply Officers' Committee? If not, to whom?

This kind of problem and the need for the closest possible co-ordination of the services has led to the suggestion that there should be a single Chief of Staff to direct the operations of all the defence forces in the same way that allied commanders in the various major theatres of war had charge of all operations. Having a single Chief of Staff might seem to solve the problem of responsibility for combined or common functions, but the advantage of having a single Chief of Staff for planning purposes would be largely lost if he became directly responsible for a large mass of administration. But differences between peacetime and wartime conditions taken together with differences in the roles of the Chief of Staff and the Commander in the field have so far led every country in its postwar organization to have separate chiefs for each service. The problem of combined or common functions might be met if the Navy, Army and Air Force were amalgamated into a single service. Combining the services has the obvious appeal of mathematical simplicity, but while it might solve some problems, it would create many new ones, besides destroying much that is valuable in the way of tradition and long-established administrative practices. It is noteworthy that complete amalgamation has not been adopted in any country.

It is believed that in Canada, however, we have already made greater progress in co-ordination than elsewhere.

Already, largely in the last six months, the following branches or functions have been amalgamated or combined under a single service head:

Dental services
Hollerith machine record (Personnel)
Printing and stationery
Mechanical transport
Blueprinting
Identification bureaus
Libraries (Ottawa only)
Public relations
Firefighting
Provost
Photostat
Communications (partial)
Food and fuel (partial)
Stores and equipment (partial)

As examples of additional inter-service activities carried on in combination, the following may be mentioned:

School of cooking
Fire protection service
Ammunition storage facilities
Film bureaus

In addition to the subjects which have been dealt with by amalgamation, some ten other subjects have been dealt with by consolidation so that there is no longer any duplication. These are the following:

Photography
Film storage
Survey — maps and charts
Communications (partial)
Training
Libraries (partial)
Water transport
Properties, building construction and maintenance
Chaplain services
Recruiting

So far it has not been considered desirable to amalgamate these services under a single head. In some cases it is desirable to have a separate branch in each service so that each will always have the organization and the administrative experience to expand to fill an essential need of each separate service in the event of emergency.

Regarding the other branches, it has been decided that a change was not desirable for military reasons or that no economy would be effected by making a change. Branches falling within these classes were:

Area unit commander
Hollerith machine records (equipment)
Intelligence
Design and development of stores and equipment
Armament and ammunition
Pay

The whole matter will be subjected to continuous review.

In connection with medical services, duplication of effort has largely been eliminated. For example, the Navy at Esquimalt and Halifax furnishes medical services and hospitalization to all three services. Medical services are supplied for all personnel by the Army at Vancouver, Calgary, Rivers, Shilo, Winnipeg, Borden, Toronto, London, Kingston, Quebec, and Valcartier and by the Air Force at Edmonton, Trenton and Rockcliffe. There is one central medical stores for the three services. The armed forces have turned over to Veterans Affairs 22 hospitals and arrangements are in effect whereby personnel of the armed forces can be hospitalized at Veterans Affairs or civilian hospitals under service, Veterans Affairs or civilian doctors. Arrangements are being extended whereby service doctors work in Veterans Affairs and civilian hospitals so as to pool resources and develop professional skills.

ORGANIZATION OF COMMANDS

In the Navy there are two major commands exercised out of Ottawa, one on the Atlantic Coast and the other on the Pacific Coast. Canadian naval vessels and personnel are evenly divided between the two coasts.

In the Army legislation enacted this year permitted the eleven military districts, dating back to before Confederation, being changed into an organization of five commands with headquarters at Halifax, Montreal, Oakville, Winnipeg and Edmonton, and additional area headquarters located at Fredericton, Quebec, Kingston, London, Regina and Vancouver.

The Air Force is organized into three commands: Central Command with headquarters at Trenton, Western with headquarters at Edmonton, and Maintenance with headquarters at Ottawa.

In order to effect maximum decentralization, officers commanding commands have been given more authority than before. In locating the commands consideration has been given to the needs of training and, if necessary, operations. Such matters will, of course, be under continuous review.

TRAINING OF OFFICERS

The young officers of today will be the leaders, the staff officers, the training cadre in any future war. The last war threw greater emphasis than ever before on the qualifications and training of officers. If there is another war, new weapons and the quickened pace of events will call for even greater qualities of imagination and adaptability as well as knowledge of military science in addition to capacity for leadership. We regard the training of officers as of primary importance. The role of the officers in modern war can only be properly discharged if they have education and standing in the community comparable to that of any of the professions as well as high qualities of character and physique.

The Royal Military College was changed from a cadet college to a staff college in 1940. At that time the need was for a large number of officers trained to meet the urgent demands of war. It was not possible to devote three years to that process, and totally different methods and a totally different curriculum were applied. Special cadet colleges were established at Brockville, Ontario, at Gordon Head, B.C., and at St. Jerome, P.Q. R.M.C. became a centre for courses for company officers, senior and junior staff officers and civil affairs administration.

Since the end of the war we have been looking into the question whether Royal Military College should be reopened and, if so, upon what basis. A committee was set up under the chairmanship of Brigadier Lett and a report was made. The present plan is that beginning in September 1947, Royal Roads will operate as a joint cadet college for the Royal Canadian Navy and Royal Canadian Air Force with a two-year course. In September 1948, Royal Roads may be extended to include army cadets as well and R.M.C. will be reopened as a cadet college on a tri-service basis with a four-year course.

In this way officer cadets of the three services will be trained together and achieve much the same educational standards which will be the highest possible. Senior matriculation or the equivalent will be required for entrance, and the curriculum will be designed so that year by year the course will be equivalent to that of the Canadian universities.

The second source of officers will be the universities. The Canadian Officers' Training Corps, the University Naval Training Divisions, and the Air Force University Summer Training Scheme will during their four year courses at the Universities take additional academic work during the college year and during each of their summer vacations do about sixteen weeks of practical work at good rates of pay. Twenty-two universities in Canada have co-operated in making arrangements under which we will in this way develop a large group of highly qualified, well educated officers who at the end of their university courses will have had additional military academic subjects and the equivalent of a year's practical work in their arm of the services. Already there are 2,700 officer candidates at the universities under these plans.

Finally, there is the third means of becoming an officer, through the lower decks or from the ranks. Plans are in preparation whereby other ranks showing the required educational qualifications and capacity for leadership will be given facilities whereby they maybe fitted into one of these plans and also given opportunities of securing in the service the required educational standing.

STAFF TRAINING

Beginning in 1948 there will be a National Defence College at Kingston where senior officers of the three services and civilian members of other government departments will receive intensive instruction in strategy, liaison and co-ordination of defence operations at the higher level. Instruction will include research needs and economic and industrial organization as well as military matters.

The three services will continue to have staff and corps courses at various levels with greater emphasis on combined operations. For example, the Air Staff College at Toronto is regularly attended by Navy and Army officers.

DEFENCE PLANNING AND DEFENCE STRATEGY

This paper deals primarily with defence needs and defence organization rather than with defence planning and strategy. The subjects of planning and strategy are subject to continuous review so as to determine the proper balance between the services and within the branches of each service so to enable us to use to best advantage the resources of our country to meet the needs as they may develop in the years ahead.

INTELLIGENCE

Intelligence activities common to the three services are being undertaken by the Joint Intelligence Bureau, which reports to the Joint Intelligence Committee, a sub-committee of the Chiefs of Staff Committee.

STRENGTH

The strength of the three services (1) before the war, (2) for which recruits are sought today, and (3) as at present, are set out in the table below:

	1939	Strength Required Now	Actual Strength
Navy	1,769	7,500	6,821
Army	4,492	18,750	13,985
Air Force	2,948	12,150	11,804
Totals	9,209	38,400	32,610

In addition there are 1990 men in the three services in the interim force or enlisted for the period of hostilities, most of whom will cease to be on strength on or before September 30,1947. About 6,000 men are needed to bring the three services to the strengths required.

In the three services the force at present envisaged will for the time being be largely concerned with training, planning, staff work, care of materials, training the reserve, etc., rather than in providing immediate operational forces, though small forces of the latter type will be organized and trained.

ESTIMATES

Reference has been made above to the appropriation for 1947-48, totalling approximately $240 millions. For purpose of comparison, this may be broken down as follows:

	In Millions
Navy	$ 47
Army	$ 80
Air Force	$ 60
Defence Research	$ 13
Alaska Highway, Northwest Staging Route, etc.	$ 15
Demobilization and reconversion	$ 25
Total	$ 240

This total may be compared to the expenditures made before the war.

Of the sums mentioned $22 millions is specially ear-marked for reserve training in the three services as compared with $ 4,215,338 in 1938-39. In addition a very considerable proportion of all expenditures on the three services have directly or indirectly to do with training reserve forces.

Nearly $3 millions is specially ear-marked for cadet training as compared with $139,500 in 1938-39, more than twenty times as much.

PAY, ALLOWANCES AND PENSIONS

As pointed out above, pay, allowances and pensions of all three services were completely revised in 1946 and put on an identical basis for equivalent ranks. At that time the aim was to give officers and men of the armed forces rates of pay which when taken in conjunction with the provision of quarters, fuel, food, clothing, dental, medical and hospital services, pensions, etc. would put them on a basis where they compared favourably with men in civilian occupations.

The rates of pay and allowances are as follows:

Table of Pay and Allowances: Monthly Rates

| Rank or Rating | | | | | | | Marriage Allowance | |
Navy	Army	Air Force	Basic Rates	After 3 yrs in Rank	After 6 yrs in Rank	S.A. (not prov with Q's and R's)	Not in Married Quarter	In Married Quarter
ordinary rating on entry	private on entry	aircraftman 2nd class on entry	50.00	...	...	45.00	20.00	10.00
ordinary rating	private (trained)	aircraftman 1st class	54.00	...	...	45.00	20.00	10.00
able rating	private 1st class	leading aircraftman	61.00	64.00	67.00	45.00	20.00	10.00
leading rating	corporal	corporal	70.00	73.00	76.00	45.00	20.00	10.00
petty officer	sergeant	sergeant	83.00	88.00	93.00	50.00	20.00	10.00
chief petty officer	staff sergeant	flight sergeant	98.00	103.00	108.00	55.00	20.00	10.00
chief petty officer (artisan)	warrant officer 2	warrant officer 2	113.00	118.00	123.00	55.00	20.00	10.00
chief petty officer (technician)	warrant officer 1	warrant officer 1	128.00	133.00	138.00	60.00	20.00	10.00

Table of Pay and Allowances: Monthly Rates

Rank or Rating							Marriage Allowance	
Navy	Army	Air Force	Basic Rates	After 3 yrs in Rank	After 6 yrs in Rank	S.A. (not prov with Q's and R's)	Not in Married Quarter	In Married Quarter
midshipman (naval service only)			75.00	...	...	45.00	...	...
acting sub-lieutenant	second lieutenant	pilot officer	135.00	...	...	45.00	30.00	20.00
sub-lieutenant	lieutenant	flying officer	160.00	175.00	190.00	60.00	30.00	20.00
warrant officer (naval service only)			175.00	190.00	205.00	60.00	30.00	20.00
officers in all services commissioned from warrant rank			180.00	195.00	210.00	60.00	30.00	20.00
lieutenant	captain	flight lieutenant	190.00	205.00	220.00	60.00	30.00	20.00
lieutenant commander	major	squadron leader	255.00	270.00	285.00	70.00	30.00	20.00
captain	colonel	group captain	420.00	455.00	490.00	80.00	30.00	20.00
commodore	brigadier	air commodore	560.00	...	...	80.00	30.00	20.00
rear admiral	major general	air vice marshall	640.00	...	...	80.00	30.00	20.00
vice admiral	lieutenant general	air marshal	725.00	...	...	80.00	30.00	20.00

The pension arrangement for the regular forces provided for by Parliament in 1946 and in effect today is the same for both officers and other ranks. If an officer or man is retired or discharged compulsorily for any reason other than his own misconduct, a pension is payable to him if he has served in the regular forces for a minimum of ten years provided that he served on active service in the last war and joins the forces prior to 31st December 1948 or becomes medically unfit. Otherwise he receives only a retiring allowance equal to two thirds of the pension which would otherwise have been payable unless he has had twenty years' service. The amount of the pension is one-fiftieth of the average annual pay and allowances received by the pensioner during the last six years of his service multiplied by the number of years he has served. Time served on active service, in the civil service and in the Royal Canadian Mounted Police and one-quarter of any time served in the reserve forces may be counted in computing the amount of the pension but not for determining eligibility for pension. Members of the forces are required to contribute annualy 5, 5½ or 6% of their pay and allowances, depending on their rate of pay, as a contribution toward their pension.

On the death of a pensioner or of an officer or man who, if compulsorily retired or discharged would have been entitled to a pension, one-half of the pension paid or payable to him may be paid to his widow for the remainder of her life together with allowances for his dependent children. If an officer or man is retired or discharged or dies without having had sufficient service to entitle him to a pension, he or his widow or dependent children may be paid a gratuity equal to one month's pay and allowances for each year's service. If an officer or man retires voluntarily or dies without leaving a widow or dependent children no pension is payable but all pension contributions are returned to him or his estate.

RESERVE TRAINING

After the last war the reserves were in poor condition. For the year ended March 31, 1921, the sum of $1,160,000 was all that was provided for reserve training for the army where the corresponding figure today is $13 millions. There was no equipment, there was very little training, there were few officers, non-commissioned officers or men. Following this war steps were taken to avoid that happening. The importance of the reserve has been shown in two wars and we should now take them for what they are — probably the most important part of the armed forces of Canada. Differentiations between the active and the reserve forces are to be wiped out.

This year we have concentrated on the organization of units, with the appointment of officers and N.C.O.s and a nucleus of men. New syllabuses and new methods of training developed during the war are provided, and every unit has full-time administrative and training personnel. This is an experiment being worked out in close co-operation with the reserve units themselves. Units are provided with modern equipment and stores on an adequate scale. In certain parts of the country reserve units feel that the progress made has not been sufficiently rapid. To them the answer may be made that only in the case of a few units have any ceilings on numbers or size proved limiting factors. Progress has been far ahead of what might be expected in less than two years after the war, immeasurably ahead of the last war. Towards the end of the summer we aim to have a campaign to assist active forces and reserve units in attaining the presently authorized strength. The challenge to reserve units is that they should be in a position by then to give useful training to the men who it is hoped and expected will be willing to serve.

The number in the reserve force of the Army at June 15, 1947, was 33,704 men (an additional 1,418 men were in the Canadian Officers' Training Corps, which does not form part of the reserve properly so-called). For those on the establishment, training is provided this year for thirty days; and in addition 10,000 are to receive fourteen days' training at summer camps. Provision is also made to give 15,000 tradesmen and specialists fifteen days' additional training at local headquarters. More training is provided for this year than ever before in peacetime.

In the Western Command a civilian committee has been set up for each reserve unit charged with the function of supporting that unit in every way possible. In the great majority of cases these civilian committees are doing useful work in support of the reserve units. We hope that the same procedure will be applied in other commands across Canada.

Arrangements for even more extended training for Naval Reserves and Air Force Auxiliaries are being provided.

To encourage participation in the reserve forces the government passed an Order-in-Council, P.C. 12/728 of July 10, 1947, providing for leave

for civil servants to undergo reserve training and it is confidently expected that other employers will make the same provision.

With the object of putting the three cadet services on a comparable
basis which would enable them to do useful work and which should lead
to the association of former cadets with the active and reserve forces, the
age limits and conditions of service for the sea cadets, army cadets and
air cadets were brought more into line. Generally speaking, the Department pays grants for training in respect of cadets in authorized corps
between the ages of 14 and 18. In Britain the age for entry into service
cadet-forces is fifteen years. Training officers and equipment are supplied, there is free transportation to camp and assistance is provided in
furnishing uniforms and bands. The numbers of cadets planned for this
year are 10,000 Sea Cadets, 50,000 Army Cadets, and 15,000 Air Cadets,
which is approximately the number of senior cadets active in these three
services today and far exceeds the number of active senior cadets before
the war. Expenditure on cadets, provided for this year of nearly $3 mil-
lions, is twenty times as great as in 1938-39.

DEFENCE RESEARCH

The Department of National Defence Act (R.S.C. 1927, c. 136) was
amended on April 1, 1947, to provide for the establishment of a Defence
Research Board as a permanent part of the department. The Board consists of five ex-officio members who are the Chiefs of Staff of the three services, the President of the National Research Council and the Deputy Minister
of National Defence. The appointed members are Professor C.H. Best of
the University of Toronto; Professor Paul Gagnon of Laval University;
Colonel R. D. Harkness of the Northern Electric Company; Professor
J.H.L. Johnstone of Dalhousie University; Professor Otto Maass of McGill
University and Professor G.M. Shrum of the University of British Columbia.

Under the guidance of this board, good progress has been made in
setting up a permanent organization for defence research. This organization is already beginning to take its place as an essential part of the defence of Canada. Defence research has been set up in Canada as a fourth
service.

The organization under the Defence Research Board will consist of
a headquarters staff, advisory committees and research establishments.

The ultimate aim of the whole organization will be to make available to the armed forces of Canada the scientific resources of Canada and of other countries. The headquarters staff will be the main link with the armed forces, getting from them their research requirements and conveying to them the latest results of scientific research. The advisory committees will serve to make available to the armed forces the best scientific advice that is available in government, university and industrial research laboratories. These committees will also help to keep the whole scientific community of the country in touch with the problems of defence to facilitate rapid mobilization in time of need.

In order to avoid any unnecessary duplication of research facilities, the research stations of the Board will deal only with those problems of the armed forces which have little or no civilian interest. In other fields, such as electronics and aeronautics, it will make use of existing research laboratories, especially those of the National Research Council.

In all its work, the Board will give priority to problems in which Canada has some special interests or for which our facilities are specially suited. Experience has already shown that well-directed defence research produces many results that are of value, both direct and indirect, to the civilian economy.

In planning this organization, the government has had in mind the vital need for continuity in research. This new organization is not a temporary addition to our armed forces. It is a fully integrated and permanent part of the defences of the country. It must be staffed and equipped to take a long term view of the scientific requirements of defence, and it must continue in being as long as there is a need for defence forces. Further, to ensure that research receives adequate consideration of the highest level, the Chairman of the Defence Research Board has been given the status of a Chief of Staff, is a member of the Chiefs of Staff Committee and Defence Council and attends meetings of the Defence Committee of the Cabinet.

INDUSTRIAL ORGANIZATION

Canada's record of production in the last war amazed the world, but those who were responsible for it would be the first to say that much more could have been done in less time had adequate plans been laid in advance.

Seventy per cent of everything we made during the war went into the pool of allied supplies. What we did was to make more of the things we could make best and exchange these for the things which other nations could make more economically or more quickly than we could. Consequently we did not make all our own arms. Much of our equipment was of British design while industrial practice and standards were North American. For this reason Canada has a special stake in standardization of arms and equipment.

Industrial organization includes planning for the development of common standards and designs, the organization of industrial development and research, the maintenance of industrial skills, and improvement in the techniques of procurement purchasing and inspection.

Following our wartime experience, defence purchasing has been put in the hands of the Canadian Commercial Corporation, staffed largely by men who gained unequalled experience in the Department of Munitions and Supply, later Reconstruction and Supply.

Canadian Arsenals Limited, a crown company, will be responsible for the production of certain types of munitions, but in addition will have important functions in connection with development and industrial organization.

Inspection, standardization and industrial organization are various aspects of the same problem of production, and all these are being worked on now on the basis of our war-won experience and in close co-operation with industrial leaders. We are in process of setting up a committee to advise the Minister and the Defence Committee of the Cabinet on matters of industrial organization. It is expected that this committee will include representatives of:

(1) the manufacturers who made munitions during the war;
(2) Canadian Arsenals Limited;
(3) Canadian Commercial Corporation;
(4) the Department of Trade and Commerce;
(5) Principal Supply Officers of the services;
(6) Defence Research.

In this way we shall be able to bring together all the forces which worked so well during the war and which it is necessary to have working together in peace.

There will be the maximum use of stocks of munitions accumulated during the war with a gradual introduction of equipment of the most modern kind. For the first time in peacetime, Canada has very considerable stores of weapons and these will not be disposed of until they can be replaced with new weapons of proven utility.

PART III

Co-operation with Other Nations

The first aim of Canadian policy is to prevent war. The Canadian Parliament and our representatives at international conferences have repeatedly affirmed our support of the United Nations as a means to this end. Moreover, to an extent not excelled by any nation in proportion to resources and population, Canada has demonstrated our determination to assist in creating the positive conditions for peace.

Canada's co-operative arrangements with other nations must be interpreted against the background of our membership in the United Nations.

These arrangements include that with the United States as stated in the Declaration of our Prime Minister and the President on February 12, 1947. The Prime Minister read the Joint Declaration in the House of Commons. The Declaration follows:

> I wish to make a statement on defence co-operation with the United States. This statement is also being made today by the government of the United States. It is regarding the results of discussions which have taken place in the Permament Joint Board on Defence on the extent to which the wartime co-operation between the armed forces of the two countries should be maintained in this post-war period. In the interests of efficiency and economy, each government has decided that its national defence establishment shall, to the extent authorized by law, continue to collaborate for peacetime joint security purposes. The collaboration will necessarily be limited and will be based on the following principles:
>
> (1) Interchange of selected individuals so as to increase the familiarity of each country's defence establishment with that of the other country.

(2) General co-operation and exchange of observers in connection with exercises and with the development and tests of material of common interest.

(3) Encouragement of common designs and standards in arms, equipment, organization, methods of training and new developments. As certain United Kingdom standards have long been in use in Canada, no radical change is contemplated or practicable and the application of this principle will be gradual.

(4) Mutual and reciprocal availability of military, naval and air facilities in each country; this principle to be applied as may be agreed in specific instances. Reciprocally each country will continue to provide with a minimum of formality, for the transit through its territory and territorial waters of military air craft and public vessels of the other country.

(5) As an underlying principle all co-operative arrangements will be without impairment of the control of either country over all activities in its territory.

While in this, as in many other matters of mutual concern, there is an identity of view and interest between the two countries, the decision of each has been taken independently in continuation of the practice developed since the establishment of the Permanent Joint Board on Defence in 1940. No treaty, executive agreement or contractual obligation has been entered into. Each country will determine the extent of its practical collaboration in respect of each and all of the foregoing principles. Either country may at any time discontinue collaboration on any or all of them. Neither country will take any action inconsistent with the Charter of the United Nations. The Charter remains the cornerstone of the foreign policy of each.

An important element in the decision of each government to authorize continued collaboration was the conviction on the part of each that in this way their obligations under the Charter of the United Nations for the maintenance of international peace and security could be fulfilled more effectively. Both governments believe that this decision is a contribution to the stability of the world and to the establishment through the United Nations of an effective system of world wide security. With this in mind each government has sent a copy of this statement to the Secretary General of the United Nations for circulation to all its members.

In August, 1940, when the creation of the Board was jointly announced by the late President Roosevelt and by myself as Prime Minister of Canada, it was stated that the Board shall commence immediate studies relating to sea, land and air problems including personnel and material. It will consider in the broad sense the defence of the north half of the western hemisphere. In discharging this continuing responsibility the Board's work led to the building up of a pattern of close defence co-operation. The principles announced today are in continuance of this co-operation. It has been the task of the governments to assure that the close security relationship between Canada and the United States in North America will in no way impair but on the contrary will strengthen the co-operation of each country within the broader framework of the United Nations.

In addition to reading the Declaration the Prime Minister made the following comments:

Co-operation between Canada and the United States in matters of defence has become increasingly effective in recent years. Among the first public statements to be made by the head of either government was the speech of the late President Roosevelt at Kingston, Ontario in 1938 when he said, 'The Dominion of Canada is part of the sisterhood of the British Empire. I give to you assurance that the people of the United States will not stand idly by if domination of Canadian soil is threatened by any other empire'. Two days later at Woodbridge, Ontario, as Prime Minister of Canada I replied, 'We, too, have our obligations as a good friendly neighbour, and one of these is to see that, at our own instance, our country is made as immune from attack or possible invasion as we can reasonably be expected to make it, and that, should the occasion ever arise, enemy forces should not be able to pursue their way, either by land, sea or air, to the United States across Canadian territory'.

It was two years later, in August 1940, that the Permanent Joint Board on Defence was created and it has met regularly ever since to discuss common problems and to make recommendations to the governments which created it. The statement made today emphasizes the desirability of continuing the co-operation between Canada and the United States in matters of defence which has developed through the years.

As the joint statement points out, the Charter of the United Nations is the cornerstone of the foreign policy of both governments. Certainly, the Canadian Government holds that its obligations to the United Nations are of overriding importance. In time, it is to be hoped that there will emerge — apart altogether from reduction and limitation of arms and elimination of weapons of mass destruction — a system of international security which will be adequate to preserve the peace of the world. The ultimate objective is not joint or regional defence, but collective international defence as the guarantee of national security.

It must be recognized, however, that much progress has still to be made before a system of international security becomes effective. Each nation must therefore consider what steps it should take in the meantime to defend itself against aggression, while bearing constantly in mind that these steps should contribute to the development of general security in accordance with the Charter of the United Nations. I should like to make it entirely clear that, so far as the Canadian government is concerned, and I am sure the United States government also, defence co-operation between Canada and the United States is intended to support and strengthen the United Nations.

It will be noted that the principles of co-operation I announced in the joint statement parallel closely the procedures which have long been applied between the nations of the British Commonwealth. Without formal agreements between governments, we have had working arrangements with the United Kingdom and other Commonwealth countries for the interchange of personnel, the exchange of observers, and so forth. The similar arrangements envisaged between Canada and the United States in no way interfere with or replace our Commonwealth connections in matters of defence training and organization. Given the geographical position of Canada, it is important that measures of co-operation should be undertaken both with the United States and the United Kingdom.

In conclusion, I should like to comment briefly on problems of northern defence. The subject has naturally engaged the attention of many people both here and abroad and some quite unfounded suggestions have been put forward. There is a persistent rumour, for example, that the United States government has asked for bases in the Canadian north. This is a rumour which I should like to deny emphatically. There has been talk of Maginot lines, of large scale defence projects, all of which is unwarranted and much of it fantastic. What we are trying to do is to view the situation soberly, realistically, and undramatically.

It is apparent to anyone who has reflected even casually on the technological advances of recent years that new geographic factors have been brought into play. The polar regions assume new importance as the shortest routes between North America and the principal centres of population of the world. In consequence, we must think and learn more about those regions. When we think of the defence of Canada, we must, in addition to looking east and west as in the past, take the north into consideration as well. Our defence forces must, of course, have experience of conditions in these regions, but it is clear that most of the things that should be done are required apart altogether from considerations of defence. We must know more about such fundamental facts as topography and weather. We must improve facilities for flying. We must develop better means of communication. The general economic development of the north will be greatly aided by tests and projects carried out by both civilian and defence services. As the government views it, our primary objective should be to expand our knowledge of the north and of the conditions necessary for life and work there with the object of developing its resources.

Canada's northern programme is thus primarily a civilian one to which contributions are made by the armed forces. This has been the pattern for many years. Thus the army years ago installed and has continued to maintain communication systems in the Northwest Territories. It is now responsible for administering the Alaska highway, now known as the Northwest Highway System, extending from Dawson Creek to the Alaska boundary. The R.C.A.F. has been responsible for taking aerial photographs to be used in the production of maps and charts. It has also been given the responsibility of administering the airfields of the northwest staging route from Edmonton north which are used for civil aviation. More recently, a small winter experimental establishment was set up at Churchill where various tests on clothing, equipment, transport, and so on, are being conducted which will be of general benefit to all who live in the north. Since the United States, as well as Canada, recognizes the need for greater familiarity with northern conditions, we have arranged for its government to participate in the work of this establishment. It may be that other tests and projects will require to be undertaken on a joint basis, in order to extend with a maximum of economy and effectiveness our knowledge of the north. Through such extension we will acquire the basic data that are needed to make more accessible the economic resources of this region and which will be more valuable for defence purposes as well.

LIAISON

In addition to the Permanent Joint Board on Defence, Canada maintains at London Joint Liaison Officers and at Washington a Joint Staff Mission representing the three services as well as Defence Research.

Pursuant to these arrangements there is an exchange of a limited number of personnel at staff and other courses as well as participation in a number of research, testing and other activities to our mutual advantage.

PURPOSE OF ORGANIZATION

This completes a summary description of the organization of the defence forces of Canada. It is believed that it is a primary importance to complete this work of organization so as to secure the utmost value for the defence dollar, provide a sound basis on which to carry on the work of the post-war forces and be the foundation for rapid expansion if that should prove necessary.

The object of this organization is to facilitate the planning, equipping, and training of Canada's armed forces to meet any need that may arise.

Defence has become a matter of major national importance. The present paper is put forward as a step towards that informed public opinion which must be the basis of all democratic action.

Introduction to
White Paper on Defence: 1964

Paul Hellyer was without doubt the most controversial minister of national defence in the post-Second World War era. His generally unpopular concept of unification would have been enough to mark him as a radical minister, but there were other ideas and aspects to his term in office that attracted attention and criticism. Hellyer was an unusual Canadian defence minister simply because he decided to direct the armed forces and to preside over the Department of National Defence. Canadians and armed forces officers were accustomed to ministers, with the exception of Brooke Claxton, who followed the status quo and rarely made decisions without lengthy consultation.

Initially, Prime Minister Lester Pearson's appointment of Hellyer as defence minister satisfied most senior officers and officials. Hellyer had been the shadow defence minister in opposition and was known to be alert to the main issues facing the armed forces. What was not well understood was that he came to the portfolio with certain instructions from the prime minister and with his own ideas about his role as minister and about defence policy and administration.

Defence policy in the early 1960s was shaped by two related events. The 1962 Cuban Missile Crisis revealed a defence establishment barely under the control of the government. It was instead sharply focused on alliance duties and largely responsive to allied commanders. When at the height of the crisis Prime Minister Diefenbaker tried to exercise control over the armed forces, he found that the central administration in Ottawa had no national plans, no intelligence capabilities, and no reliable structure for commanding and controlling the forces. That this situation was mainly the result of governments neglecting their duty to control the armed forces and to build instruments for that purpose was beside the point. In the aftermath of the Cuban Missile Crisis it was the government and not the armed forces that appeared inept.

Later the stumbling performance and inconsistency of the Diefenbaker Cabinet over nuclear weapons policy and the related decisions to acquire, but not arm, the Bomarc missile broke cabinet solidarity and further sullied the reputation of the government. To the surprise of many observers and politicians, confusion in the Cabinet over defence policy played a major part in destroying the once popular Diefenbaker regime. When Pearson won the election in 1963, he was determined that the same fate would not befall his administration. He, therefore, selected the tough-minded and ambitious Paul Hellyer to take charge of the defence establishment to make sure that what had happened to the Diefenbaker government would not happen to the Liberals. Pearson also instructed Hellyer to reduce defence expenditures quickly but quietly.

Paul Hellyer was up to the task. He believed that he was as ready as any politician had ever been to take charge of the defence portfolio. He arrived at the department with some ideas already fixed in his mind. He was determined to make a strong first impression on senior officers and officials and he did so by refusing to sign any document in his first thirty days in office. He immediately demanded a comprehensive review of defence policy and administration, rejecting recently completed internal studies such as the navy's detailed "Brock Report."[1] Hellyer suspended equipment purchases pending a defence review and cancelled outright

---

[1] *The Report of the Ad Hoc Committee on Naval Objectives,* July 1961. Department of National Defence, Directorate of History, File 81/481.

the air force's CF104 aircraft replacement program. He then revamped the Defence Council to provide what he called an internal cabinet for defence decision making. These actions, mostly unnoticed outside the defence establishment, set the stage for Hellyer's 1964 white paper on defence.

White Paper on Defence is a landmark defence document for two reasons. First, it was an attempt to build a defence policy on a Canadian foundation. While Hellyer did not reject the alliance bias underlying Canadian policy and the structure of the armed services, he insisted that the commitments that flow from the alliance be met more efficiently by constructing a strategy from a Canadian perspective. Logically, according to Hellyer, defence structure, especially as it concerned the armed services, should follow strategy. Thus the reorganization of the defence structure at the armed services and departmental levels became Hellyer's second important innovation and his most controversial decision.

Hellyer introduced his white paper on defence by reviewing what many see as the inevitable strategy for Canada, even in 1997. Defence and security "lay in collective arrangements." This notion allowed for "four parallel methods" for achieving national defence: "collective measures" as embodied in the UN; "collective defence," meaning essentially NATO; "partnership" with the United States for North American defence; and "national measures" for domestic defence. Canadian defence policy in effect became after 1949 a series of "contributions" that prompted the development of a disjointed defence establishment centred on three services each with a small operational component. Furthermore, these commitments demanded continuous activity, a move away from traditional concepts of mobilization to forces-in-being. In Hellyer's words, "a transference from credit to cash." As the services became more specialized to meet their discrete missions, they also became distant from each other, and actual defence policy became segmented and inflexible.

The world view that supported *Defence 64* was essentially pessimistic. Although nuclear war was thought to be "irrational and ... therefore, improbable," the government expected the communist countries "to continue to promote expansionist aims by measures short of all-out war." Canada, if it wished to continue to contribute to and benefit from "collective arrangements," required adequate military forces.

At this point, Hellyer introduced the idea of "a range of conflict." The idea, which according to some originated with General Jean Allard and his army staff, proposed that conflict could occur anywhere along a spectrum of warfare from nuclear exchanges to simple police actions. The policy trick was to guess which point or band on the spectrum represented the most likely future occurrence. But this was more than a parlour game because where the finger pointed had significant consequences for service programs, perhaps for their very survival.

Hellyer's argument moved from this background to strategies more or less in keeping with extant policies. He joined those who in the United States and elsewhere questioned the logic of a strategy of "massive retaliation" and opted for a strategy of "graduated defence." This strategy, when combined with the need for flexible forces to meet challenges anywhere along the range of conflict, caused Hellyer to conclude Canada's force structure must be constructed "to build in maximum flexibility." Moreover, because the armed forces would have to be ready to fight small "brush-fire wars" and because they would be versatile, it would be possible to deploy "the majority of our forces in Canada where they will be available for deployment in a variety of peacekeeping activities." This conclusion, placed in the section of the paper dealing with NATO, suggested strongly that Canada was about to radically change the disposition and capabilities of its armed forces to produce a mobile capability ready to respond quickly to new commitments. This strategy, of course, could not be accomplished without changing defence commitments and the basic structure of the armed services.

The defence minister next fired a warning shot at the chiefs of the services. In the section of the paper dealing with "the organization of the defence forces," he suggested that the "traditional pattern of organization by individual services" was no longer appropriate. Hellyer leaned on the

Glassco Commission for support by repeating their finding that the present force structure was too rigid. He went on to expose the weaknesses of the committee structure of national defence and the failures of collegial decision making.

The answer to both the need for a flexible armed forces fully responsive to the demands of government and to the problems of tri-service inefficiencies is, first, integration of the command structure and, finally, unification of the entire armed forces. Hellyer did not attempt "to set up a theoretical establishment" in this paper or initially in his dealings with officers and officials, but he expected the logic of the strategy and the assumed benefits of integration and unification to win officers and officials to his side. And there surely were some converts. However, he was at first dismayed and then angered by the resistance he encountered, and over the next four years Hellyer became more and more involved in the practical aspects of reshaping the defence establishment.

The other major innovation in Hellyer's plan for national defence was the introduction of so-called program planning. The new system would help control the random practices then in place by providing a "means of expressing force [requirements] and other military activities in terms of their immediate and long term costs." The "hope" was that "the system [would] enable defence resources to be allocated [to missions and activities] in the most effective manner ... and in accordance with a clear and detailed plan."

Defence 1964 specified the types of capabilities that Canada might develop and maintain over the next ten years. Hellyer introduced the idea of a "mobile command," signalled the end of Canada's nuclear role in Europe by hastening the "phase-in" of non-nuclear capabilities in the European-based air squadrons, hinted at the acquisition of "nuclear-powered submarines, and confirmed Canada's commitment to provide an "immediate and effective response to United Nations requirements." As important as these policies were, the real news of Hellyer's white paper had already been announced and that was his determination to reorder defence strategy and to build a force structure to accommodate it.

Hellyer's idea and policy of unification has been the centre of controversy since the first day it was introduced. It has been blamed for every failing of defence policy and the armed forces including in 1997 the disastrous Somalia campaign of 1992-93. Most of the criticism in the early days was directed at the assumption that eliminating the armed services and traditional concepts of military organization would destroy Canada's defence capabilities. Thirty years later it is safe to say, at least, that this criticism is unproved. That is because, except for the brief period between 1967 and 1972, unification as envisioned by Paul Hellyer has not been the organizing concept of the Canadian Forces, the *National Defence Act* notwithstanding. Between 1972 and 1997 the armed forces have been variously organized around the competing ideas of unification, integration, public service management, and tri-service traditions. In fact, there is no organizing concept to guide planners, so unification cannot be the cause of the ills of the armed forces today.

The capabilities of the Canadian Forces diminished or, in some cases, vanished between 1968 and 1997 for many reason. Chief among these was a steady decline in resources available to renew and build capabilities. Resources for combat capabilities withered mainly because governments reduced the defence budget, but also because officers and officials wasted monies by maintaining and supporting inefficient and ineffective procedures, policies, and organizations. The snake's nest of policies and decisions is too complex to unravel today and no one can determine if unification as envisioned in 1964-68 would have produced the results Hellyer hoped for then. Perhaps it would have, perhaps not.[2]

---

[2]See *Task Force Review on Unification* in Volume II.

But it is clear that Paul Hellyer tried to build a defence strategy for Canada on a foundation of Canadian national interests. In doing so he threatened not only the institutional interests of the service chiefs, but also the interests of officials in the Department of External Affairs who were startled by the suggestion that Canada bring its units home from Europe. Perhaps Hellyer's biggest mistake was his belief that rational ideas could move inert policies. Even before the white paper was tabled in the House of Commons, his faith in the power of logical planning was dashed by Prime Minister Lester Pearson who was not interested in revamping Canada's foreign policy and relations with allies simply to build an efficient armed force.

After Hellyer left office the spirit of unification survived for a while under the direction of Chief of the Defence Staff General Jean Allard. After Allard, however, conceptual confusion crept steadily into defence organizations and then in 1969 and with the tabling of *Defence in the 70s* all semblance of a coordinated policy joining strategy and structure disappeared.

Selected Bibliography

Jean V. Allard. (with Serge Bernier). *Memoirs of General Jean V. Allard.*
     Vancouver: University of British Columbia Press, 1988.

Leonard Beaton. "The Canadian White Paper on Defence." *International
     Journal,* 19, 3 (Summer 1964):364-70.

Douglas Bland. *The Administration of Defence Policy in Canada, 1947 to 1985.*
     Kingston: R.P. Frye Co., 1987.

_____. *Chiefs of Defence: Government and the Unified Command of the
     Canadian Armed Forces.* Toronto: Canadian Institute of Strategic Studies,
     1995.

_____. "Controlling the Defence Policy Process in Canada: White Papers on
     Defence and Bureaucratic Politics in the Department of National
     Defence." *Defence Analysis,* 5,1 (1989):3-16.

J.V. Brock. *Memoirs of a Sailor: The Thunder and the Sunshine,* Vol. II. Toronto:
     McClelland & Stewart, 1983.

David Burke. "Hellyer and Landymore: The Unification of the Canadian Armed
     Forces and an Admiral's Revolt." *American Review of Canadian Studies*
     8 (Autumn 1978):3-27.

James Eayrs. "Canada Pioneers the Single Service." *The Round Table: The
     Commonwealth Quarterly* 69 (April 1969):149-59.

Paul Hellyer. *Damn the Torpedoes: My Fight to Unify Canada's Armed Forces.*
     Toronto: McClelland & Stewart, 1990.

V.J. Kronenberg. *All Together Now: The Organization of the Department of
     National Defence in Canada, 1964-1972.* Toronto: Canadian Institute for
     International Affairs, 1973.

HOUSE OF COMMONS:
SPECIAL COMMITTEE ON DEFENCE

Minutes of Proceedings and Evidence No. 1-21, 18 June to 18 November
1963.

Interim Report of the Special Committee on Matters Relating to Defence.
Presented by Maurice Sauvé, Chairman, 20 December 1963.

Minutes of Proceedings and Evidence "Bill C90, An Act To Amend The
National Defence Act And Other Acts In Consequence Thereof." No. 1-6,
19 May to 9 June 1964.

Second Report to the House of Commons, 10 June 1964.

HOUSE OF COMMONS:
STANDING COMMITTEE ON NATIONAL DEFENCE

Minutes of Proceedings and Evidence "Bill C243, An Act To Amend The
National Defence Act and Other Acts In Consequence Thereof." No. 14-
37, 7 February to 21 March 1967.

Minutes of Proceedings and Evidence "Regulations and Orders-in-Council
Relating to the Unification of the Canadian Armed Forces." No. 1-4,
15 February to 12 March 1968.

DEPARTMENT OF NATIONAL DEFENCE:
DIRECTORATE OF HISTORY

Unification Papers, File 80/225.

WHITE PAPER ON DEFENCE

HONOURABLE PAUL HELLYER
Minister of National Defence

HONOURABLE LUCIEN CARDIN
Associate Minister of National Defence

MARCH 1964

Contents

SECTION I

INTRODUCTION

Many of the basic principles that govern Canada's defence policy are constant because they are determined by factors, such as geography and history, which are specific. Others, such as the nature and the magnitude of the threat to peace and security and the development of weapons and weapons technology, change rapidly and drastically. Therefore defence policy must adapt itself to such changes, while principles remain constant. That is why it is desirable for the government not only to provide for defence changes when they are necessary, but to keep the public informed of the nature of and the reasons for the new policies. This can be done through White Papers on Defence, debates in the House of Commons, discussions in Parliamentary Defence Committees, and in many other ways.

It is hoped that this White Paper on Defence will be helpful for this purpose.

OBJECTIVES

The objectives of Canadian defence policy, which cannot be dissociated from foreign policy, are to preserve the peace by supporting collective defence measures to deter military aggression; to support Canadian foreign policy including that arising out of our participation in international organizations, and to provide for the protection and surveillance of our territory, our air-space and our coastal waters.

Policy since 1945

POST-WAR DEVELOPMENTS AND CANADIAN POLICY

Canada's foreign and defence policies have been shaped by some of the major international developments of the post-World War II period. The first in time and importance was Canada's adherence to the Charter of the United Nations, which created an obligation to support a system of international co-operation for the maintenance of peace and security.

The second was membership in the North Atlantic Treaty Organization, which joined Western Europe and North America in a common obligation for the defence of each other's territories against aggression. NATO was necessary because there was a direct threat to the security of Europe which could not be met by United Nations or national means alone. As befitted her relatively strong post-war position, Canada played a prominent part in the formation of the Alliance.

Of even greater significance was the 1951 decision of NATO to become more than a treaty of mutual assistance by developing a system of collective military forces. This was a new experiment in international co-operation.

The advent of nuclear weapons and the development of long-range systems for their delivery introduced a new range of problems in North American defence. The decision to continue in the post-war period Canada's close military association with the United States in the defence of North America, which began with the Ogdensburg Declaration of 1940, can be seen as an aspect of Canada's conviction that security lay in collective arrangements. The emerging direct threat to North America itself, in turn, led to the concept of partnership with the United States in North American air defence, a relationship which was formalized by the signing of the North American Air Defence (NORAD) Agreement in 1958.

Parallel with the pressure from the Soviet bloc a new set of tensions developed as pre-war empires were dissolved in favour of a great number of newly independent countries. The instability inevitable in this process created a need for international peace-keeping, mainly under the United Nations, to which Canada made and continues to make an important contribution.

In these circumstances, there have developed four parallel methods by which the objectives of Canadian defence policy have been pursued. They are:

(a) *Collective Measures* for maintenance of peace and security as embodied in the Charter of the United Nations, including the search for balanced and controlled disarmament;
(b) *Collective Defence* as embodied in the North Atlantic Treaty;
(c) *Partnership with the United States* in the defence of North America;
(d) *National Measures* to discharge responsibility for the security and protection of Canada.

LIMITATIONS ON CANADIAN COMMITMENTS

Any nation must be concerned that its obligations do not outrun its capabilities. A middle power such as Canada must be particularly careful to ration its commitments. Although at the end of the war Canada could have developed the capability to manufacture nuclear weapons, it elected, as a matter of deliberate choice, not to become a nuclear power.

Also, Canada did not become a party to the inter-American defence system. And, at the conclusion of the Korean war, Canada withdrew her troops from that area. Subsequently, Canada did not assume regional defence obligations in the Pacific, such as participation in SEATO. In consequence, limits have been set to our military responsibilities.

THE POST-WAR RE-ORGANIZATION

Before 1939, the Army was the principal service, with the R.C.N. and R.C.A.F. maintaining smaller regular forces. The main role of the

Army was to train and administer the non-permanent Militia. Mobilization plans were ambitious but mobilization reserves and equipment were negligible. Nevertheless, on the basis of this rudimentary system, Canada was able, after a lengthy period of mobilization, to play an important part in World War II, as she had in World War I.

In the post-war re-organization, which took place during the years 1945-47, it was recognized that Canada could not return to its pre-war attitude to defence. Canada was then relatively strong and prosperous at a time of Soviet expansion and Western European weakness. In addition, Canada had undertaken new responsibilities through its membership in the United Nations.

Another major lesson of the war was the inadequacy of the pre-war mobilization base. After September 1939 considerable time elapsed before Canada was in a position to take a significant share in military operations. It was recognized that in any future war, such time, in all probability, would not be available. Nevertheless, the basic concept underlying the post-war re-organization was traditional: a mobilization base and a mobilization period. The primary aims of the post-war re-organization were to improve the mobilization base and to reduce the mobilization period.

POST-WAR INNOVATIONS

The post-war re-organization included, however, a number of important innovations. The R.C.N. and the R.C.A.F. achieved real, rather than nominal, equality with the Army. This development reflected lessons of the Second World War and, in particular, the importance of both air and sea power. There was a general belief that in any future war Canada's principal contribution might best be made in the air or at sea. It was argued that as a nation possessing a relatively small population but an advanced technology, with an historic objection to conscription and separated by an ocean from any probable theatre of war, Canada was well placed to supply air and naval forces but at a disadvantage in supplying large land forces.

A second significant innovation was that, in all three services, small operational components were established. This was to provide a basis for a potential military contribution to the United Nations; to enable Canada to participate in partnership with the United States in the defence of North America; to further the training of Regular Forces; and as an immediately available asset on mobilization.

In comparison with the pre-war situation, the post-war defence budget and the regular establishment were increased approximately tenfold, although primary reliance continued to be placed on mobilization. In the immediate post-war period this was a practical policy. Large reserves of equipment were retained from the Second World War, especially in the case of the Army. Probably even more important was the existence of large reserves of trained manpower.

Service mobilization plans provided for major capabilities. These included a 100,000-man Navy capable of playing an important role in the defence of North Atlantic sea communications; a field Army of six divisions, including all supporting arms and services; and a balanced Air Force. However, these plans were flexible in the sense that they provided a range of options from which, in the event of a war of some duration, the government of the day would have been able to choose.

A third important innovation was the establishment of the Joint Staff and the development of machinery for some degree of joint planning and intelligence. There was also the establishment of the National Defence College and the Service staff colleges and, eventually, participation in NATO and NORAD Commands which provided Canadian officers with wider experience in national and international staff functions. As a result, Canada was in a better position to share responsibility in the planning and direction of major military programs.

Another important change was the growth of a capability for research and development. This reflected one of the major lessons of the Second World War: that science and technology had become prime military assets equal in importance to industrial capacity and manpower. It was not expected that Canada could develop and produce the entire range of equipment required by the Canadian Armed Services. However, it was considered possible to form a technological alliance with the larger allied powers. A modest Canadian contribution in the field of research, and in appropriate cases, development, constituted Canada's membership fee.

In the immediate post-war period it was feasible to conceive of Canadian defence primarily in terms of mobilization potential. This had the very great advantage of economy in resources. It also tended to preserve flexibility. The effect of the post-war re-organization was to provide Canada with the basic elements of a modern defence establishment. It furnished the basis for the Korean War expansion which took place rapidly, and, on the whole, efficiently.

THE POST-KOREAN EXPANSION

It is now clear that decisions taken during the period 1950-53 brought about a major alteration in Canada's defence policies. The most conspicuous feature of this period was that regular manpower was increased about two-and-a-half times, while the defence budget increased almost five-fold. These developments took place under the pressures generated by four major events: the first Soviet nuclear test of September 1949 and the consequent Soviet nuclear threat to North America; membership in North Atlantic Treaty in 1949; the development of a system of collective defence under NATO; and the invasion of South Korea in June 1950.

Canada accepted specific and quite sizable operational commitments in Korea; for the defence of Northwest Europe and the western Atlantic; and for the air defence of North America. These obligations involved forces-in-being, rather than mobilization potential; in strategic terms, the equivalent of a transference from credit to cash. Canada also instituted, as part of defence policy, substantial Mutual Aid and air training programs to assist its Western European partners.

From a military point of view, the principal result was to introduce the new principle of specialization of missions. With comparatively minor exceptions, Canada's defence programs now were specific in nature and made sense only in relation to the total capabilities of the entire group of NATO nations and to the Alliance objective of creating balanced collective forces.

EVOLUTION 1954-63

Following the withdrawal of Canadian forces from Korea in 1954, there were no major changes in Canada's defence programs or commitments until 1959, when the decision was taken to convert the R.CA.F. Air Division in Europe from the air defence role to the strike and reconnaissance roles, and to re-equip it with the CF-104.

In 1959 the Department of National Defence, particularly the Army, was also assigned a role in national survival. By this time no serious attempt was being made to maintain a mobilization base. The policy was adopted of equipping to war scales only the brigade group in Germany. Troops in Canada were in future to be equipped only to training scales.

Considerations Affecting Future Policy

INTERNATIONAL OUTLOOK

Despite the evident hazards of prediction, some attempt to estimate the future evolution of world power relationships is an essential prerequisite of defence planning. Major equipment programs initiated in the near future will have to meet the requirements throughout the 70's and into the 80's. Defence-associated activities, such as research and development, will have an effect over an even longer period.

Military technology must be expected to go on changing rapidly. As long as the U.S.A. and the Soviet Union both possess the ability to inflict unacceptable damage on the other, regardless of quantitative disparities in striking power, calculated all-out thermonuclear war would be irrational and is, therefore, improbable. However, in the absence of a settlement of major East-West political problems, the maintenance by the West of the capacity to deter such thermonuclear war will remain an essential military and political necessity, with the main responsibility resting on the strategic resources of the U.S.A.

It is probable that Communist China will grow in power, and unless its national objectives change, it may also grow in menace. The production of some nuclear weapons by Communist China during the next decade cannot be discounted, but it is not likely to acquire an effective nuclear arsenal, with means of delivery, which could compare with that of the U.S.A. or the U.S.S.R. during this period.

In the same time period, failing the adoption of a self-denying ordinance by international accord, a number of additional countries may be tempted to develop an independent nuclear capability. Failure to achieve a solution to this problem, while it is still of manageable proportions, could fundamentally and dangerously alter the world security situation and render invalid many current defence assumptions.

Assumptions concerning the probable political developments over the next decade or so cannot be made with any certainty. Within the Communist world, the present trend away from a monolithic structure towards increasing diversity and individuality seems likely to continue, accompanied by a relaxation of some of the rigidities of totalitarianism and the possible adoption of less militant external policies on the part of the more affluent European Communist states. Similarly, within the Western Alliance, the resurgence of the economic strength and political influence of Europe will require some adjustment of the relationships which have characterized the post-war period.

The possession of effective deterrent forces, including nuclear weapons, by both major military groupings will probably continue to discourage military adventure and to encourage the continued search for means of reducing the possibility of war by accident, miscalculation or surprise attack. On the main East-West issues, increasing importance will probably be attached to the quest for security through negotiations of the type now being undertaken by the 18-Nation Disarmament Committee in Geneva and in bilateral discussions between the two dominant powers.

However, the Communist countries can be expected to continue to promote expansionist aims by measures short of all-out war. Tensions will persist. In the North Atlantic area there will, therefore, remain a corresponding need to maintain intact the military and political cohesion of NATO. Elsewhere in the world, Communist pressure, including the active fomenting and support of so-called "wars of liberation" in less-developed areas, may well continue and intensify. In such areas, instability will probably continue in the decade ahead and call for containment measures which do not lend themselves to Great Power or Alliance action. The peace-keeping responsibilities devolving upon the United Nations can be expected to grow correspondingly.

This does not mean that the Canadian government considers a genuine relaxation in international affairs impossible. On the contrary, the prospects of a détente in relations between the free world and the Soviet Union exist and must be encouraged in every possible way. Certainly the signing of a limited nuclear test ban agreement was a forward step in co-operation and better understanding between East and West.

There are also trends within the U.S.S.R. and other East European countries which give different and potentially more lasting motives for détente and accommodation with the non-Communist world. Most important among these are the rising expectations and demands for a better and freer life. Related to this is the profound intellectual ferment in Communist society and the desire for more open and normal relations with the West. Problems of allocating limited resources, the crisis in Communist agriculture, and in some ways the Sino-Soviet quarrel, also support the desirability from the Soviet point of view of détente with the West.

It would, however, be naive not to recognize that many Communist leaders frankly regard the policy of détente as essentially tactical and designed to buy time.

Whether the more relaxed atmosphere will prove lasting, and can be developed into a reliable basis for mutual accommodation and peace, therefore remains to be seen. Undue pessimism would be as unfounded as facile optimism. The evolution inside the Communist world will depend in part on Western policies, and our willingness to meet half-way any genuine proposals towards accommodation.

In circumstances both of cold war and of potential détente, foreign policy and diplomatic negotiation are of great importance, being vital instruments in encouraging such opportunities as may exist for accommodation and relaxation. But it is essential that a nation's diplomacy be backed up by adequate and flexible military forces to permit participation in collective security and peacekeeping, and to be ready for crises should they arise.

THE RANGE OF CONFLICT

The range of potential conflict extends from the possibility of all-out thermonuclear war, through large-scale limited war, to insurrection, guerrilla activity and political upheaval. Of these, in the scale of probability, nuclear and major non-nuclear war are the least likely provided the balance of deterrence is maintained.

As the spectrum of conflict varies, so does the method of counter-action. At the high end of the scale — the deterrence of nuclear and major non-nuclear war — the method of proven record is the association of free nations in the North Atlantic Treaty Organization. In respect of lesser conflict, the United Nations has shown itself to be a valuable stabilizing and peacekeeping influence. National forces also have been used in some circumstances.

CANADA AND THE DETERRENCE TO MAJOR WAR

The contribution Canada can make to the deterrence of war is limited by the size of our human and material resources. Nevertheless, what we can contribute is far from negligible. We have an obligation to make that contribution.

NATO STRATEGY

Strategic policies are — or ought to be — the basis of plans, military programs, major procurement decisions and the establishment of priorities for research and development. The period 1945-63 has been characterized by rapid changes in strategic concepts owing mainly to revolutionary developments in military technology and in political circumstances. This has led to the obsolescence of strategic concepts and of military equipment. Difficult adjustments have been called for on the part of all nations. It is not in Canada alone that there are differences of opinion in regard to strategy. In the Alliance as a whole there is a wide range of views.

The major difference of view is between those who advocate immediate reliance on nuclear weapons, either strategic or tactical, and those who support a strategy of options — of graduated defence. But this difference is considerably narrowed when both views are thoroughly examined. Those who support the former view cannot really expect that the response to a single rifleman or even a company of riflemen should be a world-shattering holocaust. Similarly, those who propose a strategy of options do not contemplate the sacrificing of large areas of territory before any nuclear weapons are employed for defence.

Graduated or flexible response is a reaction against the doctrine of massive retaliation. It is based upon the proposition that the Western Alliance should not be placed in a position of excessive reliance upon nuclear weapons or, more generally, of being compelled to employ force in a manner incompatible with Western aims and objectives. The principle of flexible response places increased emphasis upon the provision of conventional forces. It involves reduced dependence upon strategic and tactical nuclear weapons although it does not reduce the requirement for these capabilities.

In the belief that adequate force through a wide spectrum is essential to the deterrence of war, it is the policy of the government, in determining Canada's force structure for the balance of the decade, to build in maximum flexibility. This will permit the disposition of the majority of our forces in Canada where they will be available for deployment in a variety of peacekeeping activities.

NUCLEAR AND NON-NUCLEAR

The question of nuclear weapons involves three distinct issues: joining the so-called "nuclear club"; Canada's political responsibility as a member of a nuclear-armed alliance; and the availability of nuclear weapons to Canadian armed forces.

The first of these issues is essentially fictitious. There has never been any serious question of Canada becoming a member of the nuclear club — i.e., one of those nations which by its own national decision can launch nuclear weapons. This ability could be attained only by the national manufacture of nuclear weapons. It is not contemplated.

The question of nuclear weapons for the Canadian armed forces is subordinate to that of Canada's political responsibility as a member of a nuclear-armed alliance. NATO is a nuclear-armed defensive alliance, which dare not be otherwise as long as it is confronted by a nuclear-armed potential opponent. NATO may become less dependent upon nuclear weapons, but the alliance must continue to possess nuclear weapons in the absence of controlled disarmament and as long as hostile forces have them. Its policies must envisage that in certain circumstances such weapons would be used against aggression. A share in the responsibility for these policies is a necessary concomitant of Canada's membership in NATO. One cannot be a member of a military alliance and at the same time avoid some share of responsibility for its strategic policies.

Having accepted the responsibility for membership in a nuclear-armed alliance, the question of nuclear weapons for the Canadian armed forces is a subordinate issue. It depends on how we can most effectively contribute to collective strength.

DEFENCE OF CANADA

It is, for the foreseeable future, impossible to conceive of any significant external threat to Canada which is not also a threat to North America as a whole. It is equally inconceivable that, in resisting clear and unequivocal aggression against Canadian territory, Canada could not rely on the active support of the United States. Recognition of these facts, however, must not be permitted to obscure certain national responsibilities of which account must be taken in Canadian policy.

Canadian defence is part of the defence of North America but it is, in certain key respects, a clearly distinguishable part of the larger strategic task. One can define the defence of Canada as those aspects of North American defence which must, for reasons based upon Canadian national interests, be subject to Canadian control. The minimum requirements for the defence of Canada are: the ability to maintain surveillance of Canadian territory, airspace and territorial waters; the ability to deal with military incidents on Canadian territory; the ability to deal with incidents in the ocean areas off the Canadian coasts; and the ability to contribute, within the limit of our resources, to the defence of Canadian airspace.

There are, in addition, certain national tasks of a military or quasi-military nature for which the Department of National Defence has some responsibility. These include: survival operations; search and rescue; communications; and aid to the civil power.

NORTH AMERICAN DEFENCE

The major threat to North America at this time is from the air, and it is in the field of continental air defence that co-operation with the United States has assumed the largest proportions.

The future of continental air defence, therefore, is obviously of great concern to Canada, both because of the sizable resources devoted to it, and because of the question of nuclear warheads. While a downward trend in continental air defence forces seems likely, yet, short of total disarmament, one can not foresee the day when Canada will not be directly involved in some form of air defence operations.

Such defence, to be fully effective, involves nuclear weapons. It should be noted that these weapons could be used only in the event of a deep enemy penetration of Canadian air space.

The future of North American air defence involves a number of questions which will be of continuing concern to Canada, including the maintenance of radar and active defence components commensurate with agreed estimates of the bomber threat; possible replacement of radar and active defence systems owing to obsolescence; measures to increase the survivability of the air defence system under nuclear attack; and the implications for Canada of the possible introduction of a defence against intercontinental ballistic missiles.

Of these, the most significant is the anti-ICBM, on which the United States has devoted a considerable effort in research, with consequent heavy expenditures. While some progress has been made, it has not yet been decided to deploy such a system and any such deployment could not be expected for some time. A decision to install an AICBM system would have a profound effect on North American defence. Directly related to this decision will be the level of active air defence; the degree of passive defence and fall-out protection required; and the relevancy of a defence against missile-launching submarines. So far as this present paper is concerned, the point is that there are no major questions of policy in this area which are ready for resolution at this time.

It seems probable, however, that, failing the wide-scale deployment of AICBM, the proportion of Canada's resources directed to air defence will gradually decline through the balance of the decade.

MARITIME FORCES

Since 1939, Canadian maritime programs have been heavily concentrated upon the defence of North Atlantic sea communications against submarine attack. This concentration has been based on the importance of these communications to the entire North Atlantic Community. It has had the effect of establishing a strong Canadian presence in the approaches to the Gulf of St. Lawrence and in the waters off the Atlantic coast. At the same time an adequate anti-submarine warfare capability is being maintained on the Pacific coast.

While the relevancy of developing a capability against missile-launching submarines will be determined largely by the deployment or non-deployment of anti-ballistic missile systems, there is no doubt that maritime forces will continue to have an important role in conjunction with the strategy of flexible response.

In anti-submarine warfare, improvements in detection techniques give promise of more effective systems against both conventional and nuclear-powered submarines. There is also promise of weapons systems to make submarines increasingly vulnerable to attack. Formidable problems remain in this field, however, requiring continued emphasis on research and development.

In order to get the maximum effectiveness for our investment in the anti-submarine force, we are conducting a major study to determine the best combination of weapons systems for this task. We have the active co-operation of our allies in this research.

PEACE-KEEPING

Since the war Canada's armed forces have been increasingly engaged in peace-keeping operations mostly under the auspices of the United Nations but also under other international arrangements, as in Indo-China. These operations have varied in size and scope. One broad category has involved the use of mixed military observer teams such as those employed in Kashmir, Palestine, Lebanon and Yemen. Another has called for the deployment of substantial national contingents under United Nations command, such as those in Korea, the United Nations Emergency Force in Sinai, the United Nations operation in the Congo and, more recently, the United Nations Force in Cyprus. Canadian military personnel have participated in virtually all of the operations conducted by the United Nations.

The development of this United Nations peace-keeping role has been pragmatic, depending largely on specific conditions and prevailing political circumstances. Rarely have these been duplicated exactly. The failure of the Great Powers to agree on the enforcement measures provided for in the Charter has led to improvisations as the practical demands for United Nations assistance arose. This situation, combined with the resistance of some other member states, has rendered impracticable for the time being the establishment of a standing United Nations force. In addition, experience has taught the need for flexibility in the organization, composition and mandate of United Nations military forces.

Canada's own experience in this field points to the need for a high degree of versatility in preparing for possible United Nations service. In the past, requests from the Secretary-General for assistance have been for specialists of various kinds, mainly from the Canadian Army and the R.C.A.F. The fact that Canada is one of a small number of powers capable of and eligible for United Nations service, with a highly trained and diversified military establishment, qualifies it for varied roles in United Nations operations.

The success of United Nations peace-keeping operations may depend on the speed with which they can be established on the ground. Once there, they may be required to exercise authority with limited personnel in broad areas. Thus, there is a need for mobility as regards deployment, method of operation and logistic support. In most situations which can be foreseen, there is likely to be a need for highly mobile forces for ground observation, air surveillance, rapid transportation and reliable communications. These are among the United Nations requirements which Canadian forces have helped to meet in the past.

Preparations for United Nations service on the part of Canadian military personnel must be varied, with an emphasis on mobility. While the training and equipment of such forces may be of a special nature, the best results can be accomplished through the establishment of regular military formations, which need not be earmarked exclusively for United Nations service and which can be used for other roles as required.

The Organization of the Defence Forces

BACKGROUND

As in other Western countries, the defence forces of Canada have followed the historical division into three separate services, reflecting the traditional distinction drawn between the sea battle, the land battle, and, in more modern times, the strategy of air power.

Doubts, however, have been raised in all countries in recent years about the traditional pattern of organization by individual services. Combined operations have become commonplace, and the services have found a growing area of overlap in the tasks with which they are charged. As the Royal Commission on Government Organization noted in its report on the Department of National Defence, "Operationally, the anti-submarine forces of the R.C.A.F. bear a much more distant relationship to the Air Division in Europe or the Air Defence forces in NORAD than to the anti-submarine forces of the R.C.N.; both elements operate in the North Atlantic under the command of SACLANT."

The Royal Commissioners also pointed to the rapid development of defence technology as further diminishing any value or significance of the individual services as independent entities.

> Not only is the relative size of the 'administrative tail' growing steadily in all military forces — for budgeting, accounting, supply, construction and general administration; in addition, among the operational elements themselves there is a rapid increase in the technical content of the work, a large element being common to all three Services. Consequently, there is a growing

range of activities of common concern to the Services, for which the traditional basis of organization is unsuited. It is increasingly recognized that to maintain three separate organizations for such functions is uneconomic. Moreover, the chronic scarcity of many of the skills involved cannot be ignored.

The traditional pattern also aggravates the rigidities in the defence establishment resulting from collective arrangements. It has meant, for example, that in finding signalers for the Congo at short notice, the Canadian Army could look only to its own resources in the Royal Canadian Corps of Signals, having no access to the large reservoir of communications personnel in the other two Services.

CO-ORDINATION BY COMMITTEE

Such unity as the Canadian forces have been able to achieve has depended first and foremost on the unity of political direction which resulted from all three services being placed under the Minister of National Defence. Below the political level, however, efforts have been concentrated on achieving co-ordination rather than integration of the three services. The instrument through which co-ordination has been sought has been the Chiefs of Staff Committee.

This Committee, composed of the Chairman, the Chief of Staff of each of the three services and the Chairman of the Defence Research Board, has a collective responsibility for advising the Minister and government on matters of defence policy, for co-ordinating the efforts of the forces and for the direction of joint service organizations and operations. As was noted by the Royal Commission on Government Organization, however, the Chairman possesses no over-riding authority. Recommendations and decisions of the Committee must, in effect, be unanimous.

The report of the Commission continues —

Thus the effectiveness of the Chiefs of Staff Committee as an executive authority is, to a large extent, dependent on the personal qualities of its members, each of whom has a virtual power of veto in its deliberations. The same pattern is followed throughout the co-ordinating organization that has evolved under the Committee — encompassing more than 200 standing tri-service committees. Although the business of the Chiefs of

Staff Committee appears to be conducted with reasonable dispatch, your Commissioners observe that, in general, the system permits procrastination, and the absence of a single commanding voice may spell the difference between success or failure in any matter of joint concern to the three Services. Where an attempt is made to move beyond co-ordination to integration, the weakness of the committee basis of direction persists. When it was decided in 1953 to consolidate military medical services outside the direct authority of any one of the Chiefs of Staff, the Surgeon General was made responsible to the Personnel Members Committee comprising the Chief of Naval Personnel, the Adjutant General and the Air Member for Personnel. As an executive authority, this Committee has all the defects of the Chiefs of Staff Committee in aggravated form. Procrastination and inter-service disagreements, amounting to a virtual refusal to accept direction, have proved formidable obstacles to progress.

A similar experience is noted by your Commissioners in the report on Telecommunications, involving the unsuccessful attempt of 1950 to develop an integrated teletype relay system under tri-service committee direction; the lack of an effective executive authority in that case led to the abandonment of the attempt at consolidation and the development of three wasteful and increasingly inadequate networks.

It is the opinion of your Commissioners that effective consolidation cannot be based on joint control by the three Services with the object of preserving the traditional responsibility of the three Chiefs of Staff for the control and administration of all the Armed Forces.

INTEGRATED FORCES

Having stated the problem, the Royal Commission recommended the gradual transfer of executive control of common requirements to the Chairman, Chiefs of Staff. In the opinion of the government this solution does not adequately resolve the basic issues. If a single command structure is not established, co-ordination by the committee system will remain with all of its inevitable delays and frustrations.

The fundamental considerations are operational control and effectiveness, the streamlining of procedures and, in particular, the decision-making process, and the reduction of overhead. To the extent that operational control is exercised by Canada, it is the view of the government that it can be most effectively exercised by a single command.

The question of duplication and unnecessary overhead, too, cannot be ignored. The present headquarters organization of the Department of National Defence is far too large. The fact that our field forces are modest creates a serious imbalance between the field and headquarters branches of the service. As it appears that we will have to maintain modest forces in being for many years to come, it is apparent that a re-organization is required.

Following the most careful and thoughtful consideration, the government has decided that there is only one adequate solution. It is the integration of the Armed Forces of Canada under a single Chief of Defence Staff and a single Defence Staff. This will be the first step toward a single unified defence force for Canada. The integrated control of all aspects of planning and operations should not only produce a more effective and co-ordinated defence posture for Canada, but should also result in considerable savings. Thus, integration will result in a substantial reduction of manpower strengths in headquarters, training and related establishments, along with other operating and maintenance costs. The total savings to be effected as a result of such reductions will make available funds for capital equipment purchases, and eventually make possible more equitable distribution of the defence dollar between equipment and housekeeping costs. Sufficient savings should accrue from unification to permit a goal of 25 percent of the budget to be devoted to capital equipment being realized in the years ahead.

Two objections are given as reasons why integration should not be undertaken. First, that morale or "esprit de corps" is weakened, and second, that competition is diminished. Neither of these objections will stand against careful scrutiny. "Esprit de corps" by nature is associated with ship, or corps, or regiment, or squadron, as well as with the service. There is no thought of eliminating worthwhile traditions and there is no reason why morale should not be high — a direct result of effectiveness. Similarly, there will be no lack of competition. The sailors will press for more ships, the soldiers for more tanks and the airmen for more planes. This is as natural as breathing. Competition will not be lost but it will be contained at the service level.

THE ORGANIZATIONAL METHOD

No attempt will be made to set up a theoretical establishment to replace the existing one, nor will the details be prescribed in advance. Inevitable changes will take place under the direction of the men charged with responsibility in their various fields. Streamlined procedures will be worked out in practice. Standard policies will be based on the best available to meet functional requirements. It will be the responsibility of the Defence Staff to work out the problems but they will have the authority to do so in accordance with the chain of command unhampered by committees.

The success of the Minister in maintaining an effective civilian control raises — in the words of the Royal Commission on Government Organization — "a need for a strong staff group which is essentially civilian in character outside the framework of the Armed Forces". The government accepts and will implement the recommendation of the Commission "that the Deputy Minister be given greater responsibility for keeping under review the organization and administrative methods of the Canadian defence establishment, and assisting the Minister in the discharge of his responsibility for the control and management of the Armed Forces."

DEFENCE PROGRAMMING

It is intended to introduce into the Department of National Defence a management system for planning and controlling major Defence programs at the departmental level. This system will display various components of the long-term Defence program in suitable detail over a significant time period. The system will provide a means of expressing various force structures, weapons systems, logistic arrangements and other military activities in terms of their immediate and long-term costs.

The main objectives of the system are:

(a) to assist top management in the department in decision making by providing the means of analyzing and assessing various military programs and activities in terms which will relate military effectiveness to financial costs, manpower requirements, equipment needs, etc.

(b) to provide the type of data which will enable the effects of defence decisions to be clearly expressed in terms of forces, manpower, equipment, and money both in the short term and over a period of years.

For this purpose, the total Canadian defence structure will be grouped into a number of major programs. These programs will cover all arms of the services and will be expressed in terms of major military missions or objectives. Each program will be analyzed in appropriate detail to reflect the military and civilian manpower, the major equipments and the anticipated costs that are programmed over a period of years for the various elements of the Program. Projections of each program will be reviewed annually.

This system will enable Defence Programs to be examined and considered in relation to their overall military effectiveness from the standpoint of achieving a particular mission. It is hoped that the system will enable defence resources to be allocated to Defence Programs in the most effective manner from the point of view of ultimate military output and in accordance with a clear and detailed plan.

The Shape of Canadian Forces 1964-1974

Section III of this paper discussed the considerations affecting future defence policy, and Section IV outlined the integrated organization which contemporary defence tasks require. The question now to be resolved is the determination of the force structure which will best meet our defence needs in the face of the many uncertainties which the future holds.

Of necessity, the answer to this question is an evolutionary process. It starts with our present capabilities. These will be changed gradually in conformity to a relatively long term plan of action. To be effective, this plan, designed as a basis of development, must not be too rigid.

It is impossible to state in categorical terms exactly where and how our forces will be required and allocated in the decades ahead. However, our major defence contribution for some time will continue to be participation in collective defensive arrangements, mainly the North Atlantic Treaty Organization.

NATO EUROPE

Our present contribution to NATO in Europe is one Brigade Group stationed in Germany and one Air Division consisting of eight squadrons stationed in France and in Germany. Two brigades in Canada are intended primarily for deployment to the European theatre in the event of hostilities.

A possible course would be for Canada to withdraw from the commitment to maintain a Brigade Group on the central European front in favour of making a contribution to an air portable force based in Europe and available for employment on the NATO flanks. After the most careful consideration, it has been decided that this would not be in the best interest of Canada and the Alliance for several important reasons.

The brigade, consisting as it does of highly qualified and well trained professional soldiers, is making a useful contribution to NATO Europe at one of its most vulnerable points. Its presence, moreover, has a political significance for the Alliance, and its withdrawal from front-line positions at this time could be misinterpreted — by both our European allies and the Soviet bloc. The importance to the solidarity of the Alliance of a Canadian "presence" in the NATO defence forces is real. In consequence, it is the intention of the government to continue to employ the brigade in its present role.

It is also felt that the requirement for a mobile force can be better met by other means. Increased air transport will make it possible to move units to the European flanks, if and when required, from bases in Canada and the United States. This is more economical than stationing mobile reserves in Europe and more acceptable than withdrawing front-line battalions for mobile service on the European flanks.

A MOBILE FORCE IN CANADA

It is in respect of the two brigades kept in reserve in Canada and earmarked primarily for the European theatre that a change is proposed.

These two brigades will be re-equipped-and retrained as a mobile force as well as for rotational service with the NATO brigade. Although stationed in Canada, they will be available for use where and when required. In order to achieve maximum flexibility, these two brigades will be equipped to permit their effective deployment in circumstances ranging from service in the European theatre to United Nations peace-keeping operations.

In order to achieve a more effective use of available manpower, it is proposed to undertake a gradual conversion of the fourth brigade into a special service force. This force will be smaller than the conventional brigades and will be provided with air-portable and air-droppable equipment. It will be trained to perform a variety of military tasks.

A MOBILE FORCE FOR NATO

The Supreme Allied Commander Europe has asked Canada to make available one battalion for use as part of his mobile force. This can be done without difficulty by simply drawing on one of the Canadian-based brigades and the air transport that will be available for its deployment. When employed in the mobile role, only light equipment is required for the battalion.

AIR FORCES

As already announced, we are readjusting our air division in order to have the existing eight squadrons in Europe deployed as follows: six squadrons in Germany in the strike role and two squadrons in France in the reconnaissance role.

All eight squadrons are also being equipped for a non-nuclear attack role. This non-nuclear capacity will be phased in as quickly as possible and will give our air division maximum flexibility under varied circumstances. As follow-on CF-104 aircraft will not be acquired, the numbers of operational squadrons of this type of aircraft will decline as a result of normal attrition over the next ten years.

During the decade, we propose to give increasing emphasis to the provision of aircraft for direct support of our ground forces. We anticipate that a high performance aircraft will be available to provide sufficient flexibility for any task we might undertake from ground attack to air surveillance. These versatile tactical aircraft will possess adequate radius of action to allow rapid deployment from Canada to bases overseas. This will permit squadrons to be stationed in Canada or Europe as required.

The plan calls for the squadrons stationed in Europe to be associated, ultimately, more directly with the army brigade group. It is recognized, however, that this kind of association on a national basis may not be practical without some adjustment in the present NATO military organization in Europe. Such an adjustment, if necessary, will be the subject of consultation with NATO. Squadrons in Canada would be available for training in close association with ground forces. Thus, ground and air forces would complement each other in a manner which has not been possible in the past. Some of the squadrons stationed in Canada would also contribute to air defence as required, thereby eliminating the necessity of acquiring special aircraft for this purpose.

NORTH AMERICAN AIR DEFENCE

It is planned to continue to operate the three squadrons of CF-101's now assigned to NORAD during the life of the aircraft. Beyond this, units from the combat squadrons previously mentioned will be available if required. The two Bomarc squadrons will be operated as long as they form an integral and essential part of the NORAD system.

The radars and surveillance systems in the Canadian part of the NORAD network will be operated in accordance with the existing agreements. It is our hope, however, that there can be a gradual phasing-out as the relative threat from the manned bomber diminishes, and a gradual re-allocation of resources to other roles.

AIR TRANSPORT

As the emphasis in our force structure is on greatly increased mobility, it will be necessary to substantially augment our existing air transport capability. It is proposed to consider the possibility of utilizing the resources of the civilian air carriers in circumstances involving the transport of large numbers of personnel to areas where first-class air strips are available.

In order to have the flexibility in circumstances where improved air strips are not available, and in order to carry large quantities of stores and equipment, a considerable augmentation of the "air truck" component of the air transport fleet is being undertaken. This fleet will be available for United Nations and other requirements. It has the capability of landing both troops and equipment on improved or semi-improved air strips. This versatility will contribute much to our ability to respond to varied demands.

NATO MARITIME

It is planned to continue in the anti-submarine role. Canada has a large, capital investment in this capacity and special skills and training as well. Current developments give promise of considerable effectiveness from a "mixed" force of modest size. Studies are continuing to determine, in so far as is possible, the most effective "mix" of weapons systems. Surface ships, submarines, helicopters and fixed wing aircraft, both carrier-based and shore-based, are all useful in anti-submarine warfare. The question is to determine as precisely as is possible the proportion of weapons systems which will provide the maximum intensity of surveillance and maximum defence potential for the least cost.

In this connection, careful study is being given to the possibility of building two or three nuclear-powered submarines, which are powerful anti-submarine weapons. This is, however, a large issue and it cannot decided immediately. In any event, the requirement for naval forces will continue to be related mainly to our alliance contributions. To this end, a modern and well-equipped fleet of appropriate size is to be maintained.

CANADA AND UN REQUIREMENTS

Under the plans set out above, sizable land, air and naval forces will normally be deployed in and around Canadian territory. Additional requirements are limited fairly well to special tasks and United Nations peace-keeping operations. As indicated earlier, Canadian forces will be trained and equipped in a way which will permit immediate and effective response to United Nations requirements.

This training will include a wide variety of specialized capabilities to permit units to operate in extreme conditions from arctic to jungle, and to undertake tasks of varied complexity from firefighting to communications. The key to organization will be flexibility and mobility. The existence of adequate transport will make it possible to quickly lift units or a brigade to any trouble spot where their presence might be valuable to maintain peace or assist in the limitation of local outbreak.

In considering the areas of possible deployment in support of United Nations activities, the question of a requirement for sea-lift has been considered. Conditions may arise which will necessitate carrying heavy equipment and supplies by sea. To increase our capability, a modest additional sea-lift will be acquired either in conjunction with the anti-submarine force or independently. The combined land, sea and air forces normally stationed in Canada and at Canadian ports will be sufficiently flexible to satisfy almost any conceivable requirement for UN or other operations.

PRIORITIES

The choice of priorities outlined above is based on the following assessment:

1. Forces for the direct protection of Canada which can be deployed as required.
2. Forces-in-being as part of the deterrent in the European theatre.
3. Maritime forces-in-being as a contribution to the deterrent.
4. Forces-in-being for UN peace-keeping operations which would be included also in (1) above.
5. Reserve forces and mobilization potential.

On the basis of this assessment, major expenditures in the next few years will be designed to:

(a) re-equip the Army as a mobile force;
(b) provide an adequate air and sea lift for its immediate deployment in an emergency;
(c) acquire tactical aircraft;
(d) maintain a relatively constant improvement of maritime anti-submarine capability.

ARMED FORCES RESERVES

To assist in the primary task of re-organizing the current forces a Ministerial Commission has been set up under the chairmanship of Brigadier E. R. Suttie. It was considered advisable in order to obtain a valid perspective of both national and informed military opinion to take advantage of the judgment of a group of experienced men. The Commission has been given the task of recommending to the Minister the best means of fulfilling the militia requirements of Canadian defence policy and the changes which should be made in organization to permit the militia to carry out its revised roles more efficiently and realistically.

The primary role of the militia is to support the Regular Army. The Emergency Defence Plan calls for the withdrawal of Regular Army personnel from the Defence of Canada Forces in static installations to bring the field force up to establishment. The militia would be required to form the framework for logistics and special units which are not provided in peace time. Secondary roles include the provision of a training force which would be required in an emergency to support the field forces; internal security including the provision of trained officers and men for guarding key points; and assisting the Regular Army in its national survival responsibilities. The Ministerial Commission will advise in respect of the best organization to fulfill these roles.

Ministerial Committees have considered the question of Naval and Air Force Reserves. Naval Reserves are specifically required to release men from shore establishments in order to bring ship complements up to war time establishment in an emergency, while the Air Force Reserves have a role in support of ground forces in civil survival. The reports of these two Committees have been referred to the Suttie Commission. It will be an objective of the Commission to recommend the maximum possible degree of integration of facilities, having in mind the specific nature of the roles and to take into consideration, in the re-organization of the Reserve forces, the integration set out in Section IV.

CIVIL DEFENCE

In 1959, certain specific national survival responsibilities were assigned to the Minister of National Defence and, in turn, the Canadian Army was designated the principal Service to carry out these responsibilities. At the same time, the Emergency Measures Organization was given the overall responsibility for co-ordination at Federal, Provincial and Municipal levels. This Organization came under the jurisdiction of the Prime Minister, but in 1963 responsibility was transferred to the Minister of Defence Production.

The Canadian Army, following a study of the problems involved, has taken the following steps: a National Survival Attack Warning System was established; a Nuclear Detonation and Fallout Reporting System was designed; elements of the Army component at Federal and Provincial levels were trained to carry out damage and casualty assessment; the Army with the Emergency Measures Organization and other Federal, Provincial and Municipal agencies, developed joint plans for re-entry operations and both Regular Army and Militia Forces are being trained to carry out assigned functions in this regard; and emergency communications for continuity of government have been provided.

As has been indicated, the future priority to be assigned to civil defence measures will be influenced greatly by the decision to deploy or not to deploy an anti-ICBM system. Until this major decision has been taken it is not possible to resolve a large number of lesser policy matters in the civil defence field. In the meantime, approved projects will be completed and maintained.

MUTUAL AID AND MILITARY TRAINING ASSISTANCE

The assistance which has been given to our European Allies under the Canadian Mutual Aid Program has, in the past, been a major element of Canada's contribution to the North Atlantic Treaty Organization. The Mutual Aid Program has comprised aircrew training, transfers of equipment both from Service stocks and from new Canadian production, and Canada's contributions to the NATO Common Infrastructure Program and the budgets of the integrated NATO Military Headquarters. The total value of assistance given since the beginning of the program in 1950 will be $1,796 Million by 31 March 1964.

In recent years, the size of the Canadian Mutual Aid Program has reduced. On the one hand, the reductions have reflected the economic progress and increasing prosperity of most of our NATO allies in Europe. On the other hand, they have resulted from the end of the original NATO Aircrew Training Program, the exhaustion of equipment available for transfer from Service stocks, and the impact of costly modern reequipment programs for the Canadian Services on our ability to provide useful quantities of equipment from new Canadian production.

The Mutual Aid Program for 1964-65 totals $41.02 million. It includes the Canadian share of the costs, during the year, of the joint Canadian/ United States program of production in Canada of F104G aircraft for the Canadian Mutual Aid and U.S. Mutual Defence Assistance programs, aircrew training of Norwegian and Danish aircrew, transfers of equipment from Service stocks mainly to support equipment previously transferred, and contributions to NATO Common Infrastructure Programs and NATO Military Budgets.

Contributions by Canada to the NATO Infrastructure Programs and NATO Military Budgets will be required as long as these joint NATO undertakings continue. Apart from this, no major new programs of Canadian Mutual Aid are foreseen. Canada will, however, be prepared to continue to consider reasonable requests for assistance in military training and possibly in the provision of equipment to NATO nations which require such assistance and where it can be given by Canada with advantage to the alliance as a whole.

Canada has extended military training assistance to a number of Commonwealth countries to help them in their efforts to create armed forces sufficient to maintain stability and national independence. Canada will continue to give careful consideration to modest requests of this nature from newly independent countries.

Defence Research and Industry

RESEARCH AND SCIENCE

In this scientific era the efficient planning and provision of defence forces demands a strong contribution from defence scientists and engineers. Application of scientific research and the scientific method can provide or improve upon solutions to a wide range of technical problems that beset the military establishment. Defence research also contributes to the progressive technological development of our industry which is so essential to the production of specialized equipment for the Armed Forces. In consequence, research has a direct influence on the national economy and, thus, on the well-being of our people.

Research normally does not require large financial commitments to achieve success and, hence, Canada can make very substantial contributions to the common pool of scientific knowledge available to our allies at a reasonable cost. From this investment there are two dividends: an improvement in the collective security, and a reciprocal flow of scientific information from the much larger endeavours of some other nations of the alliance. This return on our research investment is many times greater in scientific value than the cost of our own research efforts.

The agency in the Department of National Defence responsible for scientific research is the Defence Research Board created in 1947. Since its creation the Defence Research Board has made major contributions in many defence scientific fields. The most recent example has been the production of the "Alouette" satellite which is internationally regarded as at least as successful as any other scientific satellite yet launched.

The Board's extramural research activities are carried out mainly through grants-in-aid of research to universities and by means of contracts with industry. These investigations are usually basic in nature and are carried out by university groups who seek to provide new knowledge in fields from which important military developments are likely to arise in the future.

DRB provides support to industry through a fund established to promote and strengthen the research capability of Canada's defence industry. Additionally, the research resources of industry are supported and utilized through the award of contracts to firms to undertake research required by the Defence Department.

International collaboration by DRB in the field of defence science is wide and increasing. Canada participates with the U.S. and Britain in a very active tripartite organization built up to ensure the fullest utilization of the defence scientific knowledge, resources and facilities of these countries. In addition, bilateral agreements with several NATO nations serve to enhance the interchange of defence scientific and technical knowledge. The Board provides Canadian representation on a number of specialist committees through which NATO's scientific endeavours are progressed and co-ordinated.

DEVELOPMENT

Development of military equipment within the Department of National Defence is the responsibility of the Armed Forces and represents specialized technological interests of the Services concerned. Actual development of such specific requirements, together with certain joint development projects under the auspices of standardization agreements with allied countries, is generally conducted in industry and is limited to items not available from other programs, domestic or allied. The result of conducting such development in industry is to improve industrial defence technology and thereby enhance the ability of Canadian firms to participate in co-operative development and production-sharing programs with allied countries.

With the co-operation of the Department of National Defence, the Department of Defence Production administers the Development-Sharing Assistance program in which military equipment and matériel is developed for potential use by the nations allies. The projects are conducted entirely in industry and costs are shared between the Department of Defence Production, the industrial firm conducting the development and, in many cases, the military department of the allied country having an interest in the development.

For the future, a dynamic defence research and development program is an essential element of our defence policy. It is our intention not only to support it fully, but also to implement a gradual but consistent increase in the resources made available for such a program.

INDUSTRY AND PRODUCTION-SHARING

During World War II and in the years following, Canada undertook the manufacture of a wide variety of defence equipment. This production served as a useful stimulant for Canadian industry and was beneficial in many ways to the economy as a whole.

However, since the end of the war, weapons and weapons systems have steadily become more complex and costs have mounted rapidly. Only the largest powers can economically design, develop and produce all their weapons. Therefore, there is a need for greater inter-allied co-operation to harmonize defence requirements and to co-ordinate production programs. Such co-operation was the establishment of the Canada-United States Defence Development and Production-Sharing Program.

Within the past two years efforts have been made to extend this collaboration in defence production beyond the United States to our NATO allies, and appropriate arrangements have been initiated with Britain, France and a number of other NATO countries.

It is considered that the hundreds of millions of dollars of foreign orders reaching Canada annually are evidence of progress made in co-operation with its allies in production for defence. It is in the context of these arrangements that it has been possible to justify the procurement of certain weapons developed and produced abroad.

In the broad spectrum of equipment required in an alliance there is ample room for participation by Canada in the development and manufacture of specialized equipment to meet the needs of its own forces and of allies as well. One point is most important in this regard: when Canada does succeed in establishing a breakthrough, development must be pursued with dispatch or the potential of the military and economic advantages may be dissipated.

Defence expenditures can make a contribution to the efficient development of manufacturing both for the domestic market and for export and, in so doing, contribute to the general growth of Canada. Programs to establish and improve production sources will continue. The closest co-operation between the armed services and the Department of Defence Production will be maintained in order to promote efficient purchasing practices and to see that Canadian products are used wherever that is feasible.

Conclusion

In this paper no attempt has been made to set down hard and fast rules for future policy and development. Flexibility, not rigidity, has been the keynote. The paper is a charter, a guide, not a detailed and final blueprint. The policy outlined in it is not immutable. It can be altered or adapted to meet the requirements of changing circumstances, national and international.

What those circumstances will be in the future no one can foretell. It is certain, however, that force is not the solution to the problems of peace and security in the world. Force alone, as all history shows, is not able to establish an enduring and creative peace.

Nevertheless, and regrettably, it is essential to maintain force on our side as a deterrent against attack from potential foes who are themselves heavily armed: as a means of removing the greatest temptation to an aggressor, the assurance of easy victory.

The maintenance of adequate force for the above purpose, gives us the time in which men of wisdom, persistence and goodwill can work together to build a world where peace will be secured by stronger means than force.

If we fail to take advantage of the opportunity that time gives us, then peace, and with it civilization, may be lost.

If we spare no effort in seeking for peaceful solutions to the problems that divide and embitter men, then true peace may be established and all mankind gain the victory.

In the realization of this objective, Canada, through diplomacy and defence, must continue to play a worthy part.

Introduction to Defence in the 70s

The white paper on defence presented to Parliament by defence minister Donald Macdonald in August 1971 seemed to mark a significant change from the status quo as did so many policies and attitudes of the Trudeau years. The paper was crafted by postwar politicians who had few ties to the Pearsonian internationalism that had guided defence planners for more than twenty-five years. Where Paul Hellyer had sought to reorder the way Canada delivered ongoing commitments, Macdonald sought to change, redirect, or eliminate those commitments entirely. In some sense *Defence in the 70s* ridiculed previous policies and debunked the icons of Canadian international affairs. Yet despite the apparent freshness and logic of the minister's attempt "to explain the changes taking place in defence policy," the paper illustrates, it even declares, the quandary facing anyone challenged with writing a defence policy the main purposes of which have little to do with traditional concepts of military defence. In less than two years, Trudeau's government would discover that they had far less control over defence policy than they imagined in 1970 unless they were prepared to sacrifice other interests for their ideals, and they were not.

Defence in the 70s is in important respects a companion document to a broad policy statement made by Prime Minister Trudeau on 3 April 1969. In that statement, Trudeau questioned the basic tenets of Canada's defence policy, especially as it concerned NATO. He hinted that his government would take Canada in a new and more independent direction, freeing the country, and the federal budget, from the demands of the Cold War. He identified "four major areas of activity for the Canadian Forces":

(a) ... the protection of ... [Canadian] sovereignty;

(b) the defence of North America in co-operation with U.S. forces;

(c) the fulfilment of such NATO commitments as may be agreed upon; and

(d) the performance of such international peacekeeping roles as we may from time to time assume.

The statement and the list of activities were hailed by some as new thinking that would surely result in policies more appropriate to a new era. Canada's defence would be repatriated from the demands and strictures of Cold War alliances. However, a more careful assessment of the list reveals that it need not change anything significantly. Politicians and defence planners had always maintained an identical list of defence objectives, including arguably those in power before 1945. The first two objectives are "strategic imperatives" that could not be set out in any other order. The next pair are simply a refinement of Brooke Claxton's pledge to carry out voluntary undertakings; in other words, they are "strategic choices." Everyone of experience understood that as long as the imperatives were addressed — because of the absence of threats or with appropriate resources — Canada was free to volunteer for other security missions. What Trudeau suggested was that the threat to Canada's sovereignty was so severe that the activities of the Canadian Armed Forces deployed in NATO commands and elsewhere would have to be redirected to domestic duties. Few members of the defence and foreign policy community were convinced that this assessment was true or even realistic.

By the end of the Trudeau era most Canadians realized that there was no threat to Canada's sovereignty that could be addressed by military means, but there was a continuing need for the armed forces in NATO and on peacekeeping missions. In any case, by 1979 (and much earlier by some accounts) Canada's defence policy had returned to the policy of 1969: Canada had a defence policy that was mainly a NATO policy only the forces were now seriously depleted.

Five main themes flow through *Defence in the 70s* providing its particular political hue. The paper presents a world view resigned to the strategy of deterrence based on nuclear overkill. It makes no distinction between the political motives and defence policies of the Soviet Union and the United States. Although war prevention is the necessary objective in this situation, Macdonald suggests that superpower accommodation would be preferred. Yet the paper is guardedly optimistic. It predicts that the seemingly dysfunctional bipolar system of international relations would loosen as other power centres, in China and the Pacific Rim, rose up to challenge the hegemony of the superpowers. The hint is that somehow the fact of the Cold War could be set aside, even ignored. Macdonald declares that Canada sees "greater stability [and] an increased willingness to attempt to resolve East-West issues by negotiation." This might appear odd just two years after the Soviets invaded Czechoslovakia and with a war in Vietnam that threatened to spread across southeast Asia.

The second major theme, drawn from the first, was that Europe, now reborn and prosperous, was fully capable of defending itself without the assistance of Canadian Forces stationed there. Although the minister's economic history and analysis was probably sound, he failed to understand or rejected the political and defence arguments for stationing Canadian units in Europe. The conventional idea was that Canadians fought and died in Europe and deployed forces there in peacetime to defend Canada, not as a type of mercenary force for Europeans. However, by keeping the focus on economic issues and by dismissing the alarms and warnings of the secretary of external affairs, Mitchell Sharp, Macdonald was able to rationalize the decision already taken to reduce by half the number of Canadian service persons deployed in Europe. The logic of Macdonald's analysis should have brought every Canadian rifle and airplane home, but the factor his analysis ignored, the political reaction of Europeans who valued foreign stationing, compelled him to maintain Pearson's policy, however faintheartedly.

Donald Macdonald identified new roles for the defence establishment and these were all close to home. He declared, in a third theme, that the Canadian Forces "have an important and growing role in safeguarding sovereignty and independence" at home. The emphasis he placed on this traditional role of the armed forces came from an uneasiness in government and in the public's mind that Canada was under assault from its friends and neighbours. Specifically, these challenges which were "non-military in character [included] infringements of Canadian laws" by "foreign agencies or their nationals," intrusions in the North and in coastal areas, competition for fisheries, and environmental degradations. The government's policy was to "continue effective occupation of Canadian territory" and Macdonald states that the "provision of adequate defence resources for this purpose must, therefore, be a matter of first priority" for the Canadian Forces.

Within this same theme Macdonald identifies "internal security" as another renewed and critical priority facing the armed forces. The shock of the attacks on civil order by the Front de libération du Québec (FLQ) in October 1970 clearly indicated to the government the "necessity of being able to cope effectively with any future resort to disruption, intimidation and violence as weapons of political action." This objective provided another "important and ... crucial role for the armed forces."

Macdonald broke with the idea that Canada could play an effective and important part in international peacekeeping. He remarked that the "prospects for effective international peacekeeping which were viewed with some optimism in 1964, have not developed as had been hoped."

Unfortunately, the concept was "severely hampered by inadequate terms of reference and by a lack of co-operation on the part of those involved." While the government would continue to "support the concept of peace-keeping," the message to the armed forces and the international community was that they should not count on Canada to commit significant resources to future peacekeeping operations.

Finally, *Defence in the 70s* set in train a series of actions and decisions that were to have a profound influence on civil-military relations in Canada. These initiatives began as an attempt to redirect defence decision making so as to free the minister from seeming dependence on military advice and to provide a new rational for determining "defence requirements." The white paper did not spell out how the minister would establish a new decision-making arrangement or reorder his relationship with the chief of the defence staff and the deputy minister, but he did introduce a study intended to make far-reaching inquiries of "the entire department." The "Management Review Group" would eventually produce a report that supposedly provided the rational for a wholesale reorganization of the principal apparatus for decision making in the Canadian Forces and the Department of National Defence.* The result, according to some, including the commissioners of the Inquiry into the Deployment of the Canadian Forces to Somalia, is that accountability and responsibility for defence decision making is blurred beyond recognition.

According to military doctrine, defence requirements are determined by assessing what is needed to accomplish the task at hand. That is not to say that governments would always provide what military officers thought necessary and prudent. But the process of determining requirements based on mission analysis free from political and economic constraints produced a model of what was required to do the job against which risks could be assessed if the demands of the mission were not met. Donald Macdonald

---

*"The Management of Canada's Defence." See Volume II.

introduced a contrary notion that requirements would be determined based on what was available for defence. He insisted, moreover, that the defence department present "proposed defence activities in relation to other Government programs." The weakness of this approach is that it provides no appreciation of gaps in planning because there was no abstract model on which to compare what was required with what was available for defence. Further, this process of planning from residuals stripped senior officers of one of their primary social and professional functions, to provide expert advice to governments on the means necessary to meet governments' defence objectives.

In Macdonald's opinion, "the defence budget [could] be made only in the context of the government's national priorities and in light of its consequent programs." Few officers would argue with that position. Many would argue, however, that for politicians to make a rational and reasonable decision on plans and priorities, they needed to understand the practical implications of their policies. However, the government in general, and Macdonald in particular, found the professional assessments of the requirements to meet their policies mostly unacceptable and so turned in large part to assessments made by public servants or no assessment at all.

The heart of the problem, which would only be revealed later, lay in the fact that the government had inadvertently, or so it seems, increased defence commitments without understanding the implications of doing so. At best, Macdonald had supposed that he would be able to afford new commitments at home by abandoning old commitments to NATO and the UN. In fact, he maintained the European commitment, albeit at a lower level, and added new commitments to deploy a reequipped reconnaissance formation in central Europe and two complicated army and air force formations in northern Europe. Added to these programs were others in Canada which demanded significant restructuring and reequipping of the armed forces. The government by acting without regard for military advice made commitments it could not honour because it was not prepared to pay the costs.

Defence policy and administration in the years following *Defence in the 70s* were characterized on the one hand by a scramble to make sensible plans out of incompatible policies and on the other by artful political dodging of the problem altogether. In his introductory remarks to the white paper Donald Macdonald confessed to a certain "skepticism about the traditional roles of the armed forces" and that skepticism included serious reservations about the integrity of the military profession. But the history of the Trudeau government's relations with its military advisors might best serve to illustrate the limits of political competence and the degree to which responsibility for defence policy must be shared between politicians and soldiers. Finally, the history also illustrated that Canada can perhaps survive with an incoherent defence policy or even no policy at all. The price and irony of the ideas and policies of *Defence in the 70s* was diminished sovereignty over matters that would one day seriously affect the political independence that Trudeau and Macdonald championed. They affected also, in 1984, the political fortunes of Trudeau and the Liberal Party in ways that surprised party members and many Canadians.

Selected Bibliography

J.C. Arnell and J.F. Anderson. "Program Management in the Department of National Defence." *Canadian Defence Quarterly* 1, 2 (Autumn 1971):29-34.

Douglas Bland. *The Administration of Defence Policy in Canada, 1947 to 1985.* Kingston: R.P. Frye Co., 1987.

_____. "Institutionalizing Ambiguity: The Management Review Group and the Re-shaping of the Defence Policy Process in Canada." *Canadian Public Administration* 30,4 (Winter 1987):527-49.

_____. "Controlling the Defence Policy Process in Canada: White Papers on Defence and Bureaucratic Politics in the Department of National Defence." *Defence Analysis* 5,1 (1989):3-16.

_____. *Chiefs of Defence: Government and the Unified Command of the Canadian Armed Forces.* Toronto: Canadian Institute of Strategic Studies, 1995.

R.B. Byers. "Perceptions of Parliamentary Surveillance of the Executive: The Case of Canadian Defence Policy." *Canadian Journal of Political Science* 5 (June 1972):234-50.

_____. "Structural Change and the Policy Process in the Department of National Defence: Military Perceptions." *Canadian Public Administration* 16 (Summer 1973):220-42.

_____. "Defence and Foreign Policy in the 1970s: The Demise of the Trudeau Doctrine." *International Journal* 33,2 (Spring 1978):312-38.

J.L. Granatstein and Robert Bothwell. *Pirouette: Pierre Trudeau and Canadian Foreign Policy.* Toronto: University of Toronto Press, 1990.

E. Leslie. "Too Much Management, Too Little Command." *Canadian Defence Quarterly* 2, 3 (Winter 1972/73):30-32.

P.D. Manson. "The Restructuring of National Defence Headquarters 1972-73: An Assessment." *Canadian Defence Quarterly* 3, 3 (Winter 1973/74):8-14.

J.E. Neelin and L.M. Pederson. "The Administrative Structure of the Canadian Armed Forces: Over-Centralized and Overly Staff-Ridden." *Canadian Defence Quarterly* 4, 2 (Autumn 1974):33-39.

B. Thordarson. *Trudeau and Foreign Policy.* Toronto: Oxford University Press, 1972.

DEPARTMENT OF NATIONAL DEFENCE

Report to the Minister of National Defence on the Management of Defence in Canada. Report of the Management Review Group, July 1972.

The Impact of Integration, Unification and Restructuring on the Functions and Structure of National Defence Headquarters. NDHQ Study S1/85, by D.G. Loomis *et al.* 31 July 1985.

The Canadian Forces and the Department in Peace and War. NDHQ Study S3/85, by D.G. Loomis *et al.* 15 November 1985.

DEFENCE IN THE 70s

WHITE PAPER ON DEFENCE

DONALD S. MACDONALD
Minister of National Defence

Ottawa

Shortly after I became Minister of National Defence last September, work started on this White Paper. The Government had decided that a White Paper was needed to explain the changes taking place in defence policy.

In the White Paper we have indicated the main thrust of the Government's policy thinking for the years ahead. Change in technology and the quickening pace of arms control discussions make this a particularly difficult moment for long-range defence planning. It will be appreciated, therefore, that we have not resolved all outstanding questions. In particular, there are a number of equipment options for which analysis is not far enough advanced to permit decisions to be taken at this time.

These have not been easy times for members of the Armed Forces, although this situation is not unique to Canada. There has been increasing skepticism about the traditional roles of the Armed Forces as we move further and further from the last time the Forces were engaged in combat operations. Moreover, at a time when national social and economic needs are considerable, there is substantial pressure to cut defence expenditures.

In this White Paper the Government has established what it regards as the appropriate size and structure for the Canadian Armed Forces. I feel that this White Paper emphasizes to the Armed Forces the importance the Government places on their services to Canada. They continue to serve with pride and dedication.

Donald S. Macdonald
Minister of National Defence
August, 1971

Contents

The Defence Review

WHY DEFENCE POLICY WAS REVIEWED

Important international and domestic changes have occurred since the review of defence policy which culminated in the White Paper issued in 1964. These changes have required a fundamental reappraisal of Canadian defence policy by the Government.

International Developments

The most significant changes on the international scene with consequences for Canadian defence policy have occurred in the nature of the strategic nuclear balance between the United States and the Soviet Union, and in the state of East-West political relations both in Europe and directly between the two super-powers. These changes, together with the emergence of China as a nuclear power and the growing economic strength of Europe and Japan, have resulted in a loosening of the bipolar international system. This trend is emphasized by the announcement that President Nixon of the United States will shortly be visiting the People's Republic of China, indicative of a major change in policy for both countries. On the other hand, the prospects for effective international peacekeeping, which were viewed with some optimism in 1964, have not developed as had been hoped.

National Concerns

There have been developments within Canada of particular importance to the employment of our defence forces. Defence responsibilities required re-examination as a result of Government decisions to regulate the development of the North in a manner compatible with environmental preservation, and with legislation enacted to prevent pollution in the Arctic and the Northern inland waters. Other relevant developments included the extension of Canada's territorial sea, the establishment of fisheries protection and pollution control zones on the Atlantic and Pacific coasts, and the heightened pace of exploration for offshore mineral resources. Finally, the threat to society posed by violent revolutionaries and the implications of the recent crisis — although the latter occurred well after the defence review began — merited close consideration in projecting Canadian defence activities in the 1970s.

WHY THIS PAPER WAS PRODUCED

The Government began its major defence review in 1968 and indicated the broad lines of its thinking in the policy statement made by Prime Minister Trudeau on April 3, 1969. This statement presented a new orientation in defence policy, and in particular in priorities, to accord with changes on the international and national scenes.

The White Paper on Defence is intended to explain in greater depth the decisions outlined in this policy statement, to provide a policy framework for further decisions by the Government on questions of current force posture and strategy, and to indicate the future direction of policy.

The Paper concentrates on the main policy issues, defines the approach to be taken to them, emphasizes changes which are taking place, but does not attempt to cover all areas of defence activity. Certain subsidiary questions, together with other problems of an administrative nature, will be dealt with as required in separate statements by the Minister of National Defence. Such related statements will be based upon the principles set out in this paper.

The Basis for Defence Policy in the 1970s

DEFENCE AS PART OF NATIONAL POLICY

Defence policy cannot be developed in isolation. It must reflect and serve national interests, and must be closely related to foreign policy, which the Government reviewed concurrently with defence. In the course of these reviews the principle that defence policy must be in phase with the broader external projection of national interests was underlined. In addition, internal aspects of national defence were also considered; these included aid of the civil power and assistance to the civil authorities in the furtherance of national aims.

National Aims

In the foreign policy review general national aims were defined as follows:

- that Canada will continue secure as an independent political entity;
- that Canada and all Canadians will enjoy enlarging prosperity in the widest possible sense; and
- that all Canadians will see in the life they have and the contribution they make to humanity something worthwhile preserving in identity and purpose.

Policy Themes

To achieve these aims, the themes of Canada's national policy were more specifically defined as seeking to:

- foster economic growth,
- safeguard sovereignty and independence,
- work for peace and security,
- promote social justice,
- enhance the quality of life, and
- ensure a harmonious natural environment.

The first concern of defence policy is the national aim of ensuring that Canada should continue secure as an independent political entity — an objective basic to the attainment of the other two national aims. In the policy themes flowing from the national aims, the Canadian Forces have a major part to play in the search for peace and security and also have an important and growing role in safeguarding sovereignty and independence. Accordingly it is to these two themes of national policy that the activities of the Canadian Forces are most closely related. However, defence policy can and should also be relevant to the other policy themes, and the contribution of the Department of National Defence to national development will be examined in this context.

PEACE AND SECURITY

The Changing Scene

One of the most important changes in international affairs in recent years has been the increase in stability in nuclear deterrence, and the emergence of what is, in effect, nuclear parity between the United States and the Soviet Union. Each side now has sufficient nuclear strength to assure devastating retaliation in the event of a surprise attack by the other, and thus neither could rationally consider launching a deliberate attack. There have also been qualitative changes in the composition of the nuclear balance. Of particular importance to Canada is the fact that bombers, and consequently bomber defences, have declined in relative importance in the strategic equation.

Greater stability in the last few years has been accompanied by an increased willingness to attempt to resolve East-West issues by negotiation, although it is still too early to judge the prospects for success. Formal and informal discussions are in progress between the U.S. and the U.S.S.R. on a long list of subjects, involving problems around the globe.

Of overriding importance are the current Strategic Arms Limitation Talks (SALT) where signs of agreement are emerging. Other negotiations of major importance are the Four Power Talks on Berlin in which the U.S. and U.S.S.R. are joined by Britain and France in an effort to resolve one of the main issues still outstanding from Second World War. The Federal Republic of Germany has initiated a series of negotiations fundamental to the future prospects for East-West relations, which have already yielded important agreements with the U.S.S.R. and Poland. In addition, the Government hopes it will be possible to open negotiations on Mutual and Balanced Force Reductions (MBFR) in Europe in the near future.

At the same time the nations of Western Europe are growing more prosperous and are co-operating more closely, and the likelihood has increased that the European Economic Community will be enlarged. The European members of the North Atlantic Treaty Organization (NATO) are now able to assume a greater share of the collective Alliance defence, particularly with respect to their own continent. The North Atlantic Alliance remains firm but within it there is now a more even balance between North America and Europe.

Change has been even more rapid in the Pacific area where Japan's phenomenal economic growth continues and where China's military and political power is substantially increasing. Primarily as a result of these developments in Europe and Asia, but also as a consequence of change in other parts of the world, there has been a return to a form of multi-polarity in the international system. Although the U.S. and the U.S.S.R. continue to have overwhelming military power, and in particular nuclear power, the relative ability of these two countries to influence events in the rest of the world has declined in recent years.

One other development in the international field of particular importance to Canada should be noted. In 1964 there was considerable optimism in this country concerning the scope for peacekeeping. In the intervening years the United Nations Emergency Force was compelled to leave the Middle East. Little progress has been made towards agreement on satisfactory means of international financing of peacekeeping forces. And amidst the tragedy of the Vietnam conflict, the effectiveness of the International Commission for Supervision and Control in Indo-China has further diminished. Additional observer missions were created and operated for a short time on the borders of West Pakistan and India following the border clash of 1965 and in Nigeria in 1969, but no substantial peace-keeping operation has been authorized since 1964 when the UN Force in Cyprus was established. For many reasons the scope for useful and effective peacekeeping activities now appears more modest than it did earlier, despite the persistence of widespread violence in many parts of the world.

Continuing Factors

A catastrophic war between the super powers constitutes the only major military threat to Canada. It is highly unlikely Canada would be attacked by a foreign power other than as a result of a strategic nuclear strike directed at the U.S. Our involvement would be largely a consequence of geography; Canada would not be singled out for separate attack. There is, unfortunately, not much Canada herself can do by way of effective direct defence that is of relevance against massive nuclear attack, given the present state of weapons technology, and the economic restraints on a middle power such as Canada.

Canada's overriding defence objective must therefore be the prevention of nuclear war by promoting political reconciliation to ease the underlying causes of tension, by working for arms control and disarmament agreements, and by contributing to the system of stable mutual deterrence.

Deterrence can be described in general terms as discouraging attack by demonstrating such a capability to retaliate — even after absorbing a massive surprise attack — that the possible gains of aggression would be outweighed by the losses the aggressor would sustain. The fearsome logic of mutual deterrence is clearly not a satisfactory long-term solution to the problem of preventing world conflict. But pending the establishment of a better system of security, it is the dominant factor in world politics today. Because of Canada's obvious inability to deter major nuclear war unilaterally, the Government's policy is to contribute to peace by participating in collective security arrangements. These arrangements have as their purpose the prevention or containment of conflict.

Canada's military role in North American defence involves contributing to the stability of deterrence by assisting the U.S. in operating a comprehensive system of warning, and providing some active defence against bombers and maritime forces. Canada's military role in the part of the NATO area which extends beyond the immediate North American area also constitutes a contribution to deterrence. It helps to minimize the danger of world war arising from conflict in the sensitive European and North Atlantic areas, where the super powers' interests are involved and thus the overall balance is at stake.

Canada's military role in international peacekeeping helps to prevent the outbreak or spread of hostilities in other areas of tension, so that underlying political problems can be settled through negotiation or a process of accommodation, and so that the possibility of great power involvement is minimized.

It is in Canada's interest that war should be prevented, but if unavoidable that it should be halted before it can escalate into a broader conflict which could affect the security of Canada. The Government intends therefore to maintain within feasible limits a general purpose combat capability of high professional standard within the Armed Forces, and to keep available the widest possible choice of options for responding to unforeseen international developments.

The Department of National Defence maintains a program in arms control research to support the Department of External Affairs. This has contributed to Canada's ability to make an effective contribution to the consultations held over the last two years at NATO to prepare for SALT, and to the preparations by NATO for negotiations on MBFR. It has also contributed to various other arms control proposals being discussed at the Geneva disarmament conference, on such subjects as chemical and biological warfare and a proposed comprehensive test ban treaty. Canada also played a role in the negotiations surrounding the Non-Proliferation Treaty, and the treaties banning weapons of mass destruction from outer space and the seabed.

It should be stressed that a constant criterion for evaluating all aspects of policy is the determination to avoid any suggestion of the offensive use of Canadian Forces to commit aggression, or to contribute to such action by another state. Such a possibility would be unthinkable and unacceptable. With a view to ensuring the protection of Canada and contributing to the maintenance of stable mutual deterrence, Canada's resources, its territory, and its Armed Forces will be used solely for purposes which are defensive in the judgment of the Government of Canada.

SOVEREIGNTY AND INDEPENDENCE

Canada's sovereignty and independence depend ultimately on security from armed attack. In this sense, the contribution of the Canadian Forces to the prevention of war is a vital and direct contribution to safeguarding our sovereignty and independence. Defence policy must, however, also take into account the possibility that other challenges to Canada's sovereignty and independence, mainly non-military in character, may be more likely to arise during the 1970s. They could come both from outside and from within the country, and to deal with them may in some ways be more difficult. While deterring war is not an objective Canada alone can achieve, and is therefore one which must be pursued through collective security arrangements, the other challenges to sovereignty and independence must be met exclusively by Canada. The provision of adequate Canadian defence resources for this purpose must therefore be a matter of first priority.

External Challenges

By assuming the general responsibility for surveillance and control over Canadian territory, waters and airspace, in conjunction with civil agencies, the Canadian Forces help safeguard sovereignty and independence. Challenges could occur through actions by foreign agencies or their nationals involving territorial violations or infringements of Canadian laws governing access to and activity within these areas. This is not a new role for the Canadian Forces, but its dimensions are changing.

The North, in a sense the last frontier of Canada, has a unique physical environment presenting special problems of administration and control. Modern industrial technology has in recent years stimulated a growth of commercial interest in the resource potential of the area, and contributed to a major increase in oil and gas exploration in the Territories, especially on the Arctic Islands. These activities, in which foreign as well as Canadian companies are involved, have brought with them a need to ensure that exploitation of the resources is carried out in accordance with Canada's long-term national interests. There is a danger that this increased activity with its inherent danger of oil or other pollution might disturb the finely balanced ecology of the region. The Government therefore decided to take special measures to ensure the environmental preservation of this uniquely vulnerable area, and to ensure that these measures are fully respected. Strict regulations governing land use and mineral exploration and exploitation are being brought into effect. Legislation provides for the exercise of pollution control jurisdiction in an area extending generally 100 miles from the mainland and islands of the Canadian Arctic.

Canada is a three-ocean maritime nation with one of the longest coastlines in the world, and a large portion of the trade vital to our economic strength goes by sea. The Government is concerned that Canada's many and varied interests in the waters close to our shores, on the seabed extending from our coasts, and on the high seas beyond, be protected.

The Government has taken decisions with respect to the limits of Canada's territorial sea and fishing zones off the East and West coasts. Modern fishing techniques have resulted in a concern for the conservation of fishing resources in these areas. Legislation has extended Canada's territorial sea from three to twelve miles, and the former nine-mile contiguous fishing zone has been incorporated within the extended territorial sea. At the same time, new and extensive Canadian-controlled fishing zones have been created in areas of the sea adjacent to the coast. An order-in-council has been promulgated establishing such fishing zones in Queen Charlotte Sound, Dixon Entrance and Hecate Strait on the West Coast, and the Gulf of St. Lawrence and the Bay of Fundy on the East Coast, a total area of 80,000 square miles. Against the possibility of potentially disastrous oil spills, pollution control is also to be exercised in these areas.

Exploration and exploitation of the resources of the continental shelf are regulated under the Oil and Gas Production and Conservation Act. This area extends to the limits of exploitability, which Canada interprets as comprising the submerged continental margin. Although less extensive off the West Coast, it extends hundreds of miles off the East Coast, and encompasses large areas off the Arctic mainland and islands. In recent years there has been a tremendous increase in technological capability for exploitation of this resource potential.

Departmental Responsibilities and Relationships

The Government's objective is to continue effective occupation of Canadian territory, and to have a surveillance and control capability to the extent necessary to safeguard national interests in all Canadian territory, and all airspace and waters over which Canada exercises sovereignty or jurisdiction. This involves a complex judgment on the challenges which could occur and on the surveillance and control capability required in the circumstances.

The Canadian Forces do not have sole responsibility for ensuring respect for relevant Canadian legislation but they do have a general responsibility for surveillance and control over land, sea and airspace under Canadian jurisdiction. In peacetime this role of the Forces is in many respects complementary to that of the civil authorities. The requirement for military assistance is generally greater, however, in more sparsely settled regions until a stage of economic and social development has been reached, justifying an expansion of civil agencies and resources. Similarly, where the Canadian Forces have the capability to meet a shortage in civil resources for the policing of waters off the coasts, their role can be expanded.

The area to be covered is vast. In certain regions facilities are limited and weather conditions are often adverse. The problem would perhaps be simpler if it were restricted to the more traditional security threat of direct military attack from a predictable enemy. Instead, challenges could arise in more ambiguous circumstances from private entities as well as foreign government agencies. Incidents may involve, for instance, a fishing vessel, an oil tanker or a private aircraft. But the principle involved is well established. By creating a capability for surveillance and control which is effective and visible, the intention is to discourage such challenges.

Other departments of government already have specific responsibilities in many instances for regulating activity in Canadian territory, and these lead to requirements for carrying out surveillance and exercising control. National Defence has, however, ultimate responsibility to ensure that overall an adequate Canadian surveillance and control capability exists for the protection of Canadian sovereignty and security. Consequently the Government intends to establish Canadian Forces' operations centres on the East and West coasts which will work closely with the civil departments to co-ordinate surveillance and control activities. Where required by potential challenges to our interests the Canadian Forces will carry out surveillance and exercise control in those areas not covered by the civil departments, or in which the latter require assistance in discharging their responsibilities. Close consultation between National Defence and the civil departments concerned will be maintained on a continuing basis to ensure that surveillance and control is being exercised when, where, and to the extent necessary to satisfy the Government's requirements in the most economical way.

Internal Security

The Canadian experience over the last two years clearly indicates the necessity of being able to cope effectively with any future resort to disruption, intimidation and violence as weapons of political action. The three prime instances in which the Forces were used recently in this role were during the Montreal police strike, the political kidnapping crisis of last October and the Kingston Penitentiary riots. While civil disorder should normally be contained by the civil authorities, and the strength of municipal, provincial and federal police forces should be maintained at levels sufficient for the purpose, we must nevertheless anticipate the possibility that emergencies will again arise which will necessitate the Canadian Forces coming to the aid of the civil power. It is important that the latter should be able to rely upon timely assistance from the Forces. The Forces' role in such situations is important and could be crucial.

In addition to the possibility of future crises arising in Canada, there is also the possibility that violent events elsewhere could stimulate outbreaks in Canada. This problem is therefore one with clear international ramifications. Indeed, it appears that much of the world has already moved into an era which will see established order increasingly challenged by organized violence. These are times of confrontation when growing numbers of people appear to be prepared to resort to violence with a view to destroying the democratic process.

NATIONAL DEVELOPMENT

Although maintained primarily for purposes of sovereignty and security, the Department of National Defence provides an important reservoir of skills and capabilities which in the past has been drawn upon, and which in the future can be increasingly drawn upon, to contribute to the social and economic development of Canada. By their service and devotion to duty the members of the Armed Forces, and the civilians who support them, have made a significant contribution to preserving a democratic society in Canada against the threat of external challenges.

The Armed Forces make an important contribution to Canada's unity and identity in a number of ways. They bring together Canadians from all parts of the country, from all walks of life, from the two major linguistic groups and other origins, into an activity that is truly national in scope and in purpose. They are distinctively Canadian and this is symbolized by their new uniform. A career in the Armed Forces has enabled many Canadians to advance their education and skills, whether in university, in technical specialties or in a trade. The influence of the Forces is extended to young people through cadet and militia programs, and through the work of many individual members in youth organizations. The Department continues to view its support of such activities as a vital contribution to the well-being of the youth of our country.

The inherent characteristics of the Armed Forces combine effective command and organization, high mobility, great flexibility and a range of skills and specialties broader than that of any other national organization. These provide Canada with a resource which may be used to carry out essentially non-military projects of high priority and importance to national development. The objective will be to use the Forces primarily on projects which relate to their capabilities to respond efficiently and promptly to their basic defence roles.

The Forces will be called upon, therefore, in conjunction with other government departments, to assist development in the civil sector, especially in the remote regions where disciplined task forces with wide experience in adapting to unusual or challenging circumstances are required. Where possible, the Reserves will also be used in this role. A further objective of this policy will be to promote greater involvement of the military in the community, and to ensure that the community is aware of the ways in which the military sector contributes to achieving national aims and priorities.

The Canadian Forces have made a major contribution to the development of the North. The Northwest Territories and Yukon Radio System, established in 1923, pioneered development of communications in the North. Both before Second World War and in the post-war years, the Forces carried out extensive aerial photographic and survey activities which played a key part in mapping the Arctic and in opening it up for air transportation.

The construction of defence installations in the North developed new techniques for dealing with permafrost and other Arctic conditions which have been invaluable to subsequent northern development. Much has been done to understand and deal with the special problems of communications and navigation in the Arctic. An icebreaker operated by the Forces was the first large ship to navigate the Northwest Passage. The Forces, with the help of the Defence Research Board (DRB), have been in the forefront of the opening of the North and have pioneered in finding solutions to the problems of its development. This role will be enhanced in the future, particularly where National Defence engineering and construction resources can be utilized.

The Forces will make a major contribution to the preservation of an unspoiled environment and an improved quality of life by supporting the civil agencies in exercising pollution control in the North and off Canada's coasts. The Forces and the Canada Emergency Measures Organization will continue to play an important part in providing relief and assistance in the event of natural disasters or other civil emergencies, including those resulting from oil spills or other forms of pollution.

The work of the Armed Forces, in concert with DRB as part of the Ministry of Transport Task Force during the clean-up operations after the tanker Arrow went aground in Chedabucto Bay last year, illustrates their competence in this field. The Department of National Defence provided a wide range of services and skills, including a base vessel, skilled divers, an emergency communications centre, quick-reacting transportation, special experience in civil and maritime engineering and necessary general scientific knowledge.

For many years the Forces have also assisted in flood control operations and in fighting forest fires, and have had major responsibilities for air-and-sea search and rescue activities.

The important contributions made by the Canadian Armed Forces following the recent earthquakes in Peru, their assistance in providing relief to Pakistan after the floods, and their current relief flights for the refugees in eastern India, all amply demonstrate their effectiveness in international relief operations. These operations gave support to Canadian foreign policy and enabled Canada to help the homeless and sick in vital disaster areas.

The Forces can also give further support to foreign policy objectives through increased assistance in economic aid programs. National Defence has capabilities to assist in such fields as engineering and construction, logistics policies, trades and technical training, advisory services, project analysis and air transport. The Department will work with the Canadian International Development Agency and the Department of External Affairs to study the possible use of military capabilities in support of specific aid programs or projects as the need arises.

Defence expenditure forms an important component of Federal Government expenditures and one which has considerable impact on Canada's economy. This expenditure, largely taking the form of salaries paid to military and civilian employees and of payments for goods and services, clearly has yielded important incidental benefits to economic growth.

Although the payroll to military and civilian employees is decentralized and has benefited the economies of every province in Canada, the purchases of military equipment and other supplies have tended to be concentrated in the more heavily industrialized centres. In the foreseeable future the largest volume of defence purchases will continue to be made in these industrialized areas, but to assist in the attainment of the Government's objective of regional economic equality, further decentralization of defence procurement into all regions of Canada will be encouraged whenever this can be done consistent with long-term economic efficiency.

The main economic benefits of defence activities have been scientific, technological and industrial. The requirements of the Armed Forces for effective modern equipment, and the rapid scientific and technological advances in such equipment since the Second World War, have acted as a catalyst to stimulate the introduction of new techniques into Canadian industry. The Canadian Armed Forces and the Defence Research Board have contributed many innovations, ranging from transportable housing and new methods of food processing, to navigational aids and space technology.

The Defence Industrial Research Program and programs of the Department of Industry, Trade and Commerce play an important role in maintaining a viable defence industrial base. Their financial assistance to industrial research is designed to ensure that Canadian companies can compete for research, development and ultimately, production contracts in defence and civil markets. Examples include support in the fields of digital flight simulators, short and vertical take-off aircraft and airborne doppler radar.

Research in universities also receives considerable support from DRB grants. They have been allocated in many fields, including aviation medicine and upper atmosphere and aerospace research.

Projects with a defence orientation frequently lead directly to benefits in civil areas. A major breakthrough in gas lasers by DRB has placed Canada in the forefront of this rapidly expanding field. Two Canadian companies now have licences to develop lasers using this technology for commercial use, and the simplicity of this type of laser will make low cost, high energy instruments available to a wide range of users, including small industries and laboratories. Another example is the study of underwater life support systems which has led to the development of an analogue pneumatic decompression computer, which is being produced commercially with continuing technical assistance from DRB.

The Canadian satellite program was developed principally with defence resources and skills. This has permitted Canada to stay in the forefront of this area of technology and created a foundation for a satellite program which has now been transferred to the Department of Communication. Alouette I was designed and built completely within the Defence Research Telecommunication Establishment. With Alouette II and ISIS-A the opportunity was taken to bring industry in Canada into the satellite program. As a result, skills have either been introduced or strengthened in the companies involved, and these companies are now receiving foreign contracts.

Such successes depend on the maintenance of a high level of scientific and technical expertise. Science and technology advance at an ever increasing rate, and considerable effort is required to remain competitive. Canada's participation in the international field of defence research is considered essential. In certain areas, some of which are mentioned above, Canada has been able to contribute substantially; in many others we receive much more than we contribute.

To fulfill their assigned roles, the Armed Forces need highly sophisticated and costly equipment. Our experience in 1959 with the cancellation of the Arrow interceptor aircraft firmly established that, because of the costs and the small quantities involved, such development cannot be economically undertaken by Canada acting alone. Because of costs and complexity, and the need for relatively long production runs, most countries have now accepted the need for co-operative efforts in producing their major equipment needs.

A significant portion of the capital equipment budget is thus spent abroad, largely in the United States. To ensure that Canada obtains equivalent economic, industrial and technological benefits for these expenditures, and in order to maintain a domestic defence industrial base, arrangements have been made with our allies for Canadian industry either to share in the production of equipment or to export a like value of defence products to our allies. Co-operation with the United States and other countries in development and production-sharing programs has been a significant factor in allowing the Canadian Armed Forces to purchase the best equipment at the most advantageous prices.

PRIORITIES FOR CANADIAN DEFENCE POLICY

The policy announced by the Prime Minister on April 3, 1969, initiated the process of adjusting the balance between Canadian defence activities to ensure that priorities for defence were responsive to national interests and international developments. Four major areas of activity for the Canadian Forces were identified in summary form as follows:

(a)   the surveillance of our own territory and coast-lines, i.e. the protection of our sovereignty;
(b)   the defence of North America in co-operation with U.S. forces;
(c)   the fulfilment of such NATO commitments as may be agreed upon; and
(d)   the performance of such international peacekeeping roles as we may from time to time assume.

This paper will next examine these four areas of defence policy in detail. Activity in each must be assessed in terms of the priorities which have been established, and of the cost-effectiveness and marginal return of various options. With the limited resources available for Canadian defence needs, it is desirable to have versatile forces and multi-purpose equipment rather than a high degree of specialization. Multiple tasking is also necessary in order to make the most efficient use of available resources.

Protection of Canada

Apart from aid of the civil power, which will be considered separately, the two principal aspects of this role for the Forces are surveillance and control. Surveillance requires detection and identification to obtain information on what is happening on Canada's land mass, in her airspace and on and under her coastal waters; control implies appropriate enforcement action to ensure that laws and regulations are respected.

SURVEILLANCE

Military surveillance is required for the protection of Canada and Canadian interests, but it is also an essential contribution to North American defence and, in the broader context, to the security of the North Atlantic region. In our collective security arrangements, surveillance is conducted to provide warning of potentially unfriendly acts by foreign military forces. But Canada also has a national requirement for certain surveillance activities to provide information on events of importance occurring on land, at sea and in Canadian airspace.

Air

Almost all identification of aircraft in the Canadian airspace which is under air traffic control is performed by comparing radar tracks with filed flight plans, or by ground-to-air communication through the active co-operation of the aircraft concerned. The communications network required to make flight plans available in time is of considerable complexity. Since the function of civilian air traffic control requires much of the same data as the function of identification for air defence, full civil-military co-operation is the most effective approach. There is already a considerable degree of integration and more will be possible in the future, with benefits in both areas.

Extensive surveillance systems are now operated as part of the North American Air Defence Command (NORAD) but they also serve national purposes in covering a portion of Canadian airspace. A number of radar installations, many of which were operated by the U.S., have been closed in recent years to effect economies as the bomber threat declined. The U.S. earlier this year gave Canada notice of intention to close two radar stations it operated in Canada: Melville, near Goose Bay, Labrador, and Stephenville, Newfoundland. In order to continue the radar coverage in the Labrador area which is required for adequate surveillance as well as control on the East coast, the Government decided to operate Melville as a Canadian radar site.

Maritime and Land

A substantial capability for surveillance over Canada's waters in the temperate zone is currently available. Surveillance over Arctic land and waters can be carried out by long-range patrol aircraft but at present is limited by light and weather conditions. Surveillance by ships is restricted to ice-free periods of the year. Because of the areas involved, general ground surveillance by land forces is not practicable. The Department of National Defence is assessing the challenges that might be expected in the Canadian North and, if warranted, will increase surveillance.

Surveillance over maritime and land areas is currently available from the Argus long-range patrol aircraft which was designed and bought specifically to detect and track submarines. The Tracker aircraft has similar capabilities, although its range is much shorter. Both the Argus and Tracker could be operated at least to the end of the decade, and therefore the question of a new generation of this type of aircraft need not necessarily arise for several years. The Argus would, however, have to be overhauled to ensure continued air worthiness. A comprehensive systems analysis of the alternatives is being undertaken.

The CF-5 aircraft was acquired for the non-nuclear tactical support role and will normally work with the land forces. The CF-5s will also be employed to provide a quick-response photographic reconnaissance capability in Canada and over the waters off Canadian shores. In addition, some of the CF-5s will be employed in the advanced training role now being carried out by the T-33 aircraft, thus obviating the need to acquire a new aircraft for this purpose.

Although Canada has a good capability to detect submarines in its waters in the temperate zone, it has only very limited capability to detect submarine activity in the Arctic. It might be desirable in the future to raise the level of capability so as to have subsurface perimeter surveillance, particularly to cover the channels connecting the Arctic Ocean to Baffin Bay and Baffin Bay to the Atlantic. The Government is therefore undertaking research to determine the costs and feasibility of a limited subsurface system to give warning of any unusual maritime activity. The Defence Research Board is playing an important role in these studies. If found to be desirable, the system could be operated as part of the overall surveillance of North America against unknown submarines.

The Forces already operate one submersible or miniature submarine. Submersibles could have an important role in research, and in continental shelf and seabed surveillance. In co-operation with civil agencies, the Forces and DRB will develop an undersea program of national benefit.

Assistance to the Civil Authorities

The general surveillance of Canadian airspace and waters required for national security will permit greater support to other departments. Initial consultations with the civil departments responsible by legislation for the protection of various specific interests have already indicated several areas where a greater contribution by the Armed Forces will be necessary. They will be kept under review to ensure that the total national effort is both effective and efficient in the use of available resources to meet the Government's requirements.

Some of the activities identified are:

(a) general area surveillance of foreign fishing fleets off the coasts;
(b) specific reconnaissance missions on a quick-response, short-term basis to locate those fishing fleets when they move and fail to appear where expected;
(c) area surveillance of offshore waters to detect and report suspected illegal seismic and other exploratory activities;

(d) assistance in ice reconnaissance operations;
(e) surveillance when needed of Canadian waters off the East and West coasts and in the North to detect pollution at sea;
(f) surveillance of Canadian territorial waters to detect and report foreign vessels illegally present therein;
(g) surveillance of sites of mineral exploration and exploitation projects in the North when verification of their location and status is required; and
(h) during the appropriate seasons, provision of observer space on aircraft engaged in northern surveillance operations to permit wildlife observation.

CONTROL

In addition to the requirements for surveillance a military capability for control is required as an adjunct to the other measures necessary for the protection of Canada and Canadian interests. This should include an ability to enforce these measures should laws not be respected. Such efforts to protect national interests are fully consistent with Canadian involvement in collective security against foreign military attack.

Air
Our national airspace regulations are normally enforced by taking action against the pilot or owner of an offending and non-co-operating aircraft after it lands. Occasionally, however, an aircraft is detected by radar and cannot be identified by flight plan correlation or by communication. If such aircraft cannot be identified as legitimate civil or military traffic, an interceptor aircraft must be sent up to identify it and, if necessary, force it to land.

The Government intends to use its air defence resources to the best advantage to ensure that Canadian aircraft are able to intercept and identify intruders in Canadian airspace over as wide an area as possible. At present, identification of aircraft is confined to that part of Canadian airspace covered by radar.

CF-101 (Voodoo) interceptor aircraft are operated by the Canadian Armed Forces at Chatham, New Brunswick, Bagotville (with a detachment at Val d'Or), Quebec, and Comox, British Columbia. Under the

NORAD plan the air defence needs are adequately met in areas where Canadian aircraft are not deployed, largely by interceptors flown from U.S. bases. Although from a strictly air defence point of view it may make little difference whether the aircraft is Canadian or U.S., from a national point of view the Government believes that normal peacetime identification should be performed by Canadian aircraft.

The Government has therefore decided that Canadian CF-101s should at all times be able to conduct interception and identification missions in the approaches to Eastern Canada, and appropriate arrangements will be made. The Government has decided as well to utilize CF-104 aircraft already based at Cold Lake, Alberta, in the Operational Training Squadron, so that Canada will have its own interception and identification capability in the Prairie area.

The Government will keep under review the options available for using mobile surveillance radars, either airborne or air portable, so that airspace control can be instituted where and when needed. For example, protection of Canadian interests may, in the future, require air-traffic-controlled airspace in certain parts of the North.

Maritime
Canada's sea and air maritime forces possess a considerable capability for exercising control in the territorial seas, in the fishing and pollution control zones, and in the waters above the continental shelf. It is through continuous operations and co-ordinated team efforts, often in co-operation with units of other government departments, that the necessary degree of control can be achieved. Although the present naval ships cannot operate safely in ice-covered waters, or above 65° N latitude at any time of the year, they are being employed in northern waters to a greater extent during the summer months.

The Canadian Forces are conducting an extensive test program on the hydrofoil craft, Bras d'Or, which was designed and built in Canada. A decision on procuring hydrofoil craft for surveillance and control will be based on a cost-effectiveness study. It will determine the optimum performance characteristics for this particular role, and will examine alternatives such as fast patrol boats of a normal displacement design. The study will have to be concerned with the weapons system for such craft, given their primary role of surveillance and control, and the possibilities of equipment packages to provide flexibility to meet a number of other roles. Air-cushion vehicles which might have a military role in the Arctic are being kept under review and will be considered in this study.

The possibility of the Department of National Defence providing increased support to other departments in control activities has been studied, and the results indicate a need for:

- on-call support by naval vessels on both East and West coasts to deal with incursions by fishing fleets in the Canadian territorial sea or fishing zones;
- occasional arrest within territorial waters and pollution control zones of foreign ships in breach of Canadian anti-pollution regulations.

The Forces will be prepared to respond when called upon by the appropriate authorities in such situations.

Land

The current capabilities of the Canadian Forces are generally adequate for surveillance and control. The three combat groups within Canada are air transportable and the Canadian Airborne Regiment provides a parachute-drop capability well suited for operations in the North. In the event of a requirement to defend the land mass of North America, a mutual support arrangement exists with the United States.

More emphasis is being placed on training the Armed Forces to live and operate in the Arctic. A Northern Region Headquarters has been established at Yellowknife, and there is a military liaison staff at Whitehorse. Consideration will be given to establishing other small bases in the North, particularly in the Arctic Islands, and to the desirability of reconstituting the Canadian Rangers. National Defence is also examining the desirability of establishing a special training school for all personnel assigned to the North. The adequacy of existing equipment is also being studied, with particular emphasis on over-snow vehicles.

AID OF THE CIVIL POWER

The Canadian Armed Forces, and in particular the land element, have always had a responsibility to aid the civil power whenever required, and the events of last year have shown how important this role can be. One of the tasks assigned to the three combat groups and the Airborne Regiment is to assist in internal security operations if required. Additional land forces could be made available in an emergency from the Reserves and from forces engaged in other roles. Normal military training prepares the Canadian soldier exceptionally well for this role. Discipline and restraint, which are vital when acting in such a role, are an essential part of military training.

The Defence of North America

THE NUCLEAR DETERRENT SYSTEM

The only direct external military threat to Canada's national security today is that of a large-scale nuclear attack on North America. So long as a stable strategic balance exists, the deliberate initiation of nuclear war between the U.S.S.R. and the U.S. is highly improbable; this constitutes mutual deterrence. It is far from being the theoretically ideal means of maintaining peace, but the Government, while continuing to participate in the arms control deliberations, remains convinced that there is nothing to replace it at present. Therefore, Canada must do what it can to ensure the continued effectiveness of the deterrent system.

In the defence of North America, Canada is inevitably closely associated with the United States. Even if no warheads actually landed on Canada in the event of general nuclear war, a strategic attack on the U.S., which could leave over 100 million dead, would have cataclysmic consequences for this country.

From a potential enemy's point of view, however, North America can only logically be seen as one set of targets. Canada's centres of population and industry logically form part of the major target plan for a strategic nuclear attack on North America. Most are concentrated along the St. Lawrence and in the lower Great Lakes regions, virtually all are close to the Canadian-U.S. border, and the Canadian and U.S. economies are highly integrated. Regardless of the circumstances leading up to such an attack, logically, for geographical reasons if for no other, we must plan on the basis that we shall inevitably be gravely affected.

The Government concluded in its defence review that co-operation with the United States in North American defence will remain essential so long as our joint security depends on stability in the strategic military balance. Canada's objective is to make, within the limits of our resources, an effective contribution to continued stability by assisting in the surveillance and warning systems, and in the protection of the U.S. retaliatory capability as necessary. Co-operation between Canada and the U.S. in the joint defence of North America is vital for sovereignty and security.

CANADA'S CONTRIBUTION

This paper indicates what in the Government's view would be the most appropriate and effective contribution, taking into account political, strategic, economic and military factors. Given the resources available for defence, and the almost limitless demands on them, this contribution will be directly related to the surveillance and control role for the Forces.

In air defence, Canada's part in the past has been one of contributing to the provision of interceptor aircraft, surface-to-air missiles, radars, communications and associated headquarters. These activities, conducted since 1958 under the NORAD agreement, have had three main benefits for Canada:

- they have helped to assure the protection of the U.S. deterrent against what was at one time the main threat, that of Soviet bomber attack;
- they have provided for a defence which would take place beyond the settled areas of Canada; and
- they have enhanced Canada's control over its own territory.

In maritime defence, Canada contributes forces through arrangements with the United States and assumes responsibility for ocean areas adjacent to Canada's shores. These arrangements have had two main benefits for Canada:

- they have provided surveillance over contiguous ocean areas against surface and subsurface vessels, and provided warning of a build-up of potentially hostile forces; and
- they have provided the capability necessary to cope with hostile activity.

BALLISTIC MISSILE WARNING AND DEFENCE

Warning of attack on North America by intercontinental ballistic missiles (ICBMs) is provided by a variety of surveillance systems. Although none of these is located in Canada, the communications for the Ballistic Missile Early Warning System (BMEWS) pass through Canada to the joint Canada/United States NORAD headquarters at Colorado Springs. Improvements to this system are being considered by the U.S., but none involve more extensive use of Canadian territory. The Canadian Forces also operate a Baker-Nunn camera facility at Cold Lake as part of the U.S. Space Detection and Tracking System (SPADATS).

Concern has been expressed by Canadians about the consequences of U.S. based anti-ballistic missiles (ABMs) intercepting missiles over Canadian territory. It should be understood, however, that an ABM defence in the U.S. would function only during a nuclear onslaught on North America. In these circumstances, whether interceptions took place over Canadian territory or not would make relatively little difference to the Canadian public with respect to fallout or other effects. In fact, if interceptions took place over Canada, the effects on the Canadian population would almost certainly be less than if the missiles reached their targets in the United States. The system is designed to ensure that the Spartan and Sprint missiles will not cause significant damage on the ground below the point of burst. Moreover, under current deployment plans, only the Spartan missile could carry out interceptions over Canada, and these would take place outside the atmosphere.

While the ABM question is one of obvious importance to Canada and has been closely followed by the Government, the U.S. does not depend on Canadian territory for its ABM system as it did in the 1950s and 1960s for the anti-bomber defence system, and has not requested or suggested Canadian participation.

The Strategic Arms Limitation Talks are making progress as exemplified by the fact that the U.S. and the U.S.S.R. announced an understanding on May 20, 1971, to concentrate on achieving this year an agreement on limiting deployment of ABMs. They will also agree on certain measures with respect to the limitation of offensive strategic weapons. The Canadian Government shares the conviction expressed by the two sides that this course of action will create more favourable conditions

for further negotiations to limit all strategic arms. An agreement if attained would amount to an historic turning point in efforts to curb the
nuclear arms race, and to enhance national and international security through
nuclear arms control.

MARITIME WARNING AND DEFENCE

Canada's maritime forces can detect and monitor potentially hostile
maritime operations in waters off Canada's coasts. As in air defence, this
constant surveillance contributes to international stability by demonstrating
an ability to detect any build-up by a potential aggressor. In fact, most of
Canada's maritime forces have a high degree of flexibility in the sense
that they can be employed either for North American defence or for the
protection of Canada's maritime interests through surveillance and control.

The last decade has witnessed a rapid expansion in, and a global
deployment of, Soviet naval power. The Soviet missile-firing submarine
force in particular has increased substantially in both numbers and
capability.

In 1965 the Government decided to acquire four helicopter-carrying
destroyers (DDH 280 class), two of which will be available in late 1972,
and a further two in 1973. These vessels were judged to be necessary as a
replacement for some of the ships then in service which were becoming
obsolescent. The new destroyers have a general purpose capability and
will be more flexibly employed than any of the destroyers currently in
service. They will be better able to support the activities which evolve
from the new defence priorities.

Canada now has twenty destroyers, three support ships, four submarines and several squadrons of Argus and Tracker aircraft. While this force
has considerable versatility, which will be enhanced by the four new DDHs,
it was designed as a highly specialized force to operate against submarines. Although an anti-submarine warfare (ASW) capability will be maintained as part of the general purpose maritime forces, the present degree
of emphasis on anti-submarine warfare directed against submarine-launched
ballistic missiles (SLBMs) will be reduced in favour of other maritime
roles.

The Government believes Canada's maritime forces must be reoriented
with the long term objective of providing a more versatile general purpose

capability. Versatility is required because it is not possible to be certain precisely which maritime activities will be required and which will not in the years ahead. It is therefore sensible to design a general purpose capability for Canada's maritime forces. This policy will take a long time to implement fully because of the life of current equipment, but it will govern both the acquisition of new equipment for the maritime force, and where applicable, modifications to existing equipment. This policy will also govern training for the maritime forces.

BOMBER WARNING AND DEFENCE

If a nuclear attack ever occurred, it is most probable that Soviet nuclear forces would probably be launched in a concerted program with minimal warning to achieve maximum surprise. Soviet strategic bombers, of which there are now about 150, would have a follow-on role. This is largely because of the effectiveness of NORAD's warning system. Bombers would probably be dispatched simultaneously with missiles but would reach North America several hours later, presumably to strike targets which did not require immediate attack, or which the missiles had not successfully attacked. Given this situation, the question is how much priority should be given by Canada in the future to bomber defence.

Up-to-date surveillance systems will continue to be required since, if they were not employed, bombers could approach North America undetected and add very substantially to the weight of the attack. The surveillance systems in Canada contribute to deterrence by inhibiting the Soviets from launching their bombers against North America before their missiles. This is because the NORAD detection system would signal impending attack and could invite a pre-emptive and devastating U.S. missile strike.

The time has passed, however, when a full, active anti-bomber defence is essential for the protection of the U.S. deterrent capability. The U.S.-assured destruction or retaliatory capability now resides largely in the ICBM and SLBM force. The principal threat to that force is the Soviet land-based missile force, in particular the very large SS-9 type missile.

The BOMARC missiles sited in Canada were a relatively important contribution in the days when a full anti-bomber defence existed to defend urban-industrial targets as well as to protect the deterrent which consisted largely of the U.S. bomber force. The deployment by the U.S.S.R. of a missile force numbering in the thousands has altered considerably the strategic situation. The BOMARCs have become highly vulnerable to missile attack since they cannot be dispersed like aircraft. Moreover, the Canadian BOMARCs are sited to defend the eastern part of North America whereas the preponderance of the U.S. land-based strategic retaliatory forces is located in the mid-west. Since no comprehensive defence of population against missile attack is likely to be available in the foreseeable future, the Government has concluded there is no longer sufficient reason to continue to deploy BOMARCs in Canada, and this system will therefore be retired. Arrangements will be made to minimize the economic effects of this decision.

Canada will maintain the number of interceptor aircraft at the current level to contribute to stability since Soviet bombers could considerably augment follow-on attacks on North America. The Soviets might also be tempted to rebuild their long-range bomber force if they believed there would be absolutely no defences against them. Moreover, interceptor aircraft are required for peacetime identification and sovereign control of airspace. Canadian interceptors are located so as to maximize the possibilities for conducting a defence north of heavily populated areas.

To provide effective deterrence, at the present time there is a continuing need for the integrated operational control over forces made available for the air defence of Canada and the U.S. as provided by the NORAD agreement which was signed in 1958 and renewed in 1968. The agreement does not specify any level of forces, equipment or facilities, so the nature and extent of Canada's contribution continues to be a matter for decision by the Canadian Government. The NORAD agreement will be up for renewal in 1973. The policy of the Government at that time with respect to the agreement and the interceptor force posture required will depend upon the strategic situation extant, including progress in SALT.

The Canadian Government is not therefore prepared to devote substantial sums to new equipment or facilities for use only for active antibomber defences in the future. Over the last decade the anti-bomber defences available to NORAD have been substantially reduced as a result of changes in the threat. Unless the strategic situation changes, the Government intends to update its contribution to the active anti-bomber defences of North America only to the extent that this is required for the general control of Canadian airspace.

Two systems are being developed in the U.S. primarily for the purposes of North American anti-bomber defence. They are the Over-The-Horizon (OTH) radar and the Airborne Warning and Control System (AWACS). It is possible that operating together they could replace some of the existing fixed radars and reduce the vulnerability of the system. Present indications are, however, that neither will be operational until the latter part of the decade.

The OTH radar may in the future be able to provide a surveillance capability against intruding aircraft for a large part of Canadian airspace not covered by existing radar. DRB, in co-operation with its U.S. counterpart, will be testing the operation of OTH radar in Northern Canada. The AWACS has two primary functions — warning, including surveillance, and control in terms of guidance of interceptors. It could therefore be used for patrols on a random or fixed basis, and to control intercepts if suitable aircraft were within range. The Government will keep both systems under review since they could in the future fulfill an important role in the surveillance of Canadian airspace in the North American defence context.

In air combat there is at present no alternative to equipping the CF-101s with nuclear warheads held in Canada by the U.S. under existing storage and custody arrangements. The CF-101s have a conventional air-to-air capability and are operated in this mode for peacetime interception and identification. However, to play an effective role in the defence of North America against the threat of massive nuclear attack, they require nuclear tipped air-to-air weapons. Only with such weapons would they have a reasonable prospect of destroying attacking bombers and their nuclear weapons before the latter were released.

This means that the only system still in the Canadian Forces requiring nuclear weapons will be the CF-101 Voodoo aircraft based in Canada. The Honest John surface-to-surface missile battery has been disbanded, the CF-104 will drop the nuclear strike role in Europe at the end of this year, and the BOMARC will be retired shortly.

The Government has decided that in normal peacetime circumstances the guiding principle should continue to be that, to the greatest extent feasible, defence activities on Canadian territory will be carried out by members of the Canadian Armed Forces. During periods of international crisis, however, special arrangements are required to enhance the protection of North America and contribute to the maintenance of stable mutual deterrence.

The Government is therefore prepared to continue to allow U.S. Strategic Air Command (SAC) refuelling tankers to use Goose Bay; and SAC bombers will continue to be permitted to overfly Canada on airborne alert in times of crisis, as determined by the Government. This co-operation also includes continued training flights in Canadian airspace in peacetime by SAC bombers not carrying nuclear weapons.

In addition, the Government is prepared to respond to the U.S. proposal to open negotiations with the objective of allowing U.S. interceptor aircraft to disperse to selected bases in Canada in times of crisis, as determined by the Government, if this would maximize the effectiveness of the residual anti-bomber defences. The Government is also prepared to open negotiations as proposed by the U.S. for SAC refuelling tankers to be dispersed to selected bases in Canada, should the international situation, in the Government's view, require such action.

This overall co-operation strengthens the U.S. retaliatory capability, and hence deterrence, by increasing the survivability and effectiveness of the U.S. bombers in their second strike role. Such operations bear no relationship to a first strike capability for the same reason that the Soviet bombers would not be used as a first strike weapon against the U.S. In both cases, the movement of large numbers of aircraft would be detected and would thus risk a pre-emptive missile response by the other side.

The North Atlantic Treaty Organization

Canada is one of only two partners in the NATO Alliance which station forces outside of their own continent. It is also one of only six of the 15 member nations which station forces outside their national borders for NATO purposes. It is apparent from these facts that NATO's collective defence rests primarily on defence of national homelands. An understanding of this situation is important to put in proper perspective the change in Canadian force deployment announced in April, 1969. This understanding will also dispel a widespread misconception that only the stationing of Canadian Forces in Western Europe constitutes a contribution to NATO's collective defence.

There were two main reasons for the decision to review the level of our force contribution in Europe. Economic circumstances in Europe had undergone a marked change in the nearly twenty years since Canada first stationed peacetime forces in Europe. Under the protective shield of NATO, Western Europe had succeeded in transforming the shattered economies of 1945. Since then its GNP has grown to about $600 billion per year for a population which exceeds 300 million people, and in many countries there is a high level of employment. In considering the defence implications of this phenomenal recovery, Canada concluded that its European partners were now able to provide a greater proportion of the conventional forces needed for the defence of their own region of the Alliance.

The second reason for review was that other national aims — fostering economic growth and safeguarding sovereignty and independence — dictated increased emphasis on the protection of Canadian interests at home. In addition, Government-wide financial restraints, and the resulting need for compatibility of roles and equipment for our home and overseas-based Armed Forces, dictated the need for some adjustment.

The Government reaffirmed Canada's adherence to the concept of collective security, and announced that Canada would continue to station significant though reduced forces in Europe as part of the NATO integrated force structure. Forces based in Canada for emergency deployment to Europe were not reduced. The Government reached its decision after an exhaustive examination of all factors bearing on national security. The decision did not suggest an overall reduction in NATO-wide defence, although Canada hopes that East-West negotiation will render this possible in the future. What Canada was seeking was a redistribution of effort for the defence of the European part of the Treaty area. The reductions were preceded by full consultations and implemented over a two-year period to permit internal adjustments to be made by members of the Alliance.

The decision reflected the Government's judgment that Canadian security continues to be linked to Western Europe and that Europe is still probably the most sensitive point in the East-West balance of power. It is the area from which any conflict, however limited, might most readily escalate into all-out nuclear war engulfing Canadian territory.

Western Europe has enjoyed total freedom from conflict for twenty-five years. This bears witness to the success of NATO, as does the fact that deliberate attack on Western Europe appears improbable today. Hostilities could, however, still occur there involuntarily from miscalculation in and around Berlin, or from accidental spill-over from unrest in Eastern Europe. It is in the interest of international peace, and ultimately of Canada's own security, that measures be maintained to discourage deliberate aggression in Europe, and to contain quickly any hostilities which might nevertheless occur. Canada's decision to continue to station forces in Europe, and to designate other forces in Canada for Europe in the event they should be required there, constitutes a tangible expression of Canadian support for the principle of collective security in the North Atlantic area.

Canada's military contribution in Europe reinforces its political role in the important negotiations in progress, or in prospect, designed to lead to a resolution of some of the tension-producing issues which persist from the Second World War. It would be wrong to believe that the situation in Europe is frozen or to conclude that there is no prospect of altering the

NATO/ Warsaw Pact military confrontation. Success in any of these initiatives, however, ultimately depends on the receptiveness of the other side.

The Strategic Arms Limitation Talks are extremely significant in this context, and Canada continues its efforts through consultations in NATO to provide all possible encouragement to these talks.

In addition, NATO proposed over three years ago the negotiation of an agreement on mutual and balanced force reductions (MBFR) in Europe. Finally, in the spring of this year the U.S.S.R. responded in a way which suggested that there was now a possibility of serious discussions between the two sides. Members of the Alliance are currently exploring this possibility and developing substantive and procedural approaches for force reduction talks. Canada has played an active part in the preparation and promotion of this proposal, designed to reduce tensions in Europe and to preserve present security at lower levels of manpower and cost.

NATO is the sole Western forum for consideration of all these critical political and military developments, and Canada is dependent on its membership in the Alliance for access to them.

Canadian membership in NATO can thus be justified solely on security and political grounds. Canada has in addition a direct interest in the economic well-being of Western Europe and in the preservation of trading relations with this second ranking Canadian market. In connection with the further development and probable enlargement of the European Economic Community (EEC) Canada is engaging in important negotiations with certain of our allies who are current and prospective members of the EEC. The community of interest we share with these countries through common NATO membership should be a positive factor in these negotiations.

FORCES STATIONED IN EUROPE

The reduction in the strength of the Canadian Forces assigned to Allied Command Europe forecast in April, 1969, has now been effected. The land element has been co-located with the air element in Southern Germany, with headquarters in Lahr, giving our forces in Europe a distinctive Canadian identity. Their combined strength is approximately 5,000 instead of the 10,000 formerly stationed in Europe. The Government has no plans for further reductions.

Land Component

The Canadian Government has been giving careful attention to the type of forces that should be stationed in Europe. The Government's decision in the spring of 1969 was that the land force component should be compatible with the forces based in Canada. Accordingly a number of options have been reviewed by the defence staff in consultation with the appropriate NATO authorities.

The Government has decided that the land force should be reconfigured to give it the high degree of mobility needed for tactical reconnaissance missions in a Central Region reserve role The Centurion medium tank will be retired, since this vehicle is not compatible with Canada-based forces and does not possess adequate mobility. In its place a light, tracked, direct-fire-support vehicle will be acquired as one of the main items of equipment. This vehicle, which is air portable, will be introduced later into combat groups in Canada. The result will be enhanced compatibility of Canadian and European based forces, and a lighter, more mobile land force capable of a wide range of missions.

Air Component

The Canadian air element in Europe was reduced from six to three squadrons of CF-104s in 1970, one in the reconnaissance and two in the nuclear-strike role. The nuclear-strike role will be terminated in January, 1972. It had been planned that the two nuclear-strike squadrons would be tasked to conventional attack, with the other remaining in the reconnaissance role. Because of the need for a substantial conventional ground support capability in Europe, a major element in ensuring that any hostilities could be contained without escalation to nuclear war, the plan has been changed.

The Government, after consultation with NATO, intends to employ all three squadrons in the conventional attack role in which the CF-104 is an effective aircraft. This role involves providing the tactical ground support for NATO forces in the area. The intention to task all three squadrons in this role will require minor modifications to the aircraft.

FORCES IN CANADA FOR EMPLOYMENT IN EUROPE

Canada has been committed for some time to send by air a battalion group to Allied Command Europe's Mobile Force Land (AMF(L)) if the latter is deployed to Denmark or Norway. The AMF(L) is a multi-national, quick-reaction, air-transportable force designed to act as a demonstration of allied solidarity in times of tension on the flanks of the Treaty area. Canada's battalion group commitment to the northern flank will continue. The further commitment to send the balance of an air/sea transportable combat group from Canada to the north flank in the event of an emergency will also be maintained.

Extensive trials of the CF-5 aircraft in Europe in the past year have confirmed its suitability for operational use in that theatre, particularly on the Northern flank. The Government is prepared to commit two squadrons of these aircraft to Allied Command Europe in photographic reconnaissance and ground-support roles. They would be Canada-based and flown across the Atlantic using the Forces' jet transports for in-flight refueling. One squadron would be available for the AMF(Air) in the north; the other would be in support of the Canadian air/sea transportable combat group committed to the same region. This decision will enhance NATO's deterrent strength and add to its ability to carry out the strategy of flexibility in response, which requires emphasis on conventional capability.

NATO'S MARITIME FORCES

The maritime defence of the Alliance involves employment of Canadian Forces over the Atlantic ocean areas. These operations include the sea approaches to the coast of Canada and therefore relate directly to our national security. The Canadian Government will continue to contribute to the maritime defence of the Alliance, and to earmark ships, aircraft and submarines for assignment to NATO in the event of an emergency.

In time of peace, the collective maritime power of the Alliance contributes to deterrence and thus to the security of each nation in the Alliance. This collective maritime power is embodied in various multi-national forces which reflect the solidarity and resolve of NATO. One such force is the Standing Naval Force Atlantic (STANAVFORLANT) which operates continuously under the control of the Supreme Allied Commander Atlantic (SACLANT) and Canada will continue to contribute ships to this multi-national force. This force enhances NATO's ability to respond rapidly and at an appropriate level to any developing situation.

TRAINING FORCES OF OTHER COUNTRIES IN CANADA

There has been a long history of training of forces from other countries in Canada. Notable examples were the Commonwealth Air Training Plan during the Second World War, and the NATO aircrew training in the 1950-60 period. The Canadian Forces are now conducting training programs for a small number of Danish pilots, and an agreement was recently signed with The Netherlands to conduct a pilot-training program for their Air Force beginning in late 1971.

Canada has reached an agreement with Great Britain, and is discussing with Germany the possibility of making a similar agreement, for the use of training facilities and areas in Canada. The Government believes that Canada, by providing these facilities, can make an additional valuable contribution to the effectiveness of NATO. Negotiations for such an agreement are based on the principle that the cost should be borne by the user country.

International Peacekeeping

Among the more significant achievements of the international community since the Second World War has been the development of the concept of "peacekeeping" — the use of truce supervisory bodies, military observers, or larger military forces to prevent or control conflict among nations. The concept evolved in a pragmatic and *ad hoc* fashion. Soon after the establishment of the United Nations, it became clear that fundamental political differences among great powers would preclude close co-operation among them to maintain international peace and security. In particular, these differences would prevent implementation of the collective security system based on the Security Council, foreseen in Chapter VII of the United Nations Charter. Moreover, situations detrimental to world peace arose which did not lend themselves to resolution under the terms of Chapter VII, but in which the involvement of the United Nations or other international machinery was necessary if peace was to be restored.

In these circumstances, peacekeeping techniques were developed as a means of enabling the international community, with full consent of the governments directly concerned, to take positive action in disputes threatening international peace and security. Since 1945, Canada has participated in ten United Nations peacekeeping operations. It has also been a member of the International Commissions for Supervision and Control in Indochina, which were established outside the framework of the United Nations. At the present time, approximately 625 Canadian Armed Forces personnel are serving with the United Nations Force in Cyprus, the United Nations Truce Supervision Organization (Middle East) and the United Nations Military Observer Group in India and Pakistan. Also, Canadian military and civilian personnel continue to serve with the International Commissions in Vietnam and Laos.

Canada's experience has provided it with an exceptional insight into the successes and failures of past and present international peacekeeping practices. The experience has all too often been frustrating and disillusioning. Some operations have been severely hampered by inadequate terms of reference and by a lack of co-operation on the part of those involved. Other detrimental factors have been the absence of political support of some of the great powers, and insufficient international logistic and financial resources. Certain operations have tended to become "open-ended" in the absence of a political settlement between the parties to a dispute.

Benefit can be derived from these efforts, regardless of how disappointing some of them may have been. The Government continues to support the concept of peacekeeping and will seek to utilize Canada's experience, to develop guidelines, within the United Nations and elsewhere for effective peace-keeping operations. The Government will consider constructively any request for Canadian participation in peacekeeping ventures when, in its opinion, based on the lessons of the past and the circumstances of the request, an operation holds the promise of success and Canada can play a useful role in it.

It is, of course, impossible to predict when a request will next be made and to foresee the size and scope of any future operations. Many of the conflicts likely to arise in this decade will have their roots in subversion and insurgency, and will not therefore lend themselves easily to resolution through the use of internationally constituted peacekeeping bodies.

Indo-China and the Middle East are two areas where the establishment of some kind of peacekeeping or truce supervisory operation might form part of an eventual settlement. If asked to participate in such an operation, a major factor affecting the Government's decision would be the existence of realistic terms of reference. They would have to reflect a consensus by all parties on the purposes which the operation was intended to serve and the manner in which it was to discharge its responsibilities.

A new requirement may also develop for the supervision of arms control agreements, involving the use of specialized personnel capable of inspecting, for example, installations on the seabed or the deployment of military forces.

In keeping with the Government's intention to give positive consideration, when warranted, to requests for Canadian participation in international peacekeeping, the Government intends to maintain its capability to respond quickly. A battalion group of the Canadian Armed Forces will remain on stand-by, and Canadian Forces personnel will continue to receive training to prepare them for service within peacekeeping bodies.

The Defence Department

DEFENCE BUDGET

A decision on the appropriate size of the defence budget can be made only in the context of the Government's national priorities and in the light of its consequent programs.

This Paper has set out the various ways the Canadian Forces can contribute to the fulfillment of our national aims. Properly equipped and trained, components of the Forces can be multi-tasked to several of the priorities of our defence policy.

It is not possible simply to state "defence requirements", and call that the defence budget. There is no obvious level for defence expenditures in Canada. Other countries, confronted with similar problems, attempt to allocate a certain fixed percentage of their Gross National Product for defence. The Canadian Government believes a judgment must be made on proposed defence activities in relation to other Government programs.

The Government believes that the activities described in this White Paper constitute an appropriate defence policy for Canada. Although defence expenditures will continue to be curtailed, as reflected in continuing manpower cutbacks and constraints on equipment acquisition, the Government has decided that some increase will be necessary to accommodate the following:

(a) the continued operation of the Tracker maritime patrol aircraft;
(b) the continued Operation of the Melville radar site and associated Goose Bay facilities;

(c) Canada's contribution to the NATO Integrated Communications System; and

(d) the additional roles outlined in this Paper for the CF-S aircraft.

Even with this increase, the Department's budget will remain within approximately 1% of the present ceiling. During the Fiscal Year 1972/73, the reduction of military manpower will continue down to a level fixed at 83,000.

The defence budget for the years 1973/74 and beyond will be established on the basis of program forecasts and estimates in accordance with the practice followed by other Government Departments.

CONDITIONS OF SERVICE

With a view to improving service conditions for members of the Forces, the Department of National Defence has been conducting a comprehensive study on all aspects of service life, including recruiting practices, grievance procedures, promotion and posting policies, and other factors which can affect the Forces' retention rate. One of the consequences of these studies is that the Government has concluded that career opportunities for members of the Forces should be enhanced by expanding career integration with the Public Service. The Government believes this will be to the advantage of both the members of the Forces and participating civil departments.

ORGANIZATION AND MANAGEMENT

To ensure maximum effectiveness, the Minister of National Defence has appointed a Management Review Group to examine the organization and management of the entire Department. This Group has taken over the study of ship procurement which was announced last February.

The Management Review Group is evaluating the present relationships between the military, civil and research organizations of the Department and will make recommendations to ensure there exists effective planning and control. Other areas which will be evaluated include: the relationship between Canadian Forces Headquarters and its subordinate commands; logistics and acquisition policies and associated practices in relation to time, cost and performance objectives; and the proportion of defence resources devoted to support activities.

The Group will also examine areas of inter-related responsibility with other government departments, including those of the new Department of the Environment, the Department of Supply and Services and the Department of Industry, Trade and Commerce. It is particularly important that proper arrangements exist within the Government as a whole for the Department of National Defence to exercise its responsibility for ensuring adequate surveillance and control of Canadian territory.

The Management Review Group will report directly to the Minister of National Defence. It is expected that the review will be completed during the summer of 1972, with interim progress reports being submitted periodically.

AIR TRANSPORT

The Canadian Forces' long-range, air transport component consists of Boeing 707s, and Hercules turbo-prop aircraft. In mid-1970, the Forces received the first of five Boeings now in the fleet, which replace 12 Yukon turbo-prop aircraft.

While the Forces' aircraft provide an adequate long-range air capability at this time, the requirement will be kept under review so that the sufficient capability to meet Forces' commitments is maintained. There may arise a need during periods of national and international emergency to mobilize some part of the national civil airlift resource. Accordingly, during the months ahead steps will be taken to ensure that this potential is taken into account in dealing with the airlift problem.

In addition to their long-range aircraft, the Forces have a good transport capability in a range of other aircraft including Buffaloes, Twin Otters, and transport helicopters.

PROTECTION AGAINST CHEMICAL AND BIOLOGICAL WARFARE

Methods of protection against chemical and biological weapons are subjects about which no country can risk being uninformed. Concern has, however, sometimes been expressed about the nature of Canadian participation in protection against chemical and biological agents. In 1946 Canada destroyed its stocks of lethal chemical warfare weapons and they have never been replaced. The Canadian Forces have never possessed biological weapons.

There is a distinction between chemical and biological agents in that the former can be used with some effectiveness as military weapons whereas the latter are not so adaptable to military purposes since the effects created are much less predictable. Recent discussions in the UN Disarmament Conference give reason to hope that an effective international regime may be created to control biological weapons. If Canada is to be able to play an effective role in these disarmament negotiations, and in any verification system which may result, then a minimal Canadian expertise in this field will continue to be required.

Chemical weapons pose a rather different problem for the Canadian Armed Forces. Chemical agents have been used on a number of different occasions during this century in direct support of military operations. So long as these weapons remain in the inventory of other states, then Canadian Forces should be trained in procedures and supplied with equipment to protect them against the use of these weapons.

No change will be made in the policy of not supplying the Canadian Forces with lethal chemical weapons. But the facility maintained by the Defence Research Board to advise the Forces on training and equipment needed to protect the troops against chemical agents will be continued. So long as our Forces may again be involved in operations where the opposing forces have substantial stocks of chemical weapons, it is essential that their survivability should not be jeopardized by lack of adequate preparedness.

THE RESERVE FORCE

Historically, the reserve forces have always made a significant contribution to the total strength of Canada's Armed Forces, and have played an important role in many military endeavours in both peace and war. Members of Canada's reserves have demonstrated a willingness to undergo training in peacetime to prepare themselves for active duty when called upon. The Government intends to maintain the Reserve Force at the current authorized size and to continue to depend upon it for an appropriate share of the manpower needs of the Armed Forces.

The present Reserve Force has been designated as part of the "forces in being". Therefore the composition must be adjusted from time to time to keep pace with changes in overall force manpower, and cannot be considered in isolation from the Regular Force. In addition, many members of the Reserve Force, by virtue of their civilian occupations, will not always be immediately available in time of emergency. Furthermore, only the Regulars have adequate time to train for the more sophisticated activities, and consequently the ratio of Regular to Reservist must be much higher than it has been at other times in our history.

Generally speaking, the role of the Reserves is to support the Regular Force. In particular, the Reserves provide trained officers and men for augmentation and reinforcement, and they have a particularly important role in internal security contingency plans. The Reserves also provide a base which could be expanded in an emergency. In addition to these tasks, which apply to all environments, the Naval Reserve maintains a control-of-shipping organization for operation and expansion in time of emergency. The Militia provides trained personnel for augmenting civil emergency operations, and the Air Reserve provides light, tactical air transport.

During the past year, units from all environments of the Reserves were placed under the appropriate functional commands. The Militia and Air Reserves became the responsibility of the Commander, Mobile Command, and the Naval Reserve became the responsibility of the Commander, Maritime Command. This will present more realistic and challenging training to the Reserve Force and thus increase interest and capabilities. The Reserves will be provided with the equipment they need to train adequately for their assigned tasks.

The Reserves make an important contribution to our national life by developing leaders among the young people of Canada. The Reserve training program will continue, therefore, to emphasize citizenship and leadership training.

SUMMER TRAINING FOR STUDENTS

In the past the Militia has conducted limited student training programs during the summer months. These programs were worthwhile, not only because of the valuable training received by the students, but also because they created a pool of young men whose training would make them extremely useful to the country in time of emergency. The Department of National Defence is willing to continue this type of training for even larger numbers should the demand dictate, and is willing to continue this program to encompass all three environments of the Forces.

BILINGUALISM IN THE ARMED FORCES

The Canadian Forces have a major role to play in promoting national unity. It is essential therefore that they reflect the bilingual and bicultural nature of the country. The Government realizes that although progress is being made further improvements are necessary.

The Royal Commission on Bilingualism and Biculturalism made a comprehensive study of the changes required in the Armed Forces, and the Government is in general prepared to accept their recommendations. The objectives include that the French language should increasingly become a language of the Armed Forces, in order that the military may better represent the linguistic and cultural reality of Canadian society, and that Canadians whose mother tongue is French should be adequately represented in the Armed Forces in numbers and responsibility.

The Prime Minister stated in the House of Commons on June 23, 1970, that "... equal opportunity is closely related to the merit principle which cannot be said to be fully operative unless it extends to qualified francophones, with little or no knowledge of English, a recognition equal to that which it accords to anglophones whose knowledge of French is similarly limited." The arrangements for full participation in the Armed Forces of both anglophones and francophones will be in accordance with the merit principle for recruitment and promotion.

The Armed Forces have taken steps to meet the bilingualism and biculturalism aims. Twenty-eight percent of the Canadian Forces establishment is being designated as francophone. This policy applies at all levels and in all areas of responsibility. The designation of a number of operational units as French-speaking has widened the scope of satisfactory service for francophones, while increasing the opportunity for anglophones to serve in a bilingual atmosphere. It is intended to extend this to certain headquarters units. The objective in these units will be to create eventually an environment in which members of each official language group can work in their own language.

All French-speaking recruits joining the Forces today have the opportunity of taking their basic training in the French language. Moreover, an increasing number of trades' training courses are being conducted in French, thus enhancing the career opportunities of francophones. While most notices, regulations, directives, orders and forms are now issued simultaneously in both official languages, this will be extended to other documents wherever feasible. Bilingualism objectives will also apply to the Reserves.

The mobility of serving personnel and the geographical location of military establishments present educational and linguistic problems for certain families. Among the more serious problems is the cultural readjustment required of children who are moved to other parts of the country where their first language is not generally spoken. This problem applies to both language groups, although it is more frequently felt by French-speaking children who cannot find schooling in their mother tongue outside the Province of Quebec. Under a revised Department of National Defence educational policy, an educational allowance of up to $1,700 a year is now available to allow parents or guardians to send their children away from home to study in French or English when schooling in their mother tongue is not available on or near a military base.

THE FUTURE OF THE ARMED FORCES

This White Paper has set out defence activities for the Canadian Forces in the years ahead. The Government is confident that the men and women of our Forces, Regular and Reserve, and the Cadets will respond with the same dedication, effectiveness and skill as in the past to the challenges posed to them.

For its part, the Government will ensure that Canada shall have a highly trained and well-equipped force capable of responding to the variety of challenges discussed in the Paper.

Glossary of Terms

STRATEGIC

Strategic nuclear balance: The complex relationship between the offensive and defensive capabilities of the U.S.A. and the U.S.S.R. with respect to direct nuclear attack of homeland territories.

Stable mutual deterrence: A situation in which neither side could logically see any gain in attacking the other. Stability in this context has three dimensions: first, that it is unlikely that the balance could be altered to the point that one side believed a deliberate attack would be profitable; second, that massive nuclear exchange would not develop as a result of hasty, ill-founded or desperate decisions during a crisis; and third, that the maintenance of mutual deterrence does not require a competitive resource-consuming arms race.

First Strike: A deliberate nuclear attack designed to result in a net strategic advantage to the attacker. Logically, a first strike would either have to include destruction of almost all of the other side's retaliatory capability, or be launched from behind a defensive shield of assured high effectiveness.

Second Strike: The launching of nuclear weapons in retaliation to a first strike. Since most of the offensive capability of the initial attacker would already have been used, a second strike would probably include attack of cities.

Pre-emptive Strike: A nuclear attack designed to destroy as much as possible of the other side's offensive weapons in the belief that he had begun, or was about to begin, launching a first strike.

ICBMs — Intercontinental Ballistic Missiles: Nuclear-tipped rockets which are capable, after an initial short boost to a high velocity, of "coasting" to a target about 6,000 miles or more away.

SLBMs — Submarine Launched Ballistic Missiles: Similar rockets of shorter range, capable of being launched from a submerged submarine.

ABM — Anti-Ballistic Missile: A rocket capable of intercepting and destroying an in-coming ballistic missile warhead.

SALT — Strategic Arms Limitation Talks: Negotiations being conducted by the U.S.A. and the U.S.S.R. to reach agreement on mutual limitations in their holdings of strategic weapons.

CONTINENTAL DEFENCE

NORAD Treaty — North American Air Defence Treaty: A treaty between Canada and the United States setting up a joint operational command arrangement for air defence forces.

DEW Line — Distant Early Warning Line: A chain of air defence surveillance radars spanning the North American continent just inside the Arctic Circle.

BMEWS — Ballistic Missile Early Warning System: A relatively small number of very long range radars (none of them located in Canada) capable of midcourse detection of ICBMs on a northern trajectory between the Eastern and Western Hemispheres.

ASW — Anti-Submarine Warfare: Operations directed against submarines, including surveillance, tracking, localization or destruction.

NATO

NATO — North Atlantic Treaty Organization: The political and military organizational structure operated by the fifteen nations party to the North Atlantic Treaty. Combat forces come under operational NATO military command only when authorized by individual countries during an emergency.

ACE — Allied Command Europe: The area in which SHAPE (Supreme Headquarters Allied Power Europe) would assume command of NATO military forces in an emergency.

SACLANT — Supreme Allied Commander Atlantic: The military commander of the structure which would take operational command of assigned naval forces in the North Atlantic during an emergency.

AMF(L), AMF(A) — ACE Mobile Force (Land) and (Air): Multinational forces which have been designated for rapid assembly for employment on the flanks of NATO (Denmark and Norway in the North, Greece, Turkey and Italy in the South) at times of increased international tension.

STANAVFORLANT — Standing Naval Force Atlantic: A small multi-national naval force organized and assembled in peacetime which, when authorized by the North Atlantic Council and the nations contributing ships, can respond rapidly to maritime emergencies.

MBFR — Mutual and Balanced Force Reductions: A proposal by NATO to engage in negotiations with the Warsaw Pact nations with the aim of reducing military forces in Europe while preserving security on both sides.

NATIONAL

Surveillance: Activity directed at the collection of information on what is happening in Canada's land, air, and waters.

Control: Enforcement action to ensure that Canadian laws and regulations are respected.

Continental Shelf: That portion of the seabed extending from the coast which, because of its geological characteristics, is more properly considered as part of the continental mass than as part of the deep ocean seabed.

Territorial Sea: A region of the sea extending twelve miles from straight baselines drawn from headland to headland along the coast, where Canada has full sovereignty over the seabed, the waters, and the airspace above.

Fisheries Protection or Control Zones: Regions of the sea, which can extend beyond the territorial sea, where Canada regulates and controls the exploitations of fisheries resources.

Pollution Control Zones: Regions of the sea, which can extend beyond the territorial sea, where Canada regulates and controls activities with respect to possible pollution hazards.

Cost-Effectiveness: The relationship between the benefits realized from a particular activity and the resources consumed.

Marginal Return: The incremental increase in benefits in relation to their incremental cost.

Introduction to
Challenge and Commitment:
A Defence Policy for Canada

Many observers were surprised at the vigour of the defence debate that occurred in Canada in the early 1980s. Not least of these were members of the Liberal Party who found themselves defending policies that opponents said endangered members of the Canadian Forces and embarrassed Canada generally. The centrepiece of this debate was the so-called "commitment-capability gap" characterized by the armed forces' inability to meet commitments the government had accepted because of the lack of capabilities and obvious poor state of the equipment then in service.

There was another side to the defence debate, however, and it was championed by a self-styled "peace movement." The peace movement was not so much a movement as it was a loose confederation of anti-war pacifists, anti-NATO and anti-cruise missile activists, and anti-American nationalists. The movement had no coherent policy platform nor any agreed view on all the issues, but spokespersons for the various elements commanded attention in direct proportion to the "war rhetoric" that flowed from Washington and Moscow. Ironically, one peace-movement view, that Canada needed an independent foreign policy and the military resources to back it, coincided with the view of the "hawks" who demanded of governments adequate resources to meet defence commitments. Intellectuals sniped at the government from both sides of the fence. Thus, Pierre Trudeau's government found itself in the unlikely position of having to react simultaneously to criticism of their defence policies from "hawks, doves, and owls." Suddenly, defence policy became a major issue in federal politics.

The Progressive Conservative Party and Brian Mulroney acted promptly on the opportunity the Liberals gave them. They proclaimed the sad state of the armed forces during the election campaign and promised to set things right if they were given the chance. Subsequently, after they were elected, reviewing defence policy and honouring Canada's commitments at home and abroad became a priority for the Cabinet and the new defence minister, Robert Coates.

The distance from electoral declarations to policy implementation, however, proved greater than many Conservatives had suspected. First, the choice of Coates quickly became an embarrassment for the government. Reports surfaced from inside and outside the defence department that Coates refused to listen to policy advice, made policy promises in public without consulting his cabinet colleagues, and that his personal conduct left much to be desired. When on an official trip Coates was spotted in a German sex bar, his position was completely compromised and when the incident became public he was dismissed from Cabinet. It was a situation that scandalized the chief of the defence staff and delayed for months the development of a rational Progressive Conservative defence policy.

Coates was replaced temporarily by the strong-willed Eric Nielsen who soon brought order to the portfolio and started the defence review in earnest. However, the review was complicated by several factors. The "peace movement" was growing more active and held significant rallies in several cities, but their message was still scattered and pacifist alarms, especially, were largely ignored by Canadians. Nevertheless, their opinions, reflected in the national media and supported by several prominent Canadians, could not be ignored by the Cabinet.

On the other hand, a serious policy conflict erupted inside government when defence officials began to act on the party's electoral promises. It soon became obvious to officials in the Department of Finance that the cost of meeting the defence program being developed in the Department of National Defence was not tenable. However, no one in the defence department was ready to allow what looked like a golden opportunity to slip away. The deadlock between officials naturally spread to Cabinet and for many months the two policies — an honest defence budget and fiscal responsibility — ran counter to each other.

Finally, steady, but perhaps imperceptible, changes were overtaking the Cold War balance. Under Ronald Reagan's direction the United States had set out to take the initiative from the Soviet Union in weapons development, armed forces modernization, and in arms control negotiations. The policy put enormous strains on the Soviet economy and on civil-military relations in Moscow. At the same time, the entire social structure of the Soviet Union, suffering under the weight of years of economic inefficiency, aggressive foreign policies, and social neglect, was beginning to shake. Soviet leaders tried to maintain control of the state with status quo policies while responding to demands for change, but they soon discovered (but may not have accepted) that these two objectives were incompatible. Yet, even in 1986, the Soviet Union was able to hide its internal weaknesses behind a veil of threats. Western analysts, perhaps from habit, were unable to penetrate the secrets known in Moscow and so continued to promote cold-war policies much as they had always done.

Eric Nielsen had other duties as deputy prime minister and even though he had considerable energy, he could only prepare the ground for a defence minister who could carry the portfolio full-time. Mulroney realized this and appointed Perrin Beatty defence minister in 1986. Beatty was determined to make the most of this opportunity and made the preparation of a new white paper on defence his main priority. Beatty's appointment cheered senior officers and officials at National Defence Headquarters for they saw in him a bright politician who had the backing of the prime minister. They eagerly joined with the defence minister in preparing a statement on defence that some consider the most aggressive in Canadian history.

Challenge and Commitment: A Defence Policy for Canada is the statement many thought should have been issued in 1970. Beatty's statement scoffed at the "great hopes of the early 1970s" and declared that Trudeau's promises of détente were not justified. "The realities of the present ... call for a more sober approach to international relations and the needs of security policy." Beatty confirmed the essential soundness of a security policy built on international cooperation, but affirmed that Canada must pay its way by supporting allies. These notions, a world in danger and a Canadian responsibility to respond appropriately, are the foundation of *Challenge and Commitment*.

Perrin Beatty seemed to believe that his government was committed to building a strong national defence centred on the armed forces. He listened to members of the Canadian Forces and noted in his introduction their four goals:

- Honesty. A frank admission that the Forces had to deal with serious problems which would take time to overcome.
- A contemporary and manageable mandate. A clear statement of what their Government expected them to do.
- the resources necessary to do the job.
- Perhaps most important of all, the clear moral support of Canadians for their work on behalf of Canada.

He declared boldly that "I agree fully with these priorities. This new defence policy ... provides a modern and realistic mandate to the Canadian Forces and commits the Government to giving the Forces the tools to do the job." Most members of the armed forces and many senior officers and officials took the minister at his word.

The reordering of the entire defence program and long-standing commitments seemed the logical outcome of a review that saw a growing and aggressive Soviet challenge and a Canadian Forces "in an advanced state of obsolescence or ... already obsolete." The minister considered that if "rust-out" were allowed to continue, policy would be determined by that condition alone. There were, therefore, only three options: "increase significantly the resources devoted to defence"; "reduce commitments"; or "seek some combination of these two alternatives." The government decided "to alter some commitments ... while improving the effectiveness" of others. This policy would require "a steady, predictable and honest funding program based on coherent and consistent political leadership." The minister outlined "the way ahead" as dominated by a "three ocean strategy,"* increased surveillance of Canadian territory, consolidation of European commitments, revitalization of the reserve force, and "honest funding."

Officers and officials in NDHQ began an enthusiastic review of defence policy focused mainly on ordering equipment to meet commitments as they saw them. The review, however, was fatally flawed in significant ways. First, it became a bottom-up process and few policy brakes were set against those charged with driving the defence requirements process. As a result, leaders soon realized they were faced with an enormous list of demands that outpaced the government's intentions and its budget. Unfortunately, by this time officers and officials were already being pushed to get the white paper tabled in Parliament and so the work continued unabated.

---

*This phrase was used by Admiral Brock in his naval report of 1961: *The Report of the Ad Hoc Committee on Naval Objectives*, July 1961. Department of National Defence, Directorate of History, File 81/481.

Second, the proposals conflicted with other policies and not only those in the finance department. For example, suggestions that Canada abandon some NATO commitments in northern Europe and concentrate them in central Europe surprised officials in the Department of External Affairs and in NATO. The harshness of "the threat" assessments seemed simplistic and unnatural to many outsiders, especially to those alert enough to sense the changes coming in the Soviet Union and by late 1987 the enormity of the changes was becoming increasingly obvious. The rhetoric in the white paper made the minister vulnerable to peace activists and worried his cabinet colleagues. The most controversial suggestion in the paper was the decision "to acquire a fleet of nuclear-powered submarines" and it caught most Canadians off guard.

The white paper was a clever attempt to satisfy the many conflicting demands made on ministers while supporting the promises they had made during the election and in office. The nuclear submarines, for example, could be described as serving national interests in the Arctic and bolstering Canada's NATO commitments. The revitalization of the reserves played to reservists and critics of Canada's depleted army without actually increasing the army's strength. In many ways, *Challenge and Commitment* was designed to be all things to all people.

In the end, however, the defence policy could not stand on its weak foundation. Failure to appreciate events unfolding in the Soviet Union and the end of "the threat" broke one leg off the defence stool. This instability eroded domestic political support for the policies and collapsed another leg on the stool, the financial envelop needed to support the program. Finally, the ineptness of the public relations campaign managed by senior officials in NDHQ destroyed the last leg because the very arrogance of the white paper and the apparent greediness of the armed forces cost them the support of a public that might have allowed a modest and traditional renewal of the Canadian Forces.

By 1989, *Challenge and Commitment* was a mere footnote in the history books. It failed as public policy and it was irrelevant in a world turned upside down by President Gorbachev. Nevertheless, members of the Canadian Forces who had believed they were to get the tools to do the job and "honest financing" were sorely disappointed. Many expected their leaders, beginning with the chief of the Defence Staff, General Manson, to resign. When neither he nor any other senior officer offered even a word of public criticism of the failed policy, many soldiers and officers felt betrayed.

Some observers mark the end of *Challenge and Commitment* as the beginning of the tension that eventually broke the bond between senior commanders and officers and those they led. Soldiers and junior officers may have been naive to believe in a renaissance of the armed forces, but they were led to that belief by their senior officers. When the commitment was broken yet again, they looked for someone to hold accountable and someone to express their deep disappointment, but no one was there.

After the collapse of *Challenge and Commitment,* ministers, officers, and officials tried to maintain the policy in the face of internal distrust and external disinterest. Other policy statements were prepared by other defence ministers, but they were mainly dismissed as political window dressing. Canadian defence officials were not alone in their confusion during this period. The sudden downfall of the Soviet empire and the end of the Cold War were beyond all expectations and the experience of most officials. A department that had only known how to respond to cold-war images found itself unable to response to a new situation. No one knew how to construct policy on a blank piece of paper. Defence policy, therefore, dithered and stalled while "the new world order" began to sort itself out. The new policy, however, awaited a new government with new ideas.

Selected Bibliography

Douglas Bland. "Controlling the Defence Policy Process in Canada: White Papers on Defence and Bureaucratic Politics in the Department of National Defence." *Defence Analysis* 5,1 (1989):3-16.

_____. *Chiefs of Defence: Government and the Unified Command of the Canadian Armed Forces.* Toronto: Canadian Institute of Strategic Studies, 1995.

Brian MacDonald (ed.). *Parliament and Defence Policy: Preparedness or Procrastination?* Toronto: Canadian Institute of Strategic Studies, 1982.

_____. *Canada's Defence Policy: Capabilities Versus Commitments.* Ottawa: Business Council on National Issues, 1984.

_____. *Guns and Butter: Defence and the Canadian Economy.* Toronto: Canadian Institute of Strategic Studies, 1984.

M.O. MacMillan and D.S. Sorenson (eds.). *Canada and NATO: Uneasy Past, Uncertain Future.* Waterloo: University of Waterloo Press, 1990.

Peter C. Newman. *True North, Not Strong and Free.* Toronto: McClelland & Stewart, 1983.

Erik Nielsen. *The House Is Not a Home: An Autobiography.* Toronto: Macmillan, 1989.

DEPARTMENT OF NATIONAL DEFENCE

Statement on Defence Policy. September 1991.

Canadian Defence Policy 1992. Statement by the Hon. Marcel Masse, Minister of National Defence, April 1992.

CHALLENGE AND COMMITMENT
A Defence Policy for Canada

No Government has a more important obligation than to protect the life and well-being of its people; to safeguard their values and interests. In Canada, it is time to renew that commitment.

The world has changed dramatically since the last review of Canadian defence policy. But certain truths endure. As we seek new ways to put East-West relations on a more stable footing, we must remind ourselves that stability cannot be achieved through idle dreams. Peace and stability must be earned, and earned constantly.

For Canada, this quest continues to be best pursued through co-operation with our allies. This is a recognition of our common history, our shared interests and our community of values. This unity of purpose is the very foundation of our Alliance, as important to our security as the concrete efforts we undertake to keep the peace.

Our commitments reflect a sober recognition that Canada's survival and prosperity depend not only on what we do at home but on the well being and security of the West as a whole. This White Paper responds to this reality by upgrading and consolidating our efforts to meet present circumstances and those of the future, into the next century.

But just as the Alliance can only prosper through shared effort and a common impulse, so too Canada must look to itself to safeguard its sovereignty and pursue its own interests. Only we as a nation should decide what must be done to protect our shores, our waters and our airspace. This White Paper, therefore, takes as its first priority the protection and furtherance of Canada's sovereignty as a nation.

I am confident that the measures outlined here will restore to the Canadian Forces a sense of direction and a pride born of noble purpose. Canadians will be able to hold their heads high in the knowledge that we are meeting our responsibilities to ourselves and to our children. Canada will have honoured its commitment.

Brian Mulroney
Prime Minister of Canada

Shortly after the Prime Minister asked me to become Minister of National Defence, I had the pleasure of meeting with a group of young Canadian Forces officers stationed in Germany.

These dedicated young Canadians, who will help to form the next generation of our country's military leadership, were candid about what they looked for from their Government. They listed four goals:

- Honesty. A frank admission that the Forces had to deal with serious problems which would take time to overcome.
- A contemporary and manageable mandate. A clear statement of what their Government expected them to do.
- The resources necessary to do the job, and,
- Perhaps most important of all, the clear moral support of Canadians for their work on behalf of Canada.

I agree fully with those priorities. This new defence policy, the first in 16 years, provides a modern and realistic mandate to the Canadian Forces and commits the Government to giving the Forces the tools to do the job.

For much of the 1960s and 1970s, Canada's security and our defence relationship with the other democracies were given a low priority by the Federal Government. The Forces were cut in size and much of their equipment was allowed to become obsolete. As a result, Canada's security and sovereignty were seriously weakened and both our allies and potential opponents received mixed signals about our reliability as a NATO partner.

The challenges Canadians must face between now and the next century go to the survival of humanity itself and to whether Canada will continue as a free and independent country. The new defence policy outlined in this White Paper will help ensure for our children a sovereign and free Canada in a more peaceful world.

Perrin Beatty
Minister of National Defence
June 1987

Maps, Charts and Tables

Contents

CHAPTER I

Introduction

The last White Paper on defence was issued in August, 1971. It followed on the heels of a review of foreign and defence policy that had occurred in 1968-69. That review had resulted in major reductions in the Canadian Forces, reductions of lasting effect. The only Canadian aircraft carrier, the HMCS BONAVENTURE was sold in 1970. The Canadian Forces in Europe were cut in half. The regular strength of the Canadian Forces was reduced by about 17,000. In 1967-68, about 18 per cent of the federal budget and 2.5 per cent of the Gross Domestic Product were devoted to defence. By 1971-72, these had been cut to 13 and 2 per cent, respectively.

The 1971 White Paper outlined the assumptions underlying these reductions and set the direction of policy for the future. Seen in the context of the early 1970s, it was, not surprisingly, an optimistic document that looked forward to a world in which military forces would be less relevant, at least in their traditional roles. The paper took comfort in the increasing stability of mutual deterrence between the superpowers based on an approximate parity in nuclear weapons. It saw in arms control great promise for the reduction of arms at both the nuclear and conventional levels. Citing the emergence of China as a nuclear power and the economic growth of both Europe and Japan, it anticipated a multipolar world in which power would be more diffuse and the superpowers would play less significant roles. It looked with great optimism to a future in which negotiation would resolve problems in East-West relations. This rather benign view of the world, characteristic of a period in which détente was the watchword, was offset by a real concern for internal security and social stability which obviously reflected the domestic turmoil that Canada had just experienced.

Sixteen years later, it is evident that the great hopes of the early 1970s have not been realized. As anticipated, stable mutual deterrence between the superpowers has endured, although at much higher levels of forces. The promise of arms control, as envisaged in 1971, seemed to be vindicated in the immediately ensuing years. Indeed, considerable progress was made, most notably the signing in 1972 of the first Strategic Arms Limitation Treaty (SALT 1) which included the Anti-Ballistic Missile (ABM) Treaty. Despite some initial successes, however, arms control has so far proven to be much more difficult to achieve than many had anticipated. The Mutual and Balanced Force Reductions (MBFR) talks, for example, already envisaged in 1971, have made virtually no progress.

As expected, developments in Europe and the Far East have led to a greater diffusion of power. The change, however, has not been such as to alter perceptibly the central fact of confrontation in East-West relations.

Developments during the late 1970s and the 1980s have shown that the early promise of détente was exaggerated. Events have not justified the optimism of the early 1970s that problems of East-West relations would be resolved by negotiation. While the nations of East and West have not used force directly against one another to resolve their differences, neither have they been quick to negotiate them away. Elsewhere in the world, differences between nations have been even less amenable to negotiation. Far too often, military force or the threat of military force has been the preferred tool for achieving political objectives.

The optimism of that earlier White Paper 16 years ago reflected the same hope for international peace and security which is shared by all Canadians today. The realities of the present, however, call for a more sober approach to international relations and the needs of security policy.

While Canadian security policy must be flexible enough to adapt to changing circumstances, some elements of our geostrategic situation are immutable. There is no external threat which is unique to Canada. Canada alone cannot assure its own security. As the neighbour of two heavily armed superpowers and as a country that depends on international relationships for its well-being and prosperity, if not for its survival, Canada's security ultimately requires the maintenance of a peaceful international order. In an age when a breakdown of that order could result in a nuclear holocaust, its importance is self-evident.

The first objective of Canada's security policy is to promote a stronger and more stable international environment in which our values and interests can flourish. It does so within the framework of collective security. Like each of its predecessors, this Government believes whole-heartedly that there is no acceptable alternative and rejects as naive or self-serving the arguments of those who promote neutrality or unilateral disarmament. Canada has never been neutral. We have always sought our security in a larger family of like-minded nations. In light of our position in the world, the values and traditions which have been defended steadfastly by previous generations of Canadians, and our political and economic interests, neutrality would be hypocrisy. Our security would continue to depend on the deterrence provided by our former allies, but we would have opted out of any contribution to and, equally significantly, any say in the management of that deterrent. We could turn our backs on the obligation to work for a stable world order; technology and geography would not, however, allow us to escape the consequences should that order collapse.

Canadian security policy has three major components: defence and collective security, arms control and disarmament and the peaceful resolution of disputes. This White Paper deals with the contribution of the Department of National Defence and the Canadian Forces to all aspects of that policy.

CHAPTER II

The International Environment

Canadian security policy must respond to an international environment dominated by the rivalry between East and West. These two groups of nations, each led by a superpower, are in conflict, a conflict of ideas and values. They are divided on how politics should be conducted, society ordered and economies structured. They are divided on the value of personal freedom, on the importance of the rule of law and on the proper relationship of the individual to the society. In this conflict, Canada is not neutral. Our values and our determination to defend freedom and democracy align us in the most fundamental way with other Western nations.

While the conflict between East and West is not intrinsically military, it could lead to a clash of arms. For its part, the West would resort to armed force only in its own defence. Although some would say that the same is true of the East, can Western governments responsibly base the well-being and future of their own people on expressions of goodwill and on the most optimistic interpretation of the intentions of others? It is a fact, not a matter of interpretation, that the West is faced with an ideological, political and economic adversary whose explicit long-term aim is to mould the world in its own image. That adversary has at its disposal massive military forces and a proven willingness to use force, both at home and abroad, to achieve political objectives. Perhaps this is a reflection of a deep-rooted obsession with security, well-founded on the bitter lessons of Russian history. It cannot but make everyone else feel decidedly insecure. This does not mean that war with the Soviet Union is inevitable or that mutually beneficial arrangements should not be pursued. It does mean that unless and until there is concrete progress, the West has no choice but to rely for its security on the maintenance of a rough balance of forces, backed up by nuclear deterrence

Central Europe is the geographic focus of the wider contest between East and West. It is the centre of gravity in the balance of power. The greatest concentration of military force is found here. Since the Second World War, the Soviet Union has maintained in Central Europe massive armed forces well in excess of what is reasonable for defence alone. The Western response has been to deploy forces sufficient at least to deny the Soviet Union the prospect of an easy victory. Europe is not necessarily the most likely place for a conventional conflict between East and West to begin, but it would quickly become the decisive battlefield.

A free and secure Western Europe remains critical to Canada's future. Canadian history and values owe an enormous debt to Europe. For centuries it has been the centre of the civilization of which we are a part. Not surprisingly, Canada has political, cultural and social ties with Europe unmatched by those with any other part of the world, save the United States.

Western Europe represents one of the greatest concentrations of the human and material resources of the larger community of Western nations, about one half of the population and one third of the annual gross national product. The fact that about one third of Canada's overseas trade is conducted with Western Europe is only one indicator of its importance to us.

Were Western Europe to be subverted, overrun or destroyed, what remained of the West would face a bleak future. It is difficult to imagine what place Canada would have in such a world. The context in which this nation seeks its destiny would be diminished in every respect and the most profound concerns about Canada's future as an independent nation would arise.

Canada's security in the broader sense is inseparable from that of Europe. There is nothing new in this reality. Twice in this century Canadians have fought in Europe for their freedom. Following the Second World War, successive Canadian governments have recognized the need to remain intimately engaged in European security issues. The presence of Canadian armed forces in Western Europe contributes directly to the defence of Canada, and, what is more, ensures that we will have a say in how key security issues are decided.

Canadian defence policy must also take into account the growing importance of the Asia-Pacific region. This region has, in the recent past, been undergoing more rapid change than any other part of the world. Here too, vast armed forces confront each other, particularly along the Sino-Soviet border and the Korean armistice line, while growing naval forces patrol the North Pacific. Japan may now match the Soviet Union as the world's second-largest economy. It rivals the United States in per capita income, in high technology and as the world's largest exporting nation. Japan is Canada's second-largest trading partner and a leading investor in Canada.

The Arctic Ocean, lying between the two superpowers, is also an area of growing strategic importance. In the past it served as a buffer between the Soviet Union and North America. Technology, however, is making the Arctic more accessible. Canadians cannot ignore that what was once a buffer could become a battleground.

Many parts of the world are plagued by instability and regional conflict brought about by ideological quarrels, racial strife, terrorism, territorial disputes and religious militancy. A regional conflict could provide the spark for a global conflagration. That is why Canada's security requires a forceful and effective Canadian contribution to the peaceful resolution of disputes and to peacekeeping operations.

The Canadian Government considers arms control essential to the search for a more peaceful and secure world. It offers the prospect of reducing threats, constraining the competition for military advantage, increasing stability and providing a predictable international environment. Current negotiations could lead to significant reductions in nuclear weapons, conventional forces and chemical weapons, as well as to agreements on other measures to build confidence and reduce tension. All of these possibilities are important, desirable and worthy of energetic pursuit. Progress, however, is slow and unpredictable, and there is no reason to believe that in the near future it will obviate the need for significant military forces or for deterrence based ultimately on nuclear weapons. Indeed, by increasing the need for adequate conventional forces, some of the more promising developments in arms control, such as nuclear reductions in Europe, could make Canada's contribution to collective security even more important.

Success in building a more peaceful world will lead to a reduction in the level of armaments. Until these endeavors are crowned with much greater sucess than has been enjoyed to date, the Government must ensure this country's security both at home and through contributions to collective defence efforts abroad

CHAPTER III

The Military Threat

Since the end of the Second World War, the Soviet Union has persistently expanded its military power. At the expense of the civilian economy, it has devoted vast resources to its armed forces. The result is a military establishment that has reached rough parity with the United States in strategic weapons while maintaining numerical superiority over Allied conventional forces in Europe. During the same period, it has transformed its fleet from a defensive coastal force to a powerful navy with global reach. The Soviet Union has further increased its military potential through its sponsorship and dominance of the Warsaw Pact.

NORTH AMERICA

The principal direct threat to Canada continues to be a nuclear attack on North America by the Soviet Union. Because of our geographical position, Soviet strategic planners must regard Canada and the United States as a single set of military targets no matter what political posture we might assume. Even in the unlikely event that the United States alone were attacked, geographic proximity and common interests would ensure that the effect on Canada would be devastating. Today, Soviet land-based intercontinental ballistic missiles (ICBMs) and submarine-launched ballistic missiles (SLBMs) represent the most significant threat. Their accuracy and range enable the Soviet Union to inflict enormous damage on any target, anywhere in the world.

A threat to North America from manned bombers has existed for many years. More recently, Soviet bombers have gained new importance

Strategic Nuclear Forces

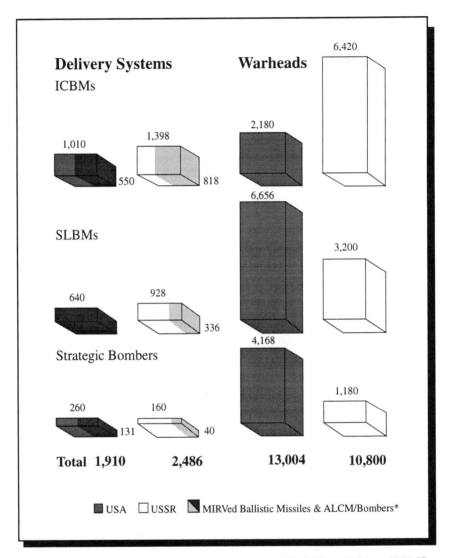

Source: The International Institute for Strategic Studies, *The Military Balance, 1986-87.*
Estimates updated to early 1987. SALT II counting rules used.
*Multiple independently targetable re-entry vehicles (MIRV) and bombers with
ALCMS are counted under a common SALT II ceiling of 1,320.

with the development and production of new models equipped with air-launched, long-range, land-attack cruise missiles (ALCMs). These cruise missiles could be launched in airborne nuclear strikes against North America from points well off the Atlantic and Pacific coasts, and from the Canadian Arctic. Anticipated improvements in cruise missile performance will make defending North America even more difficult.

Soviet bombers would acquire greater relative importance should an effective ballistic missile defence be deployed or should the superpowers agree to reduce drastically or even eliminate ballistic missiles from their arsenals. The deployment by the United States of even a partial ballistic missile defence system could lead the Soviet Union to counter, in part, by increasing its strategic bomber force.

The Soviet Union is expected to broaden its range of nuclear capabilities with the deployment in submarines of sea-launched, long-range, land-attack cruise missiles (SLCMs). Launched from offshore as far north in the Atlantic as the Labrador Sea, or in the Pacific, Soviet sea-launched cruise missiles could strike any military or industrial target in either Canada or the United States.

Although Canada is unlikely to be invaded in a conflict, limited incursions, principally to neutralize installations, or for diversionary purposes, are conceivable. Canadian airspace would almost certainly be used by manned bombers armed with cruise missiles, and, of course, space above Canada could be traversed by ballistic missiles. Canadian Arctic waters could well provide an alternate route for Soviet submarines to move from the Arctic Ocean to the Atlantic to reach cruise missile firing positions further south or to operate in more traditional roles against vital Allied shipping.

The military use of space by the Soviets has increased significantly and they now maintain about 150 operational satellites in orbit. Over 90 per cent of those satellites have military or military-related missions, including intelligence collection over Canada.

EUROPE

The Soviet Union and its Warsaw Pact allies also threaten Canadian security with their nuclear and conventionally armed forces concentrated in the European theatre. These forces are larger than defence alone requires.

In numbers of theatre nuclear-capable weapons, the Soviet Union has a decided edge. For example, the Warsaw Pact has about a three-to-one advantage over the North Atlantic Treaty Organization (NATO) in theatre nuclear ballistic missiles. At the conventional level, the Warsaw Pact maintains numerically superior forces, including about a three-to-one ratio in artillery and armed helicopters, a two-to-one ratio in main battle tanks and tactical aircraft and a similar superiority in most other categories. The Soviets and their allies also maintain a large stockpile of chemical weapons and a well-developed military capability to operate in a toxic environment. Only in the area of transport helicopters does NATO outnumber the Warsaw Pact. Confronting Western Europe as a whole are about 90 Warsaw Pact divisions. More than 2.5 million men and about 47,000 tanks stand ready for employment with minimal mobilization.

Conventional Forces in the NATO Area

		NATO[a]	Warsaw Pact
GROUND FORCES	Divisions[b]	38	90
	Manpower[c]	1,900,000	2,700,000
	Main Battle Tanks	20,000	47,000
	Artillery[d]	9,000	24,000
	Armed Helicopters	700	2,100
NAVAL FORCES[e]	Principal Surface Combatants[f]	321	196
	Attack Submarines	173	192
AIR FORCES	Land Combat Aircraft[d]	3,250	5,300

Source: The International Institute for Strategic Studies, *The Military Balance 1986-87.* Numbers are rounded.

a.   Excludes France and Spain which do not participate in NATO's integrated military structure. (French Army stationed in the Federal Republic of Germany is included).

b.   While Warsaw Pact and NATO divisions differ, they have overall firepower equivalence. Only active divisions have been included.

c.   Manpower figure is for total ground forces in Europe.

d.   Many artillery pieces and aircraft are technically dual-capable, even though operationally they may not be assigned a nuclear role.

e.   Includes NATO naval forces on both sides of the Atlantic.

f.   Light Frigates (1,000 tons) and larger ships.

Opposite the NATO area where Canadian forces are currently committed, the northern and central regions, the Warsaw Pact can readily deploy some 64 divisions, against 76 for NATO. While the Warsaw Pact would be able to select the time and place of attack and concentrate its forces accordingly, NATO, as the defender, would be obliged to thin out its divisions across the entire front. Under these circumstances, NATO maintains forces barely sufficient to cover the ground. Furthermore, the Warsaw Pact has a geographic advantage, as NATO suffers from a lack of strategic depth, and from the need for resupply and reinforcement from across the Atlantic.

In the event of war, the Warsaw Pact could be expected to use its superior numbers to overwhelm NATO defenses. In the past, NATO has been able to rely on its qualitative lead in weapons technology to compensate somewhat for the greater number of Warsaw Pact troops and equipment. As the Soviet Union continues to modernize its forces, NATO's margin of qualitative superiority is being eroded. This is particularly noticeable in tactical aircraft and tanks.

The build-up of the surface navy of the Soviet Union, both in quality and quantity over the last 20 years, has been unprecedented. It has introduced new classes of warships, like the modern KIEV class carriers, SLAVA class guided-missile cruisers, and SOVREMENNYY and UDALOY class guided-missile destroyers, and, in a striking new departure in naval policy, is now building larger aircraft carriers. All of the Soviet nuclear-powered submarines. both ballistic-missile and attack, are assigned to the two main Soviet fleets, the Northern and the Pacific. The Northern Fleet is the more important in terms of its roles, and would have a major impact on any war in Europe. Based in the Kola Peninsula, it operates extensively in the Arctic and in the Atlantic. Accordingly, 60 per cent of Soviet ballistic-missile nuclear submarines and about two thirds of their nuclear-powered attack submarines are allocated to the Northern Fleet. The Pacific Fleet has been significantly upgraded in the past decade and a half. Based principally in Vladivostok and Petropavlovsk, the Pacific Fleet makes its presence felt off the West Coast of Canada through regular patrols of ballistic-missile submarines and intelligence gathering ships, and through less regular eastern Pacific operations by surface ships and attack submarines.

The Maritime Dimension

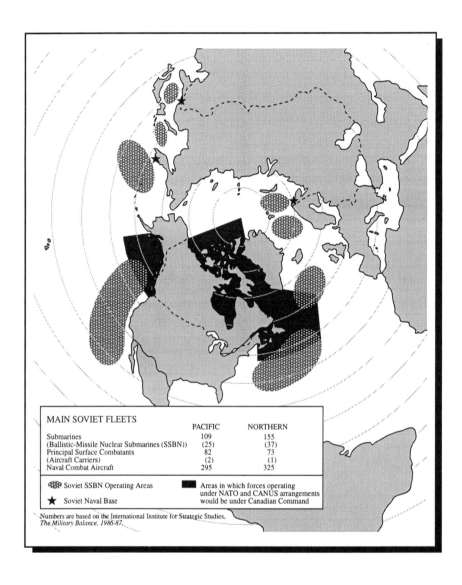

MAIN SOVIET FLEETS

	PACIFIC	NORTHERN
Submarines	109	155
(Ballistic-Missile Nuclear Submarines (SSBN))	(25)	(37)
Principal Surface Combatants	82	73
(Aircraft Carriers)	(2)	(1)
Naval Combat Aircraft	295	325

Soviet SSBN Operating Areas

★ Soviet Naval Base

Areas in which forces operating under NATO and CANUS arrangements would be under Canadian Command

Numbers are based on the International Institute for Strategic Studies, *The Military Balance, 1986-87.*

The new Soviet leadership continues to view the world as divided into two antagonistic camps. There is every reason to believe that its long-term aims continue to include the dissolution of NATO, the neutralization of non-communist Europe and the weakening of the West as a whole. Although the Soviet Union fully recognizes the dangers of aggression against NATO, it continues to seek to translate military power into political gain.

CHAPTER IV

Canadian Defence Policy

Canada has no aggressive intentions toward any country. Our objective is to deter the use of force or coercion against Canada and Canadian interests and to be able to respond adequately should deterrence fail. Such deterrence requires standing and reserve forces equipped, trained and positioned to meet any likely threat. Canada's population and resource base are not today and in the foreseeable future could not become sufficient to defend, unaided, the second-largest country in the world. The Government believes that this objective can only be met within the collective security framework provided by the North Atlantic Treaty Organization.

STRATEGIC DETERRENCE

As previously noted, the most serious direct threat to Canada is a Soviet nuclear attack on North America. Given the present balance of strategic nuclear forces, such an attack remains unlikely. Were it to occur, however, the consequences would be catastrophic. At present, the only effective counter to such a threat is a strategy of deterrence based on the maintenance of diversified nuclear forces. Such forces must be capable of surviving an attack and retaliating in a manner so devastating as to convince any potential aggressor that the penalty he risks incurring far outweighs any gain he might hope to achieve. Each superpower now has the capacity to obliterate the other, even after having absorbed a nuclear strike. For that reason, the structure of mutual deterrence today is effective and stable. The Government believes that it must remain so.

Canada does not have nuclear weapons. We have no intention of acquiring them. To deter a nuclear attack on Canada we rely on the nuclear forces of our allies. For that reason, we support the maintenance of such survivable nuclear forces as are necessary for stable and effective deterrence.

Even without nuclear weapons, Canada contributes and will continue to contribute to deterrence at the strategic level. Our role in North American Aerospace Defence (NORAD) in surveillance, warning, attack assessment and defence against air attack, and our participation in NATO and bilaterally with the United States in surveillance of Soviet submarine forces contribute to the survivability of United States strategic nuclear forces, the keystone of NATO's assured retaliatory capability. We enhance deterrence to the extent that we are able to deny any potential aggressor the use of Canadian airspace, territory or territorial waters for an attack on NATO's strategic nuclear forces.

We also contribute by making our territory and faciliteis available to our allies. For example, we have agreements with the United States which, in normal peacetime circumstances, enable unarmed aircraft of the Strategic Air Command, subject to clearance by Canada, to use Canadian military facilities and airspace for operational training. In a crisis, and if in the judgement of the Government the international situation so warranted, they would be permitted to overfly Canada with nuclear weapons and their tanker aircraft would be allowed to operate from Canadian airfields. United States interceptors and Airborne Warning and Control System (AWACS) aircraft would also be able to deploy forward to Canadain airfields to join our defence forces

Canadian airspace and military ranges and training areas are also used to test and evaluate the performance of Allied weapons, most notably the United States air-launched cruise missile. Some of these are nuclear capable, but no nuclear weapons are tested in Canada. Warships of our allies regularly visit Canadian ports. Such visits are frequently made on the occasion of exercises during which Allied ships, including Canadian warships, practice combined operations. They are a logical consequence of our membership in an alliance and of our acceptance of the protection offered by collective defence.

The United States and the Soviet Union are both conducting research into the development of strategic defences against ballistic missiles. They are also discussing the issue of strategic defence in their bilateral arms control negotiations in Geneva. Depending on a number of technical, financial and political factors. the United States may eventually begin to deploy ballistic missile defences and the Soviet Union could expand those already in place. The nature of such defences cannot now be precisely determined. The Government will follow closely the progress of such research in order to determine its implications for international security. Future decisions on Canada's role, if any, in ballistic missile defence will depend upon these developments. Such decisions will have to be considered in light of the impact ballistic missile defence could have on strategic stability and on Canadian security.

Stable deterrence at the strategic level is essential to the security of Canada. The Government will continue to contribute to the maintenance of an effective Allied deterrent according to our own independent analysis of the strategic environment.

CONVENTIONAL DEFENCE

The Soviet conventional threat to Canada and Canadian interests is often overlooked in the face of the nuclear menace. Although this aspect is most evident in Central Europe, where Warsaw Pact forces outnumber those of NATO along the frontier between East and West, it is not entirely absent wherever Canadian interests and Soviet capabilities overlap: at sea, in the Pacific, the Atlantic and the Arctic, and in the air over the approaches to North America.

Both superpowers understand the potentially apocalyptic consequences of a nuclear exchange. If hostilities were to occur, they would thus be more likely to begin at the conventional level, where the Soviet Union has its greatest advantage. Although a conventional conflict would initially put less at risk than would a nuclear war, there would be a serious risk that the hostilities would escalate to include nuclear weapons.

The most effective counter to the conventional threat is to convince any potential aggressor that the chances of an attack quickly achieving its objectives are slight and that, if he were to persist in his aggression, he would run the risk of a nuclear response. This strategy requires adequate and sustainable conventional forces trained, equipped and positioned according to the threat. It may not be necessary to match the other side weapon for weapon. but the more effective the conventional forces, the less is the reliance which has to be placed on nuclear weapons. If early resort to these weapons is to be avoided, the conventional forces in place must be able to fight over an extended period.

In an era of dramatically increasing cost and sophistication of weapons, credible conventional defence can only be maintained if all members of the Alliance work closely within the framework of collective security. Canada makes its contribution to its own security and to that of the North Atlantic Alliance through maritime forces in the Atlantic and the Pacific, through land and air forces at home and in Europe, and through NATO's common funded programs. Our current force posture is discussed in Chapter V and its future evolution in Chapter Vll.

Much of Canada's defence effort is focussed on Europe. That is where the conventional threat is concentrated and, in war, where the decisive conventional battle would be fought.

Deterrence is not divisible. If it fails in Europe, it fails everywhere. By contributing to deterrence in Europe. Canadian forces are serving Canadian interests and contributing to Canada's security.

Canada also contributes to conventional defence by providing materiel and training facilities to NATO allies. For example, we will be providing state-of the art sonar equipment to Portugal for its new frigates. There are also extensive arrangements permitting Allied forces to train in Canada or in Canadian waters, taking advantage of our relatively open spaces. The NATO Standing Naval Force Atlantic and other Allied warships regularly visit Canadian waters and exercise with Canadian maritime forces. The United Kingdom carries out army training programs at Suffield and Wainwright, Alberta. The Federal Republic of Germany conducts a similar program at Shilo, Manitoba. The United States, British and German air forces conduct low-level flying training at Goose Bay, Labrador. A similar arrangement has been made with the Netherlands for training to commence there this year. The Government will continue to promote Allied training in Canada subject to compliance with Canadian laws and approved operational, financial, social and environmental guidelines.

The Government recognizes that conventional defence must be strengthened in order to improve deterrence, reduce the likelihood of war, and raise the nuclear threshold. If our conventional forces are to deter,

Conventional Forces in Central and Northern Europe

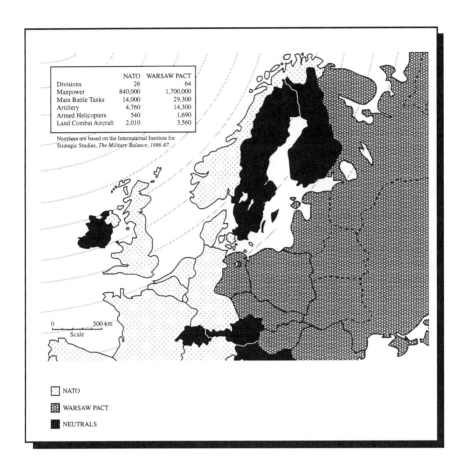

	NATO	WARSAW PACT
Divisions	26	64
Manpower	840,000	1,700,000
Main Battle Tanks	14,000	29,300
Artillery	4,760	14,300
Armed Helicopters	540	1,690
Land Combat Aircraft	2,010	3,560

Numbers are based on the International Institute for Strategic Studies, *The Military Balance, 1986-87.*

0   500 km
Scale

NATO

WARSAW PACT

NEUTRALS

they must be able to defend. If they are to defend, they must be able to fight. To do that, we must maintain their readiness and provide for their sustainment. The Government is also determined to organize and deploy these forces in such a manner as to maximize their efficiency and combat effectiveness.

SOVEREIGNTY

After the defence of the country itself. there is no issue more important to any nation than the protection of its sovereignty. The ability to exercise effective national sovereignty is the very essence of nationhood. The Canadian Forces have a particularly important, though not exclusive. role to play in this regard. The protection and control of our territory are fundamental manifestations of sovereignty. Our determination to participate fully in all collective security arrangements affecting our territory or the air or sea approaches to our country and to contribute significantly to those arrangements is an important affirmation of Canadian sovereignty.

Canada is not universally recognized as being sovereign in all of the areas that we claim. At the moment. the United States considers the Northwest Passage to be an "international strait". We regard it as "internal waters" and are engaged in discussions to see whether a solution can be reached based on mutual respect for sovereignty and our common security and other interests.

In peacetime the enforcement of Canadian laws throughout our territory is the responsibility of the civil authorities. This includes Canadian legislation on navigation and pollution in ice-covered waters, game laws in the Arctic, the regulation of fisheries and the control of air traffic in Canadian airspace. In this respect the Polar 8 Icebreaker will make a significant contribution to the maintenance of a Canadian presence and the exercise of sovereignty in Arctic waters. The military role in sovereignty is that of the ultimate coercive force available when the capabilities of the civil authorities are inadequate to enforce Canadian laws and regulations or when Canada's right to exercise jurisdiction is challenged by other states.

It follows that an important manifestation of sovereignty is the ability to monitor effectively what is happening within areas of Canadian jurisdiction, be it on land, in the air or at sea, including under the ice. But monitoring alone is not sufficient. To exercise effective control, there must also be a capability to respond with force against incursions. Such a capability represents both an earnest of the government's intent to maintain sovereignty and a deterrent to potential violators.

The Government will not allow Canadian sovereignty to be diminished in any way. Instead, it is committed to ensuring that the Canadian

Forces can operate anywhere within Canadian jurisdictional limits. Our Forces will assist civil authorities in upholding the laws and maintaining the sovereignty of Canada.

PEACEKEEPING

Conflict between NATO and the Warsaw Pact involving Canada and Canadian interests could have its genesis outside the sphere of either alliance in regions where instability and the potential for violence are widespread. As a responsible member of the world community and an active and committed member of the United Nations, Canada has a respected record of peacekeeping service and a proven capacity for difficult assignments in pursuit of the peaceful settlement of disputes. Such disputes will seldom directly involve the security of Canada. In many parts of the world, however, armed conflicts are likely to engage the interests of the Soviet Union and the United States, or their major allies, and thus potentially sow the seeds of a superpower conflict. Canada also plays a vital role in preventing a major rift between our Alliance partners by maintaining peacekeeping forces in Cyprus. In all these instances, the use of our armed forces for peacekeeping or truce supervision, under United Nations or other international auspices, serves our national interest as well as the broader community.

Each request for a Canadian contribution to peacekeeping has to be considered on its own merits. The Government's decision will be based upon the following criteria: whether there is a clear and enforceable mandate; whether the principal antagonists agree to a cease-fire and to Canada's participation in the operation; whether the arrangements are, in fact, likely to serve the cause of peace and lead to a political settlement in the long term; whether the size and international composition of the force are appropriate to the mandate and will not damage Canada's relations with other states; whether Canadian participation will jeopardize other commitments; whether there is a single identifiable authority competent to support the operation and influence the disputants; and whether participation is adequately and equitably funded and logistically supported. Moreover, each of our current commitments is routinely reviewed in light of these criteria.

Canadian military personnel have served with distinction in virtually every United Nations peacekeeping operation since the end of the Second World War. In addition, Canada makes significant financial and material resources available to the United Nations to promote peace and security. Canadian peacekeeping commitments flow from an established policy whereby up to 2,000 Canadian Forces members can be called on for peacekeeping duties at any one time. Current deployments overseas as well as standby elements in Canada are counted within this allocation.

Canada's Contribution to Peacekeeping

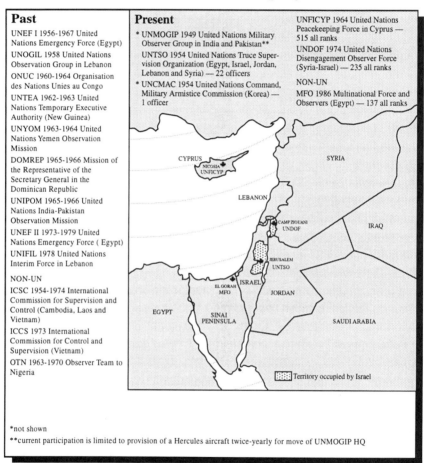

Past

UNEF I 1956-1967 United Nations Emergency Force (Egypt)

UNOGIL 1958 United Nations Observation Group in Lebanon

ONUC 1960-1964 Organisation des Nations Unies au Congo

UNTEA 1962-1963 United Nations Temporary Executive Authority (New Guinea)

UNYOM 1963-1964 United Nations Yemen Observation Mission

DOMREP 1965-1966 Mission of the Representative of the Secretary General in the Dominican Republic

UNIPOM 1965-1966 United Nations India-Pakistan Observation Mission

UNEF II 1973-1979 United Nations Emergency Force (Egypt)

UNIFIL 1978 United Nations Interim Force in Lebanon

NON-UN

ICSC 1954-1974 International Commission for Supervision and Control (Cambodia, Laos and Vietnam)

ICCS 1973 International Commission for Control and Supervision (Vietnam)

OTN 1963-1970 Observer Team to Nigeria

Present

* UNMOGIP 1949 United Nations Military Observer Group in India and Pakistan**

UNTSO 1954 United Nations Truce Supervision Organization (Egypt, Israel, Jordan, Lebanon and Syria) — 22 officers

* UNCMAC 1954 United Nations Command, Military Armistice Commission (Korea) — 1 officer

UNFICYP 1964 United Nations Peacekeeping Force in Cyprus — 515 all ranks

UNDOF 1974 United Nations Disengagement Observer Force (Syria-Israel) — 235 all ranks

NON-UN

MFO 1986 Multinational Force and Observers (Egypt) — 137 all ranks

*not shown

**current participation is limited to provision of a Hercules aircraft twice-yearly for move of UNMOGIP HQ

Our widely recognized support for the United Nations and its pursuit of global security represents an important contribution to world stability and thus to Canadian security.

ARMS CONTROL

Arms control, like defence, is one of the pillars of Canadian security policy. They are complementary, and the policies pursued in each area are consistent with the common goal of enhancing security and stability at the lowest level of forces.

Short of the utopian state of an unarmed world, arms control will never be a substitute for adequate defence. Conversely, if we are to succeed in enhancing security, we cannot rely on military force alone.

Canada has articulated the following six specific arms control goals:

- negotiated radical reductions in nuclear forces and the enhancement of strategic stability;
- maintenance and strengthening of the nuclear non-proliferation regime;
- negotiation of a global chemical weapons ban;
- support for a comprehensive test ban treaty;
- prevention of an arms race in outer space; and
- the building of confidence sufficient to facilitate the reduction of military forces in Europe and elsewhere.

Unilateral disarmament measures will not enhance Canadian security. Experience has shown that effective arms control can only be achieved through the careful negotiation of balanced and verifiable reductions or limitations. Unless such agreements are complied with fully and in good faith, they will produce neither increased stability nor the confidence necessary for improved East-West relations. That is why verification of arms control agreements is so important. Arms control negotiations require a unique blend of international diplomacy and military technical expertise. The Department of National Defence works closely with the Department of External Affairs in the formulation of arms control proposals, in the continuing dialogue with our Alliance partners and in those negotiations to which we are party.

Internationally, the Department of National Defence provides this expertise in a broad range of fora. Members of the Department participate in the Canadian delegations to the United Nations, the Conference on Security and Co-operation in Europe, and the Mutual and Balanced Force Reduction talks. They also played a role in the Stockholm Conference and will do so again in any follow-on negotiation of confidence and security building measures.

The arms control negotiations of most concern to the Department of National Defence are those with the greatest potential to affect East-West relations, the East-West military balance, or the disposition of Canadian Forces.

In the Geneva negotiations between the United States and the Soviet Union on strategic nuclear weapons, we support the current emphasis on deep reductions, concentrating on the most destabilizing systems. We believe that the limitation of long-range, air and sea-launched cruise missiles must also be addressed. In the negotiations on conventional forces in Europe, we believe the focus should be on effective confidence and security building measures and on the establishment of a more stable balance of forces so as to reduce the likelihood of war occurring as a result of miscalculation or surprise attack.

CHAPTER V

The Structure of the Forces

The Canadian Forces are committed to the direct defence of Canada, the collective defence of North America and NATO Europe, and to peacekeeping. They are organized in maritime, land, air and support forces. There are approximately 84,600 full-time (Regular) and 21,300 part-time (Primary Reserve) members of the Canadian Forces, along with 20,400 Supplementary Reservists subject to recall in a crisis. The Department of National Defence also employs 35,500 civilians.

MARITIME FORCES

The major formations of the maritime forces are naval squadrons under Maritime Command and an air group under its operational control. Maritime Command Headquarters is in Halifax, Nova Scotia.

The maritime forces on the East Coast consist of two destroyer squadrons (each with six destroyers), a submarine squadron and seven maritime air squadrons. The destroyers, with embarked helicopters, and support ships operate in anti-submarine task groups. These groups conduct surveillance operations, protect vital shipping and support other NATO maritime commitments.

The maritime forces on the West Coast consist of two destroyer squadrons (each with four destroyers) and two maritime air squadrons. They conduct surveillance operations and support joint Canada-United States security operations.

An auxiliary fleet of ocean and harbour tugs, research vessels, a coastal oiler, target-towing vessels and other craft supports both operational fleets.

Maritime Forces

Personnel

Regular	10,000
Primary Reserve	3,300

Major Operational Units

Destroyer Squadrons	4	
Submarine Squadrons	1	
Maritime Air Squadrons*	9	(1 Reserve)

Principal Equipment	*East Coast*	*West Coast*
Frigates/Destroyers	12	8
Reserve Frigates/Destroyers	1	2
Submarines	3	–
Replenishment Ships	2	1
Long Range Patrol Aircraft (Aurora)*	14	4
Med Range Patrol Aircraft (Tracker) *	15	3
Helicopters (Sea King)*	31	4
Driving Support	1	–
Training Vessels	21	10

Bases in Canada	3	

---

*operational control only (Air Command resource)

Shore infrastructure for the fleet consists of dockyards, bases, training facilities, supply depots, ammunition magazines and radio stations on both coasts.

The Naval Reserve comprises 19 divisions in cities and towns across Canada with two more planned for this year. Its primary roles are coastal defence and control of shipping in time of crisis.

LAND FORCES

The major formations of the land forces are three brigade groups and a special service force, all supported by helicopter squadrons. Land forces are deployed in Canada and Europe under the command of Mobile Command and Canadian Forces Europe, respectively. Mobile Command Headquarters is in St. Hubert, Quebec.

Land Forces

Personnel		
Regular	22,500	
Primary Reserve	15,500	

Major Operational Units		
Brigade Groups	3	
Special Service Force	1	
Task Force Headquarters	1	
Helicopter Squadrons*	11	(4 Reserve)
Major Reserve Units	106	
Minor Reserve Units	25	

Principal Equipment	In Canada	In Europe
Main Battle Tanks	37	77
Armoured Vehicles General Purpose	195	–
Armoured Personnel Carriers	891	349
Reconnaissance Vehicles	112	60
155 mm Artillery	50	26
105 mm Artillery	223	10
Anti-Tank Weapons	105	44
Tactical Helicopters (Kiowa, Twin Huey)*	88	13
Transport Helicopters (Chinook)*	7	–
Bases in Canada	8	

* operational control only (Air Command resource)

Land Forces in Canada. Mobile Command's Regular combat elements are concentrated in two brigade groups and a special service force. Brigade groups consist of battalion-sized units of armour, artillery and infantry, and engineer, signals and combat service support units. The Special Service Force is a light, air-transportable force with an airborne capability. A signals regiment, together with staff from Mobile Command HQ, is capable of establishing a task force headquarters.

One of the brigade groups, 5ᵉ Groupe-brigade du Canada (5GBC) at Valcartier, is currently designated to fulfil Canada's commitment to send an air-sea transportable (CAST) force to northern Norway in times of high East-West tension, prior to an expected attack against NATO. The other brigade group, Canadian Brigade Group (I CBG) from Calgary, is the principal source of trained manpower to bring the army elements permanently stationed in Europe up to the wartime level of forces committed by Canada to help defend against military attack in the NATO Central Region.

One infantry battalion group from the third formation, the Special Service Force, is assigned to the Allied Command Europe Mobile Force (Land), (AMF(L)), for deployment to the NATO Northern Region in times of high East-West tension, either in northern Norway or in Denmark. The Airborne Regiment of the Special Service Force is assigned to defence operations in Canada.

Canadian peacekeeping commitments are met by rotating units from each of the Canada-based elements for periods of peacekeeping duty.

The land combat elements are backed by training and support facilities: eight bases, a combat training centre. an airborne centre, an air defence school, and four regimental battle schools. Mobile Command's Regular Force strength is approximately 18,400. Land forces in Canada are supported by the helicopter squadrons of 10 Tactical Air Group.

Mobile Command's Primary Reserve is the Militia, organized into five areas, comprising 131 units and subunits. Its role is to contribute to defence of Canada missions and train replacement manpower for the Regular Force brigade groups.

Land Forces in Europe. 4 Canadian Mechanized Brigade Group (4CMBG) is stationed in the Federal Republic of Germany at Lahr and Baden-Soellingen, and forms part of Canadian Forces Europe. Its operational units consist of an armoured regiment, an artillery regiment, two mechanized infantry battalions, an engineer regiment, a signals squadron, a service battalion and a helicopter squadron. In crisis or war it would be assigned to the Central Army Group Commander's tactical reserve, performing operations in support of either II (German) Corps or VII (United States) Corps. Its current strength is approximately 4,100. In crisis, it could be augmented by 1,400 soldiers flown over from Canada.

AIR FORCES

The major formations of the air forces are air groups: six based in Canada under Air Command, and one based in Europe under Canadian

Air Forces

Personnel		
Regular	23,050	
Primary Reserve	950	

Major Operational Units		
Tactical Fighter Squadrons	8	
Maritime Squadrons*	9	(1 Reserve)
Tactical Helicopter Squadrons**	8	(4 Reserve)
Medium Transport Helicopter Squadrons**	2	
Transport and Rescue Squadrons	6	(2 Reserve)
Transport Squadrons	4	
Radar Squadrons	19	

Principal Equipment	*In Canada*	*In Europe*
Tactical Fighters (CF-18)***	60	44
Tactical Fighters (CF-5)	58	–
Maritime Aircraft*	71	–
Tactical Helicopters**	88	13
Transport Helicopters**	7	–
Tactical Transport Aircraft	46	2
Strategic Transport Aircraft	5	–
SAR Aircraft	49	–
Training Aircraft	226	5

Bases in Canada	17	

*   Squadrons under operational control of Maritime Command.
**   One squadron under command of 4CMBG; other squadrons under operational control of Mobile Command.
***   The planned procurement level for the CF-18 is 138 by September 1988.

Forces Europe. They are supported by Reserves and bases, stations, schools and other facilities.

Air Forces in Canada. Air Command provides combat-ready air forces for surveillance and control over Canadian airspace and for defence of North America. It also provides air operational and air transport support to maritime and land forces.

Air Command's Regular Force elements are organized into fighter, maritime, tactical, transport, reserve and training groups. Air Command Headquarters in Winnipeg, Manitoba provides the command and control of all air forces in Canada, with the exception of Maritime Air Group and 10 Tactical Air Group which, along with associated Air Reserve units, are under the operational control of Maritime and Mobile Commands, respectively. Two of the fighter squadrons in Canada are currently committed as rapid reinforcement forces for northern Norway in time of crisis. Functions common to all the air groups, such as maintenance, training, flight safety and standards, are centrally controlled.

The Air Reserves comprise one group headquarters, two wings, seven squadrons and nine augmentation flights.

Air Forces in Europe. The air formation in Europe, 1 Canadian Air Group (1 CAG), is a component of Canadian Forces Europe. It comprises a headquarters, three tactical fighter squadrons and an air maintenance squadron on the two bases at Lahr and Baden-Soellingen. In crisis or war, the Air Group would perform conventional air-to ground and air defence roles as part of the 4th Allied Tactical Air Force.

SUPPORT FORCES

The operational elements of the Canadian Forces depend upon support personnel who serve at military bases and facilities in Canada and overseas. Support functions comprise strategic communications, training, logistics, medical activities and personnel administration. The majority of these forces are concentrated in or directed by National Defence Headquarters, the Canadian Forces Communication Command and the Canadian Forces Training System.

Communications. Canadian Forces Communication Command provides strategic communications services to the Canadian Forces. It operates and maintains several data networks and voice communications systems. Its military personnel include a Regular Force contingency of about 3,300 members and a Communication Reserve of 1,570.

Training. The Canadian Forces Training System provides training services to the operational commands. It operates 18 schools on five training bases and three schools on other commands' bases. Its strength is 4,500 regular military personnel. Almost 2,400 members are employed as instructors. Another 500 military instructors from other commands serve as incremental staff. The training system comes under the jurisdiction of the Assistant Deputy Minister (Personnel) whose mandate also includes responsibility for the National Defence College. the Military Colleges and the Staff Colleges. The Canadian Forces also provide training for military personnel from developing countries and send training advisers abroad. At any one time, 40 to 50 students from Africa. the Middle East and the Caribbean are training in Canada.

Logistics Support. Logistics support encompasses a wide and complex spectrum of activities related to materiel acquisition, maintenance, storage, distribution and construction. Within the Canadian Forces each individual command has logistical responsibility for materiel under its operational control. At the national level this responsibility rests with the Assistant Deputy Minister (Materiel) at National Defence Headquarters. His organization is responsible for acquiring and introducing equipment into service and supporting that equipment during its service life. Given the variety and complexity of equipment used by the Canadian Forces, the logistics support group is necessarily large and technically specialized. It operates national level support units such as supply and ammunition depots, maintenance depots and workshops, test and evaluation establishments, quality assurance establishments, research establishments and movement and postal units.

CHAPTER VI

The Commitment — Capability Gap

Since coming to office, the Government has reviewed Canada's military commitments in relation to the current capabilities of the Canadian Forces and those they can be expected to possess in the future. This review has confirmed that we are not able to meet those commitments fully and effectively. After decades of neglect, there is indeed a significant "commitment-capability gap".

Even if the Canadian Forces were fully manned and had modern, state of-the-art equipment, to fulfil existing defence commitments would be a daunting challenge. The truth, however, is that much of the equipment of most elements of the Canadian Forces is in an advanced state of obsolescence or is already obsolete. Modernization programs have not kept pace with obsolescence. The maritime forces have too few operational vessels, very limited capacity to operate in the Arctic and no capability to keep Canadian waterways and harbours clear of mines. The land forces have severe equipment shortages and too few combat-ready soldiers, and the Militia is too small, ill-equipped and insufficiently trained to make up the difference. The air forces suffer from a serious shortage of air transport to move troops and equipment to Europe in times of tension and to sustain them during hostilities. They have too few maritime patrol aircraft. They lack sufficient numbers of modern weapons for the CF-18 and have no replacement for CF-18 aircraft lost in peacetime. Nowhere, however, is the gap more evident than in the lack of logistic and medical support for our forces committed to Europe.

The root of the problem is the level of funding available to defence over the last 25 years. There has been a long-term trend towards spending

Canada's Defence Effort

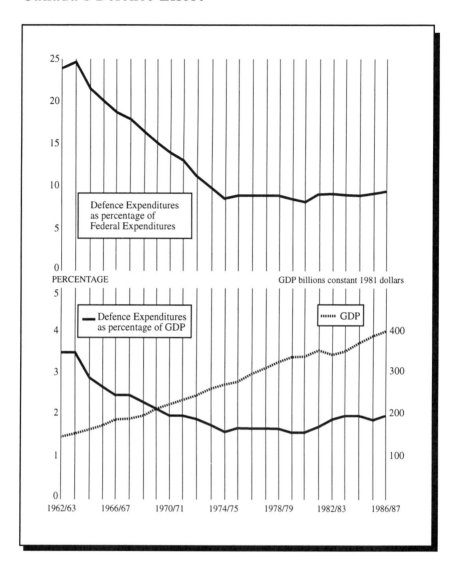

smaller percentages of the federal budget and of Canada's Gross Domestic Product on defence. In some of those 25 years, defence spending actually fell. In many others, it did not keep pace with inflation. Inevitably, the portion of the defence budget that suffered most from this neglect was that used to buy new equipment. In 1962-63, more than 20 per cent of the budget was spent on capital projects. This level generally declined throughout the 1960s until it reached a low point of about 9 per cent in 1972-73. It began to increase thereafter, but it was not until 1982-83 that it went above 20 per cent again. In 1985, NATO countries spent, on average, about 25 per cent of their defence budgets on equipment acquisition.

Underfunding inevitably took its toll on the equipment used by the Canadian Forces. Purchases were deferred or spread over a longer period of time. It became normal to replace equipment on a less than one-for-one basis and to reduce modernization programs, even though there might be no military logic for doing so. As a result, the navy today relies exclusively on vessels in commission or under construction in 1971. The newest ship is already 14 years old. The oldest, at 31 years, is older than most of those who sail in her. In 1963 there were 45 major warships and 10 minesweepers in commission. Today there are only 26 warships and no minesweepers. Since 1971 the air force has acquired only two new militarily significant aircraft systems, the CF-18 fighter and the CP-140 Aurora long-range patrol aircraft. In both cases, fewer aircraft were acquired than those they replaced. The air force now has about 75 per cent of the aircraft, fixed-wing and helicopter, that it had in 1971. The army was able to replace a number of items of equipment. Once again, most, including its major acquisition, the Leopard tank, were in considerably smaller numbers than those they replaced.

In recent years more money has been spent to purchase equipment. The results will eventually be seen in the form of new frigates, low-level air defence batteries and many other essential but less significant improvements. Nevertheless, even this funding is insufficient to overcome the "bow wave" of deferred equipment acquisition built up since the 1960s. If this condition were allowed to continue unaltered, it would soon lead to "rust-out", the unplanned and pervasive deterioration in the military capabilities of the Canadian Forces.

Capital Program

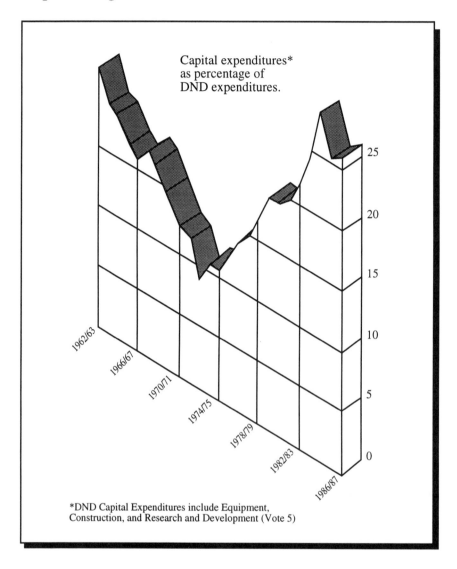

Capital expenditures*
as percentage of
DND expenditures.

*DND Capital Expenditures include Equipment,
Construction, and Research and Development (Vote 5)

Eventually our commitments could not be safely maintained and, finally, even any illusion that we were contributing to collective security would disappear. Our forces stationed in Germany would cease to be effective in combat and would have to be withdrawn by the mid-1990s. Despite the ongoing delivery of the CF-18, without the purchase of additional aircraft to replace those lost through peacetime attrition, there would be insufficient fighters in Europe or Canada to maintain our commitments beyond the late 1990s. Although the Canadian Patrol Frigate Program is underway and the Tribal class is being updated, the rest of our maritime forces will soon be beyond the point where they are effective and will have to be withdrawn in the mid-1990s.

If "rust-out" were permitted to occur either by intent or neglect, the loss of equipment in the 1990s would by itself dictate a new, greatly diminished, defence role. In order to avoid having a policy determined by the process of obsolescence, there were really only three approaches the Government could take over a reasonable period of time:

- increase significantly the resources devoted to defence so that, over a period of 10 to 15 years, the Canadian Forces would become capable of meeting current commitments;
- reduce commitments to the point where those remaining could be carried out by existing forces, within existing resources; or
- seek some combination of these two alternatives.

Each of these approaches posed difficult choices. The first was the only one by which Canada's present commitments could credibly be met. This approach would not preclude reorienting Canada's present alliance commitments over a period of years. Indeed, changes in commitments are more easily negotiated when they are part of a strong and growing defence performance. Our effort would, of course, have to increase substantially. Defence expenditures would have to rise in real terms at a rate so dramatic as to be beyond Canada's ability to pay.

The second approach would require massive cuts in our military commitments. A reduction sufficient to eliminate the gap would have major repercussions on our relations with the United States and our Western European allies. It would represent a retreat from our undertakings within

Canada's Comparative Defence Effort* – 1985

GROSS DOMESTIC PRODUCT ($ billion)		PER CAPITA DEFENCE EXPENDITURE ($)	
United States	3841	United States	1114
Federal Republic of Germany	622	United Kingdom	448
France	510	Norway	433
United Kingdom	451	France	376
Italy	359	Federal Republic of Germany	327
Canada	342	Canada	292
Spain	168	Netherlands	275
Netherlands	125	Belgium	273
Belgium	79	Denmark	254
Denmark	58	Greece	234
Norway	55	Italy	166
Turkey	53	Spain	124
Greece	33	Luxembourg	107
Portugal	21	Portugal	61
Luxembourg	3.6	Turkey	46
Iceland	2.5	Iceland	0
NATO Europe	2539	NATO Europe (average)	256

TOTAL DEFENCE EXPENDITURE ($ billion)		DEFENCE EXPENDITURE AS % OF GDP	
United States	267.0	Greece	7.1
United Kingdom	25.4	United States	6.9
France	20.7	United Kingdom	5.6
Federal Republic of Germany	19.9	Turkey	4.4
Italy	9.5	France	4.1
Canada	7.4	Belgium	3.4
Spain	4.8	Norway	3.3
Netherlands	4.0	Federal Republic of Germany	3.2
Belgium	2.7	Netherlands	3.2
Greece	2.3	Portugal	3.0
Turkey	2.3	Spain	2.9
Norway	1.8	Italy	2.6
Denmark	1.3	Denmark	2.2
Portugal	0.63	Canada	2.2
Luxembourg	0.039	Luxembourg	1.1
		Iceland	0
NATO Europe	95	NATO Europe (average)	3.8

*All figures are in 1985 US dollars.
NATO definition of defence expenditure used except for Spain where only national data were available.

NATO, would be read by our allies as shirking our common defence responsibilities and would threaten the cohesion of the Alliance.

Shrinking our undertakings to existing levels of resources would markedly affect the nature of our commitments abroad. It would also have far-reaching implications for the forces in Canada and would harm the local economies where military bases are now located.

As a result of its defence review, the Government has decided to alter some commitments to bring them more into line with resources, while improving the effectiveness with which the remaining commitments are carried out. At the same time spending will be increased in a determined fashion to make the defence effort more responsive to the challenges of the 1990s and beyond. The results of decades of neglect can be overcome, but it will require a long-term solution: a steady, predictable and honest funding program based on coherent and consistent political leadership.

CHAPTER VII

The Way Ahead

Canadian defence policy will continue to be based on a strategy of collective security within the framework of the North Atlantic Alliance, including the continental defence partnership with the United States. Within this broad framework, defence policy will contribute to:

- maintenance of strategic deterrence,
- credible conventional defence,
- protection of Canadian sovereignty,
- peaceful settlement of international disputes, and
- effective arms control.

Canada will continue to participate in collective deterrence and defence in North America, in Western Europe and at sea.

In charting the way ahead, the Government will take a number of strategically coherent and militarily sound initiatives. These changes will be apparent in both national and alliance contexts and will, collectively, represent a significant and visible increase in the overall effectiveness of the Canadian Forces. We will provide the navy with modern, capable vessels for operations in the three oceans contiguous to our territory: the Atlantic, the Pacific and the Arctic. Our ability to survey and defend Canadian territory will be bolstered. Our land and air commitments in Europe will be consolidated on the central front in order to provide a credible and more sustainable Canadian contribution. The Reserves will be revitalized and enlarged to assume a greater role in the defence of Canada. These initiatives, when combined with what is already being done, will produce over time the best force structure within available resources and a level of military capability sufficient to meet our commitments effectively. With these changes, Canada will be a more responsible partner. And, we will be more honest with our allies, with our citizens, and with the men and women of the Canadian Forces who risk their lives in our defence.

THREE OCEANS

Canada is a maritime nation with a proud sea-going tradition. The three oceans off our shores are sources of natural wealth, which we are only beginning to tap, and avenues for the growing international trade upon which we are dependent for our well-being.

Strategically, the sea is neutral. Sufficient naval forces, properly deployed, can keep an opponent at arm's length, thus providing strategic depth. Alternatively, an opponent can use the sea to get in close and attack targets of his own choosing. Canadian naval forces must be able to respond to challenges within our own waters, if necessary denying their use to an enemy. We must also contribute to the collective maritime strength of the Alliance.

The Atlantic is the ocean of primary strategic importance to Canada and its NATO allies. It is essential to deterrence, particularly deterrence of conventional aggression in Europe, that the vital sea lines be maintained in order to resupply and reinforce Western Europe. With sufficient naval forces, the Atlantic is a bridge linking the two halves of the Alliance. In their absence, it is a barrier. Our opponents have a natural advantage: it is easier to threaten shipping than to ensure its safety. Canadian maritime forces — aircraft, surface ships and submarines — by contributing to the security of the Atlantic sea lines of communication, and thus to the support of our land forces, enhance deterrence

The strategic significance of the northeast Pacific has become increasingly apparent in light of the growing reach of the Soviet Navy. The shortest sea lines linking North America with the key trading nations of the western Pacific pass through this area, as do the shipping lanes between Alaska and the United States West Coast. The Strait of Juan de Fuca is a major shipping artery giving the ports of southern British Columbia and Puget Sound access to the Pacific. Its seaward end is important as a focal point for commercial shipping and as an egress for Canadian and United States naval forces. Additionally, Soviet submarine operations in the northeast Pacific have been increasing. The growing strategic importance of this area, for which Canada has specific responsibilities under bilateral agreements with the United States, underlines the need for a more effective Canadian naval force on the West Coast.

Over the past two decades, with the development of nuclear power, the Arctic has become an operating area for submarines. Deep channels through the Canadian Arctic offer a means of passing between the Arctic and Atlantic oceans. In a period of tension or war, Soviet submarines could seek to operate off the deep channels of the Canadian Archipelago to intercept Allied submarines entering the Arctic. Moreover, the Soviets might use these channels in war to reach patrol areas in the North Atlantic, including the Labrador Sea. In light of these circumstances, the Canadian navy must be able to determine what is happening under the ice in the Canadian Arctic, and to deter hostile or potentially hostile intrusions.

At present, the Canadian navy cannot carry out in the Arctic these roles essential to our security and sovereignty. Some have suggested that the use of mines would be sufficient to counter the submarine threat. Canada, however, has no stocks of mines and no infrastructure to support mine warfare. Moreover, Western nations have no mines designed specifically for the Arctic. Such capabilities could be acquired, but they would be costly and, in light of their specialized purpose, neither flexible nor cost-effective. Even then, how would mines be laid in channels which are covered with ice? Once there, could control over them be maintained in light of the ever-present danger that ice movement would alter their location? When necessary, could they be removed, as is required by the 1907 Hague Convention? Could any Canadian government responsibly accept the risk of inadvertently sinking a neutral or friendly vessel?

While there is little to recommend the use of mines defensively in the Arctic, an enemy could use them against us to good effect in our more southern waters. Canada's ports and internal waters are vulnerable to closure or disruption in war by mines laid by enemy ships, submarines or aircraft. Because Canada has no effective means of clearing mines, even a small number could close a port or waterway. Modern mines could be easily and surreptitiously laid just prior to hostilities, and activated when needed. Our current inability to meet this threat must be rectified.

244 Canada's National Defence

Canada's areas of maritime interest are vast and our resources limited. No single system is capable of handling by itself the range of our maritime requirements. Aircraft, ships and submarines all have unique advantages which must be combined so that their strengths reinforce each other to produce a balanced, effective force. Our existing naval vessels are obsolete and insufficient to perform today's tasks, let alone those forecast for the next 15 years. Accordingly, the Government will pursue a vigorous naval modernization program. The goal will be greater flexibility, a more appropriate balance among air, surface, and underwater assets and the reorientation of Canadian naval forces toward effective operations in the Atlantic, the Pacific and the Arctic oceans.

Such a fleet will be created by continuing current programs and initiating others. The four newest destroyers now in service, the TRIBAL class (on average, 15 years old), are being modernized under a program announced in June, 1985. They will provide an area air defence capability and state-of-the-art command and control for our anti-submarine warfare task groups. This modernization will enable these destroyers, the ALGONQUIN, ATHABASKAN, HURON and IROQUOIS, to remain effective beyond the turn of the century.

To strengthen naval capabilities in the Atlantic and Pacific, replacement of surface warships will continue beyond the six Canadian patrol frigates currently under construction with a second batch of six frigates. These ships will carry modern helicopters to extend the distance and speed at which they can pursue submarines. The Sea King helicopters now in service are already at the end of their useful life and a process to select a new shipborne aircraft, to be produced in Canada, is currently underway. To ensure our ports and waterways remain open, mine countermeasures vessels and equipment will also be acquired.

In all three oceans, underwater surveillance is essential to monitor the activities of potentially hostile submarines. Greater emphasis will be placed on underwater detection by continuing to develop Canadian sonar systems, by acquiring array-towing vessels to provide an area surveillance capability in the northeast Pacific and northwest Atlantic, and by deploying fixed sonar systems in the Canadian Arctic.

Submarines are essential to meet current and evolving long-range ocean surveillance and control requirements in the Atlantic and Pacific as well as in the Arctic. Nuclear-powered submarines (SSNs) are uniquely capable anti-submarine platforms. In contrast to a diesel submarine, the

Sea Ice Coverage

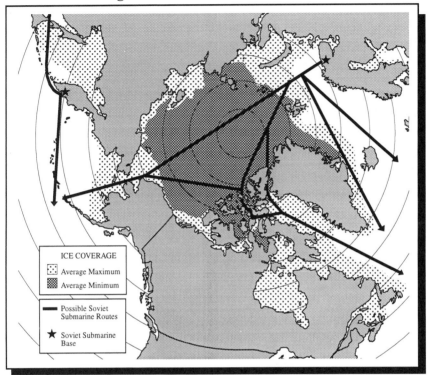

Soviet nuclear submarines can reach the Atlantic and the Pacific by travelling under the Arctic icecap.

SSN can maintain high speed for long periods. It can, therefore, reach its operational patrol area faster and stay there longer. The SSN can also shift more rapidly from one area to another to meet changing circumstances. Essentially it is a vehicle of manoeuvre while the diesel submarine is one of position. Given the vast distances in the three ocean areas in which Canada requires maritime forces and the SSN's unlimited endurance and flexibility, the Government has decided to acquire a fleet of nuclear-powered submarines to enhance the overall effectiveness of the Canadian navy.

Through their mere presence, nuclear-powered submarines can deny an opponent the use of sea areas. They are the only proven vehicle, today or for the foreseeable future, capable of sustained operation under the ice. A program of 10 to 12 will permit submarines to be on station on a continuing basis in the Canadian areas of responsibility in the northeast

Pacific, the North Atlantic and the Canadian Arctic. There they will be employed in essentially the same role now assigned to our diesel submarines. A fleet of nuclear-powered submarines is the best way to achieve the required operational capabilities in the vast Pacific and Atlantic oceans. In addition, the SSN is the only vessel able to exercise surveillance and control in northern Canadian ice-covered waters. SSNs will complement aircraft, destroyers and frigates in a vivid demonstration of Canadian determination to meet challenges in all three oceans. Such a highly capable, significant and versatile force will help to restore the effectiveness of the Canadian navy and prepare it to meet Canada's naval requirements well into the next century.

Fleet Composition

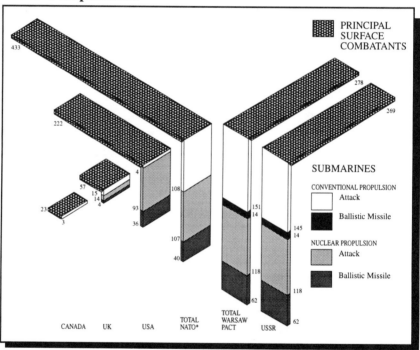

Source: The International Institute for Strategic Studies, *The Military Balance, 1986-87.*
*Excludes France and Spain which do not participate in NATO's integrated military structure. France has 46 principal surface combatants and 23 submarines (6 SSBN, 2 SSN, 15 conventional). Spain has 23 principal surface combatants and 8 conventional submarines.

The acquisition of nuclear-powered submarines has been given careful study, both in terms of cost and of the mix between surface ships and submarines. A suitable SSN for Canada would be comparable in cost to an air defence frigate, but more expensive than a diesel submarine. The projected cost of replacing the current diesel submarines and acquiring a third batch of air defence frigates would, however, be roughly equal to a 10 to 12 nuclear-powered submarine program over the next 20 years. Consequently, since the SSN is a more capable anti-submarine platform for all three oceans, it is deemed to be the best investment for the navy. Thus, although the number of surface ships will be allowed to decrease slightly, the resulting naval force will be more balanced.

Nuclear propulsion for submarines is technologically mature and extremely safe. Half of NATO's attack submarines are nuclear-powered, and the proportion is almost the same for the Soviet Union. Current nuclear-powered warships and their reactors are designed to the most exacting standards and are operated by highly trained crews using rigorously applied procedures. For example, after 34 years and more than 3,000 reactor-years of operating experience, the United States Navy has had no nuclear accidents. Similarly, there have been no known safety hazards associated with the design and operation of British and French nuclear submarines. In the Canadian nuclear-powered submarine program, similar control processes and standards, including stringent national acceptance and operating criteria, will be applied.

Our nuclear-powered submarines will not be nuclear-armed. Their acquisition will be compatible with the positions that Canada has taken on the non-proliferation of nuclear weapons and with Canadian environmental protection laws and regulations. While it is likely that we will build these submarines in Canada on the basis of a proven design now in service with the naval forces of one of our allies, we will be fortunate in being able to rely on the proven competence, expertise and enviable safety record of the Canadian nuclear industry.

A phased acquisition of nuclear-powered submarines, underwater surveillance capabilities, 12 new frigates and modern shipborne aircraft, the update of the TRIBAL Class destroyers, and a mine countermeasures capability will provide Canada with a credible navy capable of monitoring activity in its three contiguous oceans and of deterring their use by adversaries

SURVEILLANCE

The Canadian Forces conduct surveillance of Canadian air, land and sea jurisdictions in order to provide warning, assessment, and defence against hostile activity. Surveillance is an affirmation of Canadian sovereignty and a contribution to Canadian and collective security. Given the size of our territory and the limited resources available, effective surveillance calls for the imaginative use of new technology.

In protecting against the air threat, we have traditionally seen the North American continent as a single strategic entity and have co-operated with the United States through NORAD in the warning, assessment and defence against air attack. Recently, we have undertaken the North American Air Defence Modernization Program in partnership with the United States. The result will be a significant improvement in our capability to identify and intercept aircraft and cruise missiles around the periphery of North America. Modern radar systems will detect and track intruders so our tactical fighters can identify and, if necessary, engage them.

The North American Air Defence Modernization Program involves several new radar systems. The North Warning System, replacing the Distant Early Warning Line, will stretch from Alaska across the Canadian Arctic at approximately the 70th parallel and extend down the East Coast to Labrador. It will consist of minimally manned, long-range radar and unmanned, short-range, gap-filler radars. Over-the-Horizon Backscatter radars located in the United States will provide detection and tracking at very long range off the East and West coasts and to the south. The CADIN/ Pinetree radars are obsolete and, in most cases, no longer needed. To complete and modernize radar coverage of coastal airspace, retention of three sites on the East Coast and one on the West Coast is being considered as well as installation of additional radars along the West Coast and the Alaska Panhandle.

The other components of the airspace surveillance system, the Canadian NORAD Region Operations Control Centre, the CF-18 fighters and the associated communications, are all part of the modernization program. We will be upgrading five existing airfields in the North to function as Forward Operating Locations for interceptors from Cold Lake and Bagotville. As recently announced, the new Forward Operating Locations will be Yellowknife, Inuvik, Rankin Inlet, Kuujjuaq and Iqaluit, where preconstruction preparations will begin this summer, with construction following in 1990. In addition, other airfields will be upgraded to serve as Dispersed Operating Bases for the Airborne Warning and Control System (AWACS) aircraft. We are increasing the number of Canadian Forces personnel in certain NORAD positions, such as at Over-the Horizon Backscatter radar sites and as crew members on United States AWACS aircraft, components of NORAD which have been funded by the United States alone. We will maintain the strength of our fleet of CF-18s and arm them effectively. We also plan to participate in the United States Air Defense Initiative.

Surveillance on and beneath the sea will be substantially enhanced by the naval programs already discussed. Even those naval assets, however, will not be sufficient to conduct year-round surveillance of the three oceans contiguous to our territory. Our capabilities are currently limited by the number of our long-range patrol aircraft. The flying time available from the present fleet of 18 Aurora aircraft is insufficient. Effective surveillance on the Atlantic Coast with 14 Auroras is barely achieved. On the Pacific, with only four Auroras, it is less than adequate. Our surveillance of the Arctic has increased, but we are still only able to launch a three-day patrol approximately once every three weeks. To remedy this situation we shall acquire at least six additional long-range patrol aircraft and will modernize our fleet of Tracker medium-range aircraft.

Our ability to detect, track and identify potentially threatening surface activity on land and at sea is limited not only by the size of our forces but also by the technology available to them. It is possible that, in the short term, we will be able to increase considerably our surveillance capability by installing synthetic aperture radar in existing aircraft. This technology offers considerable potential for all-weather surveillance of surface targets. Our Defence Research Establishments are already investigating this potential with industry.

Looking ahead to the end of the century and beyond, space will increasingly be utilized in support of national defence aims. Canada's priorities for military space activity — surveillance, communications, navigation and search and rescue — flow naturally from our geography. Parliamentary committees of both the Senate and the House have in recent years recommended that Canada establish a national military space program. The Department is conscious of the need to co-ordinate its efforts with Canada's civilian space endeavours, both in government and in industry, to ensure that possibilities for co-operation and mutual support are fully exploited.

Canada will be exploring the use of space-based systems for many of its surveillance requirements. Space-based systems offer the promise of far more effective surveillance of activity on land and on the surface of the sea. Although technologically more challenging, these systems will, in time, replace the ground-based radars of the North Warning System to provide a detection capability adequate against the bomber and cruise missile forces of the future. Only space-based surveillance has the potential for complete coverage of Canadian territory and adjoining air and sea space.

The Canadian Forces use satellites for communications and in search and rescue. A program is already underway to introduce equipment which will use the United States Satellite Global Positioning System for highly accurate navigation. The Department is conducting research on extremely high frequency satellite communications in order to send more information, more securely. It has also initiated a major five-year research program on space-based radar for the detection and tracking of aircraft and cruise missiles. Two concept and feasibility studies have already been completed by leading Canadian aerospace firms. Canada will also participate, along with other allies, in the United States TEAL RUBY experiments on space-based, infra-red surveillance. We are working with the United States in the bilateral Aerospace Defence Advanced Technology Working Group to identify advanced technology relevant to our future defence needs.

Should the results of our studies and those of the United States show that space-based radar is feasible, practical and affordable, the Department will have to devote, over the next 15 years, significant resources to the establishment of a space-based surveillance system for North American air defence. Decisions regarding our contribution to a joint space-based radar system, or the development of a national system, if a co-operative endeavour is not possible, will have to be taken in the course of the next 5 to 10 years. Failure to meet this challenge could mean forfeiting the responsibility for surveillance of Canadian airspace to the United States.

Canadian participation in the NORAD role of surveillance of objects in space began with the installation of a Baker-Nunn optical tracking system in Cold Lake in 1961. Our tracking systems are now out of date and are being phased out. Nevertheless, it is prudent, in light of the growing use of space for civil and military purposes and consequently the growing number of objects in space, that we remain involved in space surveillance. For this reason we will be examining options for continuing activity in this area after the closure of the existing facilities.

In developing space-based or space-related systems, Canada will continue to co-operate and share costs, experience, technology and responsibilities with the United States, as we have done for almost 30 years in NORAD. In air defence the nature and cost of technology have demonstrated the logic of a continental defence partnership. The same logic applies to space. We therefore anticipate continuing participation with the United States in all forms of early warning and surveillance relevant to North American air defence, whether the means be ground. air or space-based.

Perceptions on the military use of space have increasingly been affected by the American and Soviet research programs into strategic defence and the question this has raised as to the future relationship between the offensive and defensive elements in the nuclear balance. These developments should not obscure the fact that, regardless of the outcome of this research and debate, Canada will still require a capacity to exercise effective surveillance and control over its air, land and sea space. Such a capacity is important for our sovereignty as well as for our security. Our investigations into space activity are in furtherance of this goal and fully consonant with our security and arms control policies. Space is not and should not be the exclusive presence of the super-powers. We are prepared to use it in pursuit of defence and other national objectives and in conformity with our international obligations.

TERRITORIAL DEFENCE

The responsibility of the Canadian Forces does not end with the detection and assessment of threatening or hostile activity. Defence requires an ability to meet force with force. Fighter squadrons equipped with the

CF-18 provide that capability in the air. Naval assets will provide an analogous capacity at sea. We must also have appropriate land forces to demonstrate presence, authority and effective defence within Canada in peacetime and to defend against incursions and sabotage in war.

Canada needs well-trained and well-equipped land forces, comprising both Regulars and Reservists, to protect military vital points and to deploy rapidly to deal with threats in any part of the country. Land forces now fail short of these requirements. Aside from the quick response capability of the Canadian Airborne Regiment, and the valuable but limited surveillance in the Arctic provided by the Canadian Rangers, there is insufficient trained manpower or suitable equipment earmarked specifically for these missions.

In response, we will create additional brigades, mainly from the Reserves, to improve the land force's capability to undertake operations in the defence of Canada. There will also be a minimally-trained guard force created to protect vital military locations. These formations will supplement the present Special Service Force. They will be organized, for purposes of command, control and support, into a task force structure and provided with modern equipment. In addition, the Canadian Rangers will be expanded and their equipment improved.

We will also establish a northern training centre in the 1990s to ensure that forces for the defence of Canada are maintained at an appropriate level of combat readiness. We are seeking a location that comprises all the essential elements for our military purposes and for support of sea, land and air training in Arctic conditions. The selection of the site for the centre will take into account the views of native peoples, existing facilities and local land use.

We will continue, under the Canada-United States defence agreements, to address the conventional threat in its broader North American context. This goal will be achieved by contributing naval, land and air forces to joint training and operations.

CONSOLIDATION IN EUROPE

The current Canadian military commitments in Europe are spread over two widely separated regions. The 4 Canadian Mechanized Brigade Group and the 1 Canadian Air Group are stationed in southern Germany.

The Canadian Air-Sea Transportable (CAST) Brigade Group and two Rapid Reinforcement fighter squadrons, stationed in Canada, are committed to northern Norway in time of crisis.

Canada has also undertaken to provide a battalion group to the Allied Command Europe Mobile Force (Land) (AMF(L)), and a fighter squadron to the Allied Command Europe Mobile Force (Air) (AMF(A)), for deployment to NATO's Northern Region. Both the battalion group and the fighter squadron are stationed in Canada. The latter is one of the two Rapid Reinforcement squadrons already committed, as cited above, to northern Norway. During the past two years Canada has increased its forces stationed in Europe by about 1,500 and the number will grow further with improvements such as low-level air defence.

It has been obvious for some time that these widespread land and air force commitments in Europe represent a dilution of valuable combat resources, and cannot reasonably be supported or sustained from an ocean away in the event of hostilities. They force us to maintain widely separated lines of communication for which we have insufficient strategic transport. We also lack the theatre-level logistics and medical formations to support and maintain these commitments. There are particularly severe problems associated with the deployment of the CAST Brigade to northern Norway. The force requires some weeks to reach Norway, making timely deployment questionable, and it cannot make an opposed landing. Moreover, once deployed, it would be extremely difficult to reinforce and resupply, particularly after the start of hostilities. The result is that, even if successfully deployed, the brigade could rapidly find itself in an untenable position.

The same difficulties with reinforcement and resupply affect our fighter squadrons assigned to northern Norway. They can deploy quickly and perform well, but this is also a small force which would be much more effectively employed as part of a concentrated air commitment in those locations where we have already made large investments in survivable support facilities tailored to the unique requirements of the CF-18.

If these commitments in northern Norway were to be met fully and effectively, the deficiencies cited above would have to be rectified. This could only be done at great cost. If they were not corrected, it would be as obvious to our opponents as it is to us and, consequently, these commitments would contribute little to deterrence.

The Government has concluded that consolidation in southern Germany is the best way to achieve a more credible, effective and sustainable contribution to the common defence in Europe. Consolidation will reduce, although not eliminate, the critical logistic and medical support problems posed by our current commitments. It will ensure that in time of need there will be an identifiable, operational and sustainable Canadian force in Europe.

The task of the Canada-based CAST Brigade Group will, therefore, be shifted from northern Norway to the central front, thus enabling the Canadian army to field a division-sized force in a crisis. The resulting combat power will be enhanced and made more effective than what could have been achieved by two separately deployed brigades. Consolidation will thus be of significant value to NATO s Central Army Group, as the size of its operational reserve will be doubled.

For the division to be fully effective in a two-brigade posture, a number of other improvements will be necessary. Over time, a large part of the Canada-based brigade's equipment and supplies must be pre-positioned in Europe. Even more important will be the acquisition of new tanks. Part of the division headquarters and some other divisional troop elements will be stationed in Europe. The logistics and medical elements necessary to support our European commitments will be provided along with additional airlift capability. The creation of the necessary support structure will require material and personnel resources, the latter being drawn chiefly from the Reserves, with an appropriate cadre of regulars stationed in Europe.

Canada will also shift the commitment of the two Canada-based Rapid Reinforcement fighter squadrons from northern Norway to southern Germany. The concentration of five fighter squadrons on our two existing air bases there will enable us to make more effective use of those facilities and will significantly increase Canada's contribution to the 4th Allied Tactical Air Force. Operating from airfields protected by Low-Level Air Defence units and equipped with hardened aircraft shelters, Canada will contribute an Air Division capable of multi-role operations.

The decision to shift the commitment of the CAST Brigade and the two fighter squadrons from northern Norway has not been taken lightly. Great care has been and will continue to be taken to ensure that our decision will not be strategically or militarily damaging to Norway or to the

Alliance. To this end, the Minister of National Defence has conducted an extensive series of discussions with the Secretary General of NATO, the Norwegian Minister of Defence and other Allied defence ministers, and the Major NATO Commanders.

Most recently, we have consulted NATO formally, as nations undertake to do when contemplating a change in their commitments to the Alliance. We did not expect unanimous support for our proposals, but are confident, from the assessment which NATO has offered, that satisfactory alternative arrangements for the defence of northern Norway are in hand. We are also discussing with the Norwegian government other ways of continuing our very close and rewarding bilateral military relationship.

Those consulted understand that Canada wants to increase its contribution to the conventional deterrent to make it more effective and thereby contribute to raising the nuclear threshold. They understand that, by concentrating and streamlining combat forces and their associated support, supply and sustainment arrangements in one area, we will make the Canadian Forces in Europe more effective and thus enhance our contribution to collective defence.

Canada will, however, maintain the existing battalion group commitment to the AMF(L) for service on the northern flank. The AMF is a small, mobile, multinational task force which could be sent, at short notice, to any threatened flank of Allied Command Europe. It is a jointly organized and supported NATO unit available to the Supreme Allied Commander, Europe (SACEUR) to demonstrate solidarity and the Alliance's ability and determination to defend itself against aggression. As such, it does not pose problems of logistics support of the magnitude encountered with the CAST commitment. Additionally, the Government believes that Canadian participation remains a useful and valuable contribution to deterrence in Europe.

While Canada has indicated that it could not provide a battalion group for operations in NATO's Southern Region, there are two possibilities for deployment should the AMF(L) be assigned to the Northern Region. One is in precisely the same area in which Canadian Forces have trained for the CAST commitment. To simplify deployment, we will leave, for the use of our AMF(L) battalion, much of the equipment now pre-positioned for the CAST Brigade Group. The other possibility is to deploy the AMF(L) to Denmark in order to defend the Baltic approaches

To facilitate the adjustment of our commitments to Central Europe and to increase the overall effectiveness of our forces, modest changes will be required in the posture of our forces stationed in southern Germany. In the long run, we must reduce the mutual interference of collocated land and air forces on our bases at Lahr and Baden-Soellingen. We must improve the deployment of the land forces relative to their wartime missions and make provision for the medical and logistics support which has been ignored for so long. Significant improvement in combat effectiveness cannot occur without the early conclusion of satisfactory arrangements with our allies to provide needed facilities and host-nation support.

Over the longer term, we will be prepared to discuss with our allies and with SACEUR possible alternative locations for our land forces in Germany on the understanding that the considerable costs associated with any change in our current posture would not be our responsibility. In the meantime, however, we will consolidate around the existing facilities in which we have invested so heavily over the years.

THE RESERVES

In the early days of the nuclear threat, Canada's naval, land, and air reserves were cut dramatically. It was commonly believed that any war would be short, and the relative value of reserves, which would take some time to mobilize, was therefore seriously questioned. By the 1970s, the Reserves had little capacity to contribute usefully to the country's defence. This situation has been exacerbated by budgetary stringency, which limited the resources available to the Reserves even more than those for the Regular Force. In most NATO countries reserve forces outnumber their regular force counterparts. Canada stands out as a glaring exception, with only one quarter as many active Reservists as Regulars.

It is now clear that it is both impractical and undesirable to try to meet all of our personnel requirements through the Regular Force. The costs attached to an all-volunteer, full-time military force have become too high. In many cases, the tasks which the Regulars are called upon to undertake can be carried out by trained Reserve personnel. Furthermore, we will be able to address the serious multiple-tasking problems now facing the Regular Force if appropriate numbers of trained Reservists are available.

If the Reserve Force is to be used fully and effectively, the distinction between Regular and Reserve personnel must be greatly reduced. Their responsibilities must be integrated into a Total Force Concept. For example, a unit responding to an emergency could be manned by any mix of Regulars and Reservists. The proper ratio for a specific commitment would be determined by the type of unit, the reaction time and the skills needed. If we are to rely to a greater degree on the Reserves to augment the Regular Force, the size of the Reserves will have to be significantly increased and their training and equipment substantially improved.

At present, the Reserve Force is divided into a number of subcomponents. The largest of these is the Primary Reserve, which comprises formed units that train frequently. Another subcomponent, the Supplementary Reserve, is made up of former Regulars and Primary Reservists, who may serve voluntarily or be placed on active service in an emergency, but who are not required to take continuous training. The Supplementary Reserve must also be revitalized to permit it to make up most of the balance of reserve requirements beyond the Primary Reserve.

The other two elements of the Reserve Force are the Cadet Instructor List and the Canadian Rangers. The size and role of the Cadet Instructor List, a group which provides the command structure and most of the instructors for the Sea, Army and Air Cadets, will remain as they are. However, while the role of the Canadian Rangers will remain basically unchanged, its significance as a surveillance force and as a visible expression of Canadian sovereignty in the North requires its expansion and an improvement in the equipment, training and support it receives

In a Total Force structure, the Reserve Force will be developed not only to augment the Regular Force but also to take on other specific tasks. The Naval Reserve will have two wartime functions of its own: Naval Control of Shipping and Maritime Coastal Defence, including the clearing of mines. The Militia will contribute to defence operations in Canada and elsewhere in North America, and will train replacements for land forces deployed overseas. The Militia will also establish a relatively large force of lightly armed guards to protect military vital points, and make a major contribution to the logistic and medical organizations required to support our consolidated European commitments. The Air Reserve will be more closely associated with the regular air force through the establishment of a number of Integrated Regular-Reserve units. The

Communication Reserve will continue to contribute to the provision of strategic and tactical communications. All of this will, of course, require a significant increase in strength as well as new and improved equipment.

The opening phase of Reserve modernization is already under way and will be pursued with vigour. It will greatly improve the equipment.

Regular & Reserve Personnel

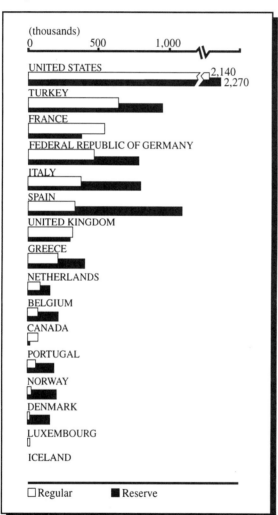

(thousands)

UNITED STATES — 2,140 / 2,270
TURKEY
FRANCE
FEDERAL REPUBLIC OF GERMANY
ITALY
SPAIN
UNITED KINGDOM
GREECE
NETHERLANDS
BELGIUM
CANADA
PORTUGAL
NORWAY
DENMARK
LUXEMBOURG
ICELAND

□ Regular   ■ Reserve

*Estimates based on The International Institute for Strategic Studies, *The Military Balance, 1986-87*, p. 215, except for Canadian data.

and training of the Primary Reserve It will then be better able to fulfil many of our high-priority commitments, including maritime and NORAD operations in Canada and land and air missions in Europe. In the longer term, it will be necessary to implement a complete Reserve Force Development Plan. As a result, Reserve strength will increase to about 90,000. The revitalization of our Reserves will contribute enormously to our ability to meet fully and effectively all our military commitments. The Government recognizes the value of retaining Reserve units in their traditional locales and will make every effort to do so.

Reserve expansion will require a larger pool of trained officers. For this reason, we will study the reactivation of university training programs like those which existed before 1970, the Canadian Officers' Training Corps, the University Reserve Training Plan and the University Naval Training Divisions.

In order to achieve these objectives, pay and benefits will have to be improved. Resources to increase Reserve recruiting will also be required. Terms and conditions of service must be altered to make it easier for members to serve and employers will be encouraged to support Reserve service by members of their work force.

The Canadian Forces must have a highly motivated, well-trained, properly equipped Reserve to be able to meet Canada's defence commitments and to provide a base for expansion whenever that may be required.

FUNDING THE DEFENCE PROGRAM

This White Paper establishes a blueprint and sets the direction of defence policy to the end of the century. Implementing this new defence policy will be expensive and will pose a significant challenge for this and future governments. It has never been easy for democratic governments to find, in peacetime, the resources necessary for defence. It is certainly not easy now. The pressures for economic and social programs designed to bring prosperity and to provide opportunities for fuller and richer lives make defence spending seem, at least to some, an unattractive use of national resources. Social benefits, however, are the fruits of a secure and free society. This Government accepts the preservation of such a society as its fundamental responsibility and will, therefore, provide the resources necessary to make the Canadian Forces operationally effective and responsive to the challenges of the 1990s and beyond.

Defence planning is, by its very nature, long-term. Most major defence projects, whether they concern new ships, aircraft, or other weaponry, take at least ten years to produce results. To provide a planning framework in which equipment decisions respond to, rather than lead, policy, the Government has developed a new long-term planning and funding process. A rolling five-year funding plan will be introduced within a fifteen-year planning framework. An annual Cabinet review, each autumn, will establish firm budgets for the following five-year period, and planning guidance for the remaining ten years.

The Government is committed to a base rate of annual real growth in the defence budget of two per cent per year after inflation, for the fifteen-year planning period. Increased resources over those provided by this planned funding floor will be necessary in some years as major projects forecast in this White Paper are introduced. The first annual review of the defence program will be conducted in September, 1987, at which time the second phase of the Ship Replacement Program will be examined to determine the annual level of incremental funding required over the two per cent base line for the first five-year period.

The new planning system will enable the Government, on an annual basis, to make adjustments to the defence program reflecting changes in military, technological, strategic and fiscal circumstances. Such adjustments will be explained and reflected when the annual departmental estimates are tabled.

CHAPTER VIII

Foundations for Defence

The men and women of the Canadian Forces form the front line of Canada's defence. They can only be effective, however, if their efforts are based on firm foundations. They require the leadership that comes from effective command and control. The Government must have in place organizational structures which will make it possible, in a crisis, to mobilize the human and material resources of the country. It must also have the legal authority to respond appropriately in crisis or war. The armed forces must have the industrial base to supply them with essential equipment and materiel. Moreover, all aspects of defence policy must be supported by vigorous research and development in order to maximize our defence effort.

COMMAND AND CONTROL

The present structure for the administration of defence policy and the command and control of the Canadian Forces is the result of a long evolution. Today we have a defence structure that is distinctly Canadian, has served us well and is essentially sound.

In the post-war years, Canada's three services became increasingly integrated. In 1964 the responsibility for their command and control was vested in the newly created position of Chief of the Defence Staff. This decision was followed by the Canadian Forces Reorganization Act in 1967, which unified the services into a single Canadian Armed Forces. In 1972 a Management Review Group recommendation led to the amalgamation of the Canadian Forces military headquarters and the departmental headquarters. The new structure enabled military officers and civilian officials to develop advice for ministers more effectively.

The unification of command responsibilities under the Chief of the Defence Staff has made a major contribution to the formulation of defence policy. The Chief of the Defence Staff provides a single source of military advice to the Government and, as the leader of the military profession in Canada, he is ultimately responsible for the operational command and control and logistic support of all Canadian Forces.

The Chief of the Defence Staff receives essential support from his senior advisers, the commanders of the functional commands. A recently strengthened Armed Forces Council is the forum through which the commanders and senior staff officers help develop policy advice for the Chief of the Defence Staff. This change will re-emphasize operational effectiveness and focus attention on the enhancement of our defence capabilities.

When the three services were unified, the commands were organized by function, such as air transport, training, and air defence. Previously, however, the army had been structured on a geographical basis. The great distances between units required the delegation of specific authority and responsibility to regional commanders

In an attempt to maintain the functional concept and to react to regional responsibilities, the Canadian Forces eventually adopted a combined functional and regional command structure. Nevertheless, regional operations continued to depend largely on army units and consequently required, in most emergencies, the transfer of command of troops and resources among commands.

It has become evident that in a crisis our present structure would not suffice and would have to be reorganized at precisely the moment when continuity would be essential. In order to simplify and strengthen Canada's defence structure, the Government intends to establish a geographically oriented regional command structure under the Commander, Mobile Command. He will be responsible for aid of the civil power and assistance to civil authorities, co-ordinating support to the Militia, and the operation of army mobilization in each region.

This new structure will be developed from existing resources. Where appropriate, air and naval officers will be assigned to regional headquarters. Separating functional and regional responsibilities will simplify the chain of command and relieve National Defence Headquarters and other command headquarters of detailed regional responsibilities.

Morale and esprit de corps are important components of service life and are vital to the cohesion of units under stress in crisis and war. These factors and the essential differences in operational environments must be acknowledged in the structure of the Canadian Forces. It was towards this end that the promise to issue three distinct uniforms was promptly put into effect by this Government. In the future we shall ensure that the maintenance of morale and the special needs of service life are recognized and respected. We must produce a defence structure that is resilient and able to exploit Canada's defence potential.

MOBILIZATION PLANNING AND PREPAREDNESS

The mobilization of human and material resources of the country in time of crisis must receive more attention. Preparations need to be made in the areas of transportation, communications, energy, food supply, medical services and construction. During the past two years, the Government has increased the emergency planning staffs in the key civil departments concerned with mobilization planning. The Provinces are participating fully in the planning process and discussions are proceeding with the private sector.

The Government will emphasize the importance of emergency planning by all departments. In addition, legislation will be introduced to establish formally and give a clear mandate to Emergency Preparedness Canada, the agency responsible for co-ordinating the civil aspects of government-wide mobilization planning.

In an international crisis, national emergency agencies will be responsible for the rapid mobilization of Canada's civil potential. The Government might, for example, need to direct the use of sea, land and air transport for the movement of military personnel and supplies, as well as to take special measures to accelerate defence production. Measures might be required to control and regulate the production and distribution of energy and foodstuffs, to redirect strategic materials and to provide for the early and orderly mobilization of the Reserves. The authority for implementing such measures and for activating the national emergency agencies will be contained in new emergencies legislation.

NEW EMERGENCIES LEGISLATION

Canada is one of the very few developed nations without comprehensive emergencies legislation. The broad and sweeping powers of the *War Measures Act* are excessive in relation to national emergencies in peacetime. While the *War Measures Act* is certainly adequate for war or invasion, it incorporates few safeguards against abuse. Other statutes with emergency provisions provide little more than an incomplete patchwork of inadequately safeguarded emergency measures. In addition, existing emergencies legislation does not adequately recognize either the role or the legitimate interests of the Provinces in providing a national response to national emergencies.

The alternatives to comprehensive emergencies legislation are of doubtful value. The Crown prerogative and the common law doctrine of "necessity" provide, at best, a shaky and uncertain basis for effective action in an emergency. Reliance on ad hoc legislation enacted in the heat of a crisis could lead to less balanced and restrained measures than those based on legislation carefully considered by Parliament during normal times. Furthermore, such an ad hoc approach could delay the response if Parliament were not in session, and would be impossible if Parliament were dissolved when the emergency arose.

Therefore, to ensure that it will be in a position to provide adequately for the safety and security of the Canadian people, the Government intends to introduce comprehensive legislation to deal with the full range of possible national emergencies.

The new Emergencies Act will authorize the Government, in a national emergency, to take the necessary, special, temporary measures. The legislation will include adequate safeguards to protect fundamental rights and freedoms and to limit both the duration and the substance of exceptional measures to no more than is needed. It will also respect the interests of the Provinces, and provide for Parliamentary review when the legislation is invoked and at every stage while it is in effect. The existing *War Measures Act* will be repealed.

In the context of national security, the Emergencies Act will provide the legal authority for the Government to respond to an international crisis or war. The Act will enable the Government to implement preparatory and preventive measures, in concert with Canada's allies and in an orderly and non-provocative way. The Government will be able to begin civil mobilization to prepare the nation for war. Such a capability to demonstrate readiness and resolve is an important part of the strategy of deterrence.

DEFENCE INDUSTRIAL PREPAREDNESS

Maintaining the conventional forces of NATO as a credible deterrent requires that our industrial base be able to respond to the needs of our armed forces and those of our allies, both for initial readiness and for follow-on sustainment.

A key element of both readiness and sustainment is the ability to equip and resupply military forces. Sustainment requires an assured source of materiel well in excess of affordable stockpiles. In July 1987, a departmental task force will make specific proposals to enhance defence industrial preparedness planning. The task force, in conjunction with the departments of Supply and Services, Regional Industrial Expansion, External Affairs and others, is developing a method of measuring the ability of defence industry to provide assured support to critical operational items used by the Canadian Forces.

Extensive study within NATO, particularly by the United States, has shown that carefully planned investment in industry significantly increases preparedness. Examples include the advance procurement of critical components or test equipment and improvements in manufacturing technology. On a continuing basis and as determined through extensive study, industrial preparedness measures will be pursued by the Government to enhance the responsiveness of the defence industrial base.

The increasing complexity and high cost of modern weapons systems are such that it is not feasible for Canada to undertake most major defence development projects on its own. Rising costs and growing technological complexity are forcing many nations to view co-operative research, development, production and support as a logical complement to collective defence. It is in our national interest to pursue armaments co-operation through arrangements with other nations both within and outside the NATO Alliance. Where major equipment must be procured offshore, the Government will promote teaming arrangements with Canadian industry to foster technology transfer and the creation of an indigenous support base. Canada also recognizes the military and economic advantages

266 Canada's National Defence

of co-operating with other nations in fulfilling mutual defence equipment requirements. Bilateral research, development and production agreements have been made with the United Kingdom, the Federal Republic of Germany, the Netherlands, France, Italy, Denmark and Norway as well as with Sweden.

In acquiring equipment, the Government will pay greater attention to the long-term industrial implications. For example, the need for indigenous support and repair and overhaul capability for new equipment will be addressed from the beginning. To increase consultation with industry, a Defence Industrial Preparedness Advisory Committee, composed of industrialists and academics, has recently been established. This forum affords the defence industrial community an opportunity to develop innovative approaches to defence industrial preparedness.

We will continue, within the Alliance, to increase efficiency by consolidating Allied requirements where possible and sharing production for common use. Canadian industry is an important element of the North American Defence Industrial Base. Through participation in Canada-United States Defence Development and Defence Production-Sharing Arrangements, Canada co-operates with the United States in the development and production of defence equipment. These programs allow Canadian industry to specialize in selected areas through access to the American military market. We will continue to work closely with the United States in an effort to foster the common use of this base.

There is a high degree of commonality between our critical operational items and those of the United States. Security of supply could be greatly enhanced through co-production arrangements. For example, a recently completed Canada-United States study has concluded that the capability to increase production of conventional precision-guided munitions in an emergency could be significantly improved by further developing Canadian sources of critical components within the North American Defence Industrial Base. Other initiatives in progress will contribute to the strengthening of that base. These include participation by government and industry in both countries in analysing a variety of production capabilities to better satisfy mutual defence needs. The gas turbine engine, which Canadian industry produces for aircraft, ships and vehicles, is but one example. The growing importance of Canadian industry to the overall North American Defence Industrial Base and the need to enhance further Canada-United States co-operation were recognized at the March 1985 summit between the Prime Minister of Canada and the President of the United States. In their joint release, they stated that further measures could be taken "... to facilitate defence economic and trade co-operation and joint participation in major defence programs."

The implementation of the equipment and facility acquisition programs required to give effect to the policies and commitments proposed in this paper will significantly increase procurement by the Department of National Defence. A concerted effort to find and train additional specialized people to manage effectively the new acquisition programs will be needed. This procurement will also place additional strain on other departments and on our existing defence industrial base. Both government and industry will need to ensure that appropriate resources are allocated to the task.

RESEARCH AND DEVELOPMENT

Modern armed forces are dependent upon advanced technology for effective military operations. Consequently, advances in science and technology are key considerations in strategic policy, equipment purchases, military doctrine and operations, equipment development and maintainability, and the selection, protection, performance and training of military personnel. In the last decade there have been major advances in computers, software, integrated circuits, sensors, propulsion, materials and other technologies that now form the foundation for the next generation of defence systems. These advances are changing the nature of military science to a degree unparalleled in history.

The current technological advantage enjoyed by the West is a direct result of earlier investments in research and development and the continuing search for advanced technologies by industry, universities and defence laboratories. However, this technological edge has been diminishing as a result of declining R&D efforts in the West and of massive Soviet efforts to develop new technologies and to copy Western technology. For example, recent estimates give the Soviet Union a two-to-one advantage over the United States in the numbers of scientists and engineers employed in research and development. The Government will make every effort to eliminate the illegal transfer of technology to Warsaw Pact nations.

The transfer of defence research and, particularly, development to the private sector is important for the application of new technologies to Western defence. The Department of National Defence has been steadily increasing the funds contracted to Canadian industry for R&D: in the 10-year period 1977-1987, the expansion has been almost sevenfold. Such contracting will continue to increase. In addition, the Government is considering a Defence Industrial Research program to help domestic industry establish a technology base from which to meet the Canadian Forces' requirements for new equipment, resupply and life-cycle support. The program would help mobilize those areas where Canadian industry has strengths and would serve as a channel for information exchange and technology transfer between the Canadian Defence Research Establishments and the defence industrial community.

In co-operation with other departments the Department of National Defence will pursue policies to increase R&D capability and expertise in Canada. The Defence Industry Productivity Program of the Department of Regional Industrial Expansion is an example of such an initiative. Canadian technology will be incorporated into National Defence operations and plans wherever possible in order to help strengthen Canada's defence industrial capability.

The development and production of competitive defence equipment for Canadian and Allied forces will require the judicious employment of emerging technologies to provide the necessary military capability at affordable cost. For this purpose a broad base of scientific and engineering expertise is maintained at a level sufficient to understand, compare and assess the capabilities of the most advanced products available and to judge the potential applications of new technologies. This level of knowledge is derived from defence research and development in government, industrial and university laboratories. The information obtained is pooled with our allies through a number of bilateral and multilateral agreements. In return we gain access to a volume of knowledge far beyond that which can be created at home.

In addition to providing the technology to meet the needs of the Canadian Forces, the R&D activities of the Department have made significant contributions to meeting civilian needs and to the Canadian economy. Designed and constructed in Canadian defence laboratories, the Alouette ionospheric research satellite made Canada the third country in space and laid the foundation for the Canadian space industry. The Department's leadership in space continues with the international Search and Rescue satellite program, which has dramatically aided in the localization of both air and sea emergencies, and with new initiatives on extra high frequency communications and space-based surveillance technology.

The Department has also supported the aircraft industry in Canada by assisting in the establishment of the technology base in computer-aided design, small turbine jet engines and composite materials. Another field that has benefited from technology transfer from defence laboratories is lasers. The rise of Canadian industry as a supplier of laser systems internationally rests on the technology of the carbon dioxide laser which was invented at the Defence Research Establishment, Valcartier.

Defence research extends well beyond the direct application of engineering, physics and chemistry to hardware design. The ability of humans to cope with complex defence systems under continuous operational conditions will be a key determinant of future military effectiveness. Meeting these challenges will require new research in information, command and control, and all of the attendant aspects of human performance and behaviour.

Operational research is fundamental to the improvement of tactics and logistics. It enables optimum use to be made of equipment in service, and helps ensure the best plans for acquisition of new equipment.

To broaden the understanding of defence problems and to stimulate systematic research by well-qualified scholars, the Department maintains a Military and Strategic Studies program in a number of Canadian universities. To date, teaching and research have emphasized the more classical areas of strategic studies, dealing with international relations, political trends and the balance of power. The Department will broaden its support to encourage teaching and research in other areas important to defence analysis, such as the economics of defence, operational research and systems analysis and the implications for security of technological developments.

CHAPTER IX

The Armed Forces and Society

In their primary role, the Canadian Forces make a vital contribution to keeping Canada a free, peaceful and democratic society. The Canadian Forces make other valuable contributions to society in ways that are not always obvious or fully understood. In living the concept of service before self, members of the Forces and their families develop to a particularly fine degree those qualities of citizenship and community service that bind us as a nation and focus our national identity. Through application of skill, determination and discipline, Canadian service personnel have earned an international reputation as exemplary soldiers and citizens. Canada's participation in peacekeeping has earned us a reputation as responsible, reliable and trustworthy members of the world community. The Forces enrich the civilian labour force through the addition of trained, motivated and educated individuals. In the normal course of their professional duties they offer emergency assistance to the public. In private life they are well-known for support of community activities.

The Canadian Forces are an integral part of our society, yet, in a sense, they remain somewhat separate from it. Their duties and rules of daily behaviour set them apart from their fellow citizens. There is a risk that this separation could lead to estrangement. The Canadian Forces tend to be concentrated in only a few areas of the country, which are often distant from large urban centres. The Reserves, which once were the major link between the Forces and society, have been allowed to run down. Moreover, attitudes of the public toward defence have doubtless been affected by concern about, or even distaste for, some of the unpleasant realities of international security.

It must be recalled, however, that Canada's military experience has made a unique and dramatic contribution to our national development. In this spring of 1987 it is fitting to recall that 70 years ago, at Vimy Ridge, Canadians from all parts of this country and from all walks of life, working together as a superb fighting machine, won one of the greatest victories of the First World War. From a comradeship born of shared experience in the face of adversity, sacrifice and danger, blossomed a sense of self-confidence, unity and maturity; in short, a new sense of nation

Despite justifiable pride in past military accomplishments, Canadians find the prospect of war ever more abhorrent, a feeling that has been reinforced by the losses suffered in two world wars and the Korean conflict. The advent of nuclear weapons has only added to the concern with which they view the possibility that Canada could again be caught up in a major armed struggle. Canadian security policy and the roles of the Forces must be widely and well understood, if the Forces are to enjoy the support they require.

To this end the Department has taken a number of steps to make more information more accessible to the public. It has established a National Defence Speakers Bureau, comprising senior military commanders, departmental managers and other experts. The Department is producing informational material on defence issues and ensuring that it is effectively distributed. To bring Canadian Forces bases into closer contact with a greater number of Canadian communities, the Department has developed an expanded community relations program. The goal is to ensure that the facts on security are available to the Canadian public.

The Government's decision to put greater emphasis on the Reserves will build a more effective bridge between the Forces and society and tap a larger personnel pool. Revitalizing the Reserves will, in addition, provide young Canadians with skills and work experience, increasing their employment opportunities.

Since the Second World War, Canada has become much more diverse, both ethnically and culturally. The Canadian Forces, an institution which should be broadly representative of society as a whole, must reflect this diversity. The Department will continue to encourage participation in the Forces from all segments of society.

The Department must be institutionally bilingual and representative of both official language communities in Canada. Significant progress has been made over the past 16 years in providing a more balanced representation, both within the Canadian Forces and within the civilian component of the Department. Communication with the public in either official language is now generally available. Yet much more remains to be done, particularly in the language of work, before all employees can enjoy full and equitable career opportunities.

Changes in social roles, expectations and values pose enormous challenges to the Canadian Forces in their need to maintain discipline and cohesion. The Department of National Defence is in the forefront of responding to those developments. For example, three quarters of the military occupations are now open to women. There are approximately 7,800 women in the Regular Force. They represent a higher percentage than in any other NATO country except the United States. A further 4,200 are in the Primary Reserve. Moreover, the Government firmly believes that every Canadian must have equal rights and responsibilities in the defence of Canada. As announced in February, the Department is conducting a series of trials to determine how, when, and in which occupations and units the remaining restrictions on the employment of women in the Canadian Forces can be removed.

The proclamation of the Canadian Charter of Rights and Freedoms has contributed to an increased awareness, among all Canadians, of issues of individual rights and freedoms. The Department of National Defence has taken steps to ensure that its policies and practices comply with the Charter. Within the Canadian Forces, substantial changes have been made to the Code of Service Discipline to conform to the Charter based legal rights. Major efforts have been made, and are continuing, to accommodate the equal rights guaranteed by the Charter. However, while society has become more concerned with individual rights and freedoms, the cohesive team effort required for successful military operations frequently demands that the needs of the group take precedence. Thus, a careful balance must be found, within the law, between respect for individual rights and the needs of national security.

The Canadian Forces, while clearly having a distinct and different ethos, do reflect many of the tensions present in Canadian society. Pressures for social change and requirements for operational effectiveness are not always in harmony. While this is not necessarily a new phenomenon, the Government will strive to develop closer relations between the Forces and society at large.

DEFENCE AND THE ECONOMY

Defence expenditures in Canada contribute economic benefits to all sectors of Canadian society. In fiscal year 1985-86, Canadian defence spending accounted for approximately $12 billion of the Gross Domestic Product. It produced $1.6 billion in taxes and generated approximately 294,000 jobs, 178,000 in the private sector.

The impact of defence spending is not confined to one area or sector, or to a narrow band of economic activity. It is, instead, felt throughout the entire economy and in all parts of the country. While it is true that at any given time a particular project may create more employment in, for example, the shipbuilding industry rather than the aircraft industry, an evaluation of economic and regional impact over time indicates that defence expenditures benefit all regions and economic sectors of the country.

Jobs in the Private Sector (1985/86)

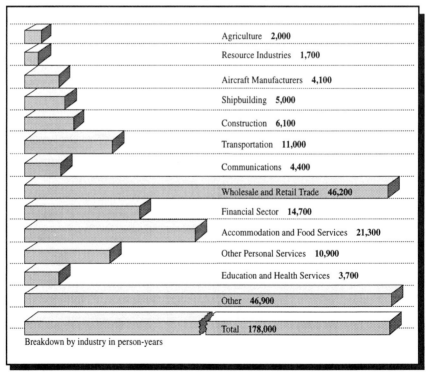

Agriculture **2,000**

Resource Industries **1,700**

Aircraft Manufacturers **4,100**

Shipbuilding **5,000**

Construction **6,100**

Transportation **11,000**

Communications **4,400**

Wholesale and Retail Trade **46,200**

Financial Sector **14,700**

Accommodation and Food Services **21,300**

Other Personal Services **10,900**

Education and Health Services **3,700**

Other **46,900**

Total **178,000**

Breakdown by industry in person-years

As an illustration of the extent to which defence projects create jobs, it is anticipated that the current Canadian Patrol Frigate (CPF) and Tribal Update and Modernization (TRUMP) programs will generate about 34,100 person-years of employment between 1984 and 1992. Canadian firms, particularly the shipbuilding and electronics industries, will do about two thirds of the work. These programs will result in the development of new technical skills and contribute to the growth of small business jobs in Canada.

Examples of Jobs Generated by Defence Projects

(Person Years)	*CPF*	*TRUMP*
Project Management	3,000	800
Electronic Systems	6,000	4,000
Marine Systems	5,000	3,500
Shipbuilding	7,100	4,700
TOTAL	21,100	13,000

The Department of National Defence is both a producer and a consumer in the Canadian economy. Canadian defence spending contributes significantly to the maintenance of a robust and flexible economic environment. Defence purchases contribute to the development of internationally competitive Canadian industries.

By enhancing Canadian international competitiveness, defence expenditures allow us to take advantage of economic opportunities abroad in both defence and parallel non-defence industries. At the same time, the Department's participation in international trade gives Canadian manufacturers a channel to advertise Canada's capacity to produce the high-quality goods demanded by foreign buyers. Because of the pervasive nature of Canadian defence activity, Canada has an entree into a wide variety of foreign research, development and manufacturing processes.

The education and training of highly skilled workers essential to the operation of a modern economy is a further benefit of Canada's defence industrial base. In a situation where the demand for skilled personnel often exceeds supply, the Canadian Forces provide capable, experienced and disciplined individuals who can play vital roles in the civilian economy following their military service.

Defence programs also make a significant contribution to overcoming regional economic disparities. Over the years, it has frequently been possible to use scarce defence dollars to strengthen local and regional economies while at the same time satisfying defence requirements.

SEARCH AND RESCUE

Following the Second World War, the Government assigned to the Royal Canadian Air Force the responsibility for Search and Rescue. The Canadian Forces now provide resources for both air and marine Search and Rescue operations and co-ordinate the response to all distress incidents in Canada and the surrounding ocean areas.

The National Search and Rescue System is responsible for an area of over 15 million square kilometres. At present, Rescue Co-ordination Centres are located in Halifax, Trenton, Edmonton and Victoria, and are staffed by Canadian Forces personnel and Canadian Coast Guard officers. These centres have at their disposal dedicated resources, which include specially equipped Canadian Forces fixed-wing aircraft and helicopters, ground search parties at specified Canadian Forces bases and stations, and Canadian Coast Guard surface vessels and hovercraft. Other resources include Regular and Reserve squadron aircraft and ships of the Canadian Forces, and vessels of the Department of Fisheries and Oceans. Additionally, the Royal Canadian Mounted Police, the Department of Indian and Northern Affairs and the Department of Energy Mines and Resources also assist in Search and Rescue operations when feasible, as do numerous individuals and private organizations.

The Canadian Forces constantly improve their all-weather search and rescue capability. The Search and Rescue Satellite-Aided Tracking System (COSPAS/SARSAT) is an international space-based distress signal detection system involving France, the United States, the Soviet Union, Canada and others. This system, which has strong Canadian support and industrial participation, has already been credited with saving more than 700 lives worldwide. In addition to improving equipment and exploiting new technologies, the Search and Rescue program is more effectively utilizing national resources through such organizations as the Civil Air Search and Rescue Association and the Canadian Marine Rescue Auxiliary. The Canadian Forces will continue to play a central role in the National Search and Rescue System.

FOREIGN DISASTER AND HUMANITARIAN RELIEF

The Canadian Forces have, on request, provided humanitarian and philanthropic assistance to those in need in a number of Third World countries. This aid has been given primarily through the transport of needed supplies, such as powdered milk, medical and dental supplies, ambulances, clothing and school books. It has also included mercy flights, medical evacuations and specialized search and rescue personnel.

The humanitarian assistance provided in the past has been an important contribution to the alleviation of human suffering. More needs to be done. Accordingly, the Government intends to be even more active in using the Canadian Forces for humanitarian disaster relief abroad. In conjunction with the Department of External Affairs or the Canadian International Development Agency, the Department of National Defence will consider requests from governments of countries where disasters have occurred, and will be prepared to provide support in the form of air and sea transport, helicopters, tents, field hospitals, medical supplies, portable communications equipment and other emergency items. Canadian Forces personnel will also be made available to provide engineering, medical and other specialized services, and to operate equipment.

ASSISTANCE TO CIVIL AUTHORITIES AND CIVILIAN ORGANIZATIONS

The Canadian Forces play an important role in supporting civil authorities charged with enforcing Canadian laws. For example, they assist the Department of Fisheries and Oceans in the surveillance of the 200-mile Extended Fishing Zone and the enforcement of Canadian Fisheries laws in that zone when coercive assistance is required. Arrangements exist to provide a similar service to the RCMP in their role of interdicting illegal drugs. The Canadian Forces are also called upon to provide emergency assistance to Canadians in cases of disaster such as floods, forest fires and landslides. The Department of National Defence is working with other departments to improve the availability and effective employment of the Canadian Forces in these roles.

CADETS

The Department of National Defence operates and supports organizations for both male and female cadets between the ages of 12 and 19. It does so in partnership with the Navy League, the Army Cadet League and the Air Cadet League of Canada. There are about 60,000 Royal Canadian Sea, Army and Air Cadets in 1,090 cadet corps and squadrons spread across the country. Approximately 22,000 of these cadets acquire leadership and specialty training skills each summer at camps in Canada and overseas.

The cadet organizations provide young Canadians with excellent training emphasizing leadership, physical fitness and service to the community. In fostering civic responsibility, cadet training makes an invaluable contribution to the nation and one which the Department will continue to support to the full.

CHAPTER X

Conclusion

"...three elements are indispensable to a nation: people, territory and a navy. But military strength is the keystone that is essential to the structure."

George-Étienne Cartier

Canadians have been blessed by geography and history. It has been more than 170 years since this country was invaded by a foreign power. Canada as a nation has never suffered occupation. In war, we have always shared in the fruits of victory and have been spared the bitter taste of defeat. Canadian reactions to international security issues have been conditioned by these geographic and historical realities.

Canadians tend to approach international relations optimistically, assuming the best of others. Few Canadians feel militarily threatened and most have difficulty imagining anyone as an enemy. While accepting the necessity of a defence effort, we do not expect to have to resort to force of arms to resolve our problems.

This White Paper has sought to remind Canadians that the world is not always as benign or predictable as we would wish, that the spectre, if not the reality, of violence is ever-present and that those who do not look to their own military forces can become the victims of the forces of others.

Since coming to office, the Government has reviewed our defence effort. This review has confirmed that Canadian defence policy, as it has evolved since the Second World War, is essentially sound. That policy will continue to be based on a strategy of collective security within the framework of the North Atlantic Alliance, including the continental defence partnership with the United States. Canada will continue to support that strategy through military contributions in North America, in Western Europe and at sea.

Our examination revealed that the primary means with which Canadian security policy is implemented, the Canadian Forces, have been sadly neglected. Failure to provide modern equipment has undercut the credibility of the Canadian Forces, weakening Canada's contribution to deterrence and collective defence. Moreover, if Canadian men and women ever had to go into combat with the aged equipment they currently possess, lives would be needlessly lost.

Decades of neglect must be overcome. The Government is determined to do so through coherent and consistent leadership and by a steady, predictable and honest funding program. For the future, we will take a number of initiatives which will represent a significant and visible increase in the effectiveness of the Canadian Forces. We will create a modern navy capable of operating in the Atlantic, the Pacific and the Arctic. We will bolster our capacity for surveillance and defence of Canadian territory. We will revitalize and enlarge the Reserves so that they can assume a greater role in the defence of Canada. We will consolidate our land and air commitments in Europe on the central front, thereby providing a more credible and sustainable contribution to collective security.

The Government will implement this program vigorously. Over time, our endeavours will produce a defence posture responsive to the challenges of the 1990s and beyond. Canadian security and sovereignty will be better served. Canada will become a more responsible ally. We will then have a firmer basis from which to contribute to peace and freedom.

Introduction to
1994 Defence White Paper

In the first Liberal white paper on defence since 1971, the government tried to dance between two contrary objectives. It hoped to convince Canadians, members of the armed forces, and allies that "Canada continues to have a vital interest in doing its part to ensure global security," while it cut deeply into the capabilities that provide the means for "doing its part." Consequently, *1994 Defence White Paper* is long on rhetoric, but short on specifics, especially about future Canadian military capabilities.

In 1992 the Progressive Conservative government declared that there were only two certainties in the defence field: uncertainty and lower expenditures. David Collenette confirmed these facts by marking 1993-94 as "a significant turning point [for defence policy].... Responding to a fundamental reordering of international affairs and the need to confront important economic realities at home." The aim of the government's defence program was to create "an effective, realistic and affordable policy" but the outcome hung on defining what was effective and affordable.

The preparation of the white paper on defence in circumstances of fundamental change spurred a serious and prolonged debate in Canada about the aims and means of national defence. The government aided this debate by establishing a Special Joint Committee of the Senate and House of Commons (SJC) to consult with Canadians on all aspects of national defence policy. The committee met in Ottawa and travelled across

Canada and to Canadian Forces units overseas to gather opinions and recommendations from interest groups and individuals who wished to express ideas and views on defence policy.

The debate, generally, exposed two approaches to restructuring the armed forces for the future. On the one hand stood those, mostly from within the defence establishment, who wanted to retain traditional cold-war "general purpose forces" capable of engaging in classical total war military activities. On the other hand, others, mostly from outside the defence establishment, proposed that Canada develop military capabilities especially suited to a world characterized by regional conflicts and low-level military operations. The debate became unusually pointed because many interests, institutions, and costly programs rested on whose view prevailed in the Cabinet.

Although Collenette acknowledged the breadth of the debate in his opening remarks and elsewhere in the white paper, the focus of the white paper came mainly from the SJC report. The defence minister stated in his introduction to *1994 Defence White Paper* that "virtually all [the SJC] recommendations are reflected in this White Paper." However, he emphasized that the "Committee's recommendation concerning the size of the Regular Forces was judged to be inconsistent with the financial parameters within which the Department of National Defence must operate." In effect, the government accepted the recommendations to substantially rebuild the armed forces, but rejected the obvious need to pay for the renewal.

The white paper accepted the world view of those proposing radical changes in defence organization. Canada faced, according to the white paper, "a safer world ... balanced by the persistence of conflict within and between states [and] we can expect pockets of chaos and instability that will threaten international peace and security." Canada faced no immediate threats and the prospects for the type of interstate war the armed forces had prepared for over more than forty years was minimal. The main cause of future conflicts would not come from "balance of power" struggles between the superpowers, but from a variety of persistent social stresses. Population explosions, refugees, "failed states," "resurgence of old hatreds," and weapons proliferation were cited as the primary threats to international security. Therefore, Canada's armed forces would not need to be prepared for the types of missions it had assumed during the Cold War, but it must have the means to guard "essential Canadian values and vital interests, at home and abroad." These values and vital interests were, however, left undefined.

The second major factor determining Canada's defence policy was "domestic considerations," which would bring significant and continuing reductions in all sectors of the defence budget. Collenette announced that "defence spending in the year 2000 ... in real terms would be less than 60 percent of that assumed in the 1987 Defence White Paper." The effect of this target was felt immediately in the defence department when programs were cancelled and bases and organizations closed.

Despite these significant changes in basic policy assumptions, the minister, under considerable pressure from his military advisers and their supporters in industry and the defence community at large, encouraged traditional defence views. He spoke of "prudent levels of military force" and a "capability to generate forces" for national defence "should the need arise." Collenette hinted that the government was committed to making "the required investment in our armed forces" because the government had concluded that "the maintenance of multi-purpose, combat capable forces is in the national interest.... The challenge [would] be to design a defence program that will deliver capable armed forces within the limits of our resources."

Many officers and commentators seized this rhetoric as a commitment by the government to parry the views of those who had suggested that Canada cut its defence uniform to suit the logic of the new strategic challenges and lower expenditures. The minister's support for the slogan "multi-purpose, combat-capable forces" seemed a straw stout enough to float every traditionalist, despite the government's obvious intent to provide just enough funds to keep the barest defence force from drowning.

1994 Defence White Paper departed from other defence policy papers in another important aspect. For the first time since Claxton's statement, there was no mention of priorities nor any listing of defence objectives. Rather, the government committed itself to the idea of "collective security" linked firmly to the United Nations. While not dismissing "collective defence" and allies, NATO was not placed in its usual separate chapter, but bunched into the category of missions related to "contributing to international security." Collenette seemed to reject long-standing NATO commitments when he stated that "Canada is not obliged to take on a major portion of every operation or to contribute forces for longer than seems reasonable." In the future, Canada would only commit forces "if suitable resources are available and if our personnel can be appropriately armed." The emphasis was towards the UN and its needs and away from the type of expensive, open-ended commitments that characterized Canadian defence policy between 1950 and 1992.

The minister, in search of savings, directed a full review of defence spending across the department and the armed forces. This direction, at times, met considerable resistence, again because it upset the usual ways of doing things. Headquarters were ordered closed, commanders were moved, bases were closed or reduced, and major procurement policies were changed.

For officers and officials accustomed to the predictability of the Cold War and the commitments that flowed from it, change was not easy. The tension in National Defence Headquarters created by the minister's determination to reorder defence policy and create a new strategy was intense. The minister, reportedly, rejected several drafts of the white paper because they failed to respond appropriately to his ideas and directions. This was no simple clash over the allocation of the defence budget, it was a radical imposition of new ideas, ideas that struck at institutions and the preferences of senior officers and officials in the defence establishment.

When David Collenette stated that this was "a significant turning point in the history of the Department of Defence and the Canadian Forces," some people might have thought that he was being melodramatic. Others might have thought that he was referring only to the changes that ended the Cold War. What he meant, however, was that the way Canadians thought about national defence and how it would be achieved would be changed completely. Imposing the new order meant turning away from established ways of doing things, from allies, institutions, capabilities, and traditions.

After he tabled *1994 Defence White Paper*, Collenette became increasingly embroiled in the so-called Somalia Affair and he was not able to devote his full attention to managing defence policy. He found, as other ministers found before him, that bureaucracies can bide their time and retrace steps to turning points. Senior officers and officials have made meaningful changes to the way the armed forces does business, mainly because they had no choice given the reduced defence budget. But they did not and have not accepted the "collective security" notion at the heart of the white paper. Nor have they abandoned their ambitions to build a force with the capabilities of the forces of major states, if only in miniature. Even though the armed forces are continually engaged in small operations that demand army units and equipment suited to low-level combat, senior leaders still try to find reasons for building "general-purpose combat forces" suited to major international warfare.

The minister snared his policies in his own tangled rhetoric, and he left an opportunity for leaders with other ideas to return to their own preferences. *1994 Defence White Paper* was a bold attempt by the minister of defence to rescue defence policy from the dictates of the Cold War and officers and officials conditioned by that singular event. Whether the ministers can sustain a new strategy in face of inherent bureaucratic resistence to change and whether the Canadian Forces will respond logically and practically to the reordered world remains to be seen. However, from the perspective of mid-1997, the omens are not good. When there is no consensus between ministers, officials, and officers about the situation, objectives, and the resources needed for national defence, the usual outcome is confusion and confusion might be the chief characteristic of Canadian defence policy today.

Selected Bibliography

Douglas Bland. "A Strategy of Choice: Preparing the Canadian Armed Forces for the 21st Century." *Canadian Foreign Policy* II,1 (Spring 1994):109-136
_____. *Chiefs of Defence: Government and the Unified Command of the Canadian Armed Forces.* Toronto: Canadian Institute of Strategic Studies, 1995.

C.R. Nixon. "A Point of View -V." *The Defence Association National Network News* Vol.1/12, 15 July 1993.

Canada 21: Canada and Common Security in the Twenty-First Century. Toronto: Centre for International Studies, University of Toronto, 1994.

Janice Stein. "Canada 21: A Moment and a Model." *Canadian Foreign Policy* 2,1 (Spring 1994): 9-13

Joel L. Sokolsky. "A Seat at the Table: Canada and Its Alliances." *Armed Forces and Society* 16, 1 (Fall 1989): 11-35.

_____. "Canadian Forces: Organization and Equipment for the Modern World." *Forum* 8, 2 (April 1993): 36-43.

G.C.E. Thériault. "Reflections on Canadian Defence Policy and its Underlying Structural Problems." *Canadian Defence Quarterly* 22, 6 (July 1993), 3-10.

HOUSE OF COMMONS/SENATE

Security in a Changing World: The Report of the Special Joint Committee on Canada's Defence Policy. 1994.

CONFERENCE OF DEFENCE ASSOCIATIONS

The Future of Canada's Air Force. Ottawa, 1990.

Canadian Security: A Policy for the 21st Century. Ottawa, 1993.

1994 DEFENCE WHITE PAPER

Contents

Introduction

The past year has marked a significant turning point in the history of the Department of National Defence and the Canadian Forces. Responding to a fundamental reordering of international affairs and the need to confront important economic realities at home, the Prime Minister announced in November 1993 a comprehensive review of Canadian defence policy. In February 1994, a Special Joint Committee of the Senate and House of Commons was established to consult Canadians on all aspects of this issue. With the new defence policy outlined in this White Paper, the Government has fulfilled its commitment.

The Special Joint Committee on Canada's Defence Policy travelled across the country listening to the views of ordinary citizens, defence experts, disarmament advocates and non-governmental organizations. It sought the advice of our allies and saw at first hand the tasks performed by our forces in Canada, in support of NORAD and NATO, and on peacekeeping and humanitarian operations abroad.

Beyond the work of the Committee, the Government made a concerted effort to involve Parliament in the formulation of defence policy. During the past year, Parliament held special debates on issues such as peacekeeping and cruise missile testing, ensuring that our decisions took full account of the concerns of Canadians from across the political spectrum.

As Minister of National Defence, I conducted a personal policy review by meeting with interested groups, giving a number of speeches and interviews, and responding to many enquiries from citizens who expressed their opinions on defence issues.

I co-chaired, with my colleagues the Ministers of Foreign Affairs and of International Trade, a National Forum on Canada's International Relations. Together, we established a process that allowed the Foreign Policy Review and Defence Policy Review to proceed in harmony. I followed closely the work of the Special Joint Committee Reviewing Canada's Foreign Policy, whose recommendations have been carefully assessed in preparing this White Paper. The Prime Minister, the Minister of Foreign Affairs and I also exchanged views with our Alliance partners, both on a bilateral basis and at NATO meetings.

Within the Department of National Defence, I sought the advice of civilian officials and military commanders. Senior members of the Department and the armed forces appeared before the Special Joint Committee. In addition, Canadian Forces bases and stations across the country held open houses, informing local communities about the review of defence policy and encouraging their participation.

The Report of the Special Joint Committee played an integral role in shaping Canada's new defence policy. Virtually all its recommendations are reflected in this White Paper. In a few cases, after further examination, the Government has preferred to adopt an alternate approach, but the intent of the Committee is met. The Committee's recommendation concerning the size of the Regular Forces was judged to be inconsistent with the financial parameters within which the Department of National Defence must operate. Cuts to the defence budget deeper than those envisioned by the Committee will be required to meet the Government's deficit reduction targets.

The defence of Canada and Canadian interests and values is first and foremost a domestic concern. The primary obligation of the Department of National Defence and the Canadian Forces is to protect the country and its citizens from challenges to their security. For the men and women who defend Canada, ultimately with their lives, this entails a level of responsibility and sacrifice that far surpasses that of most other professions. In putting service before self, the Canadian Forces, drawn from all walks of life and every region of the country, exemplify the high ideals of our society and demonstrate how we can come together to solve common problems. At a time when the continued existence of the nation is being debated and national symbols take on more importance than ever, the unifying role of the Department and the Forces can only help to build a stronger, more dynamic and prosperous country.

In the final analysis, it may be said that a nation not worth defending is a nation not worth preserving.

The consensus achieved on the way ahead — an effective, realistic and affordable policy, one that calls for multi-purpose, combat-capable armed forces able to meet the challenges to Canada's security both at home and abroad — will serve to guide the work of the Department and the Forces into the next century. Together, we can take pride in a new defence policy that meets Canada's needs and fulfils our obligations, both to the nation and to our men and women in uniform.

The Honourable David Collenette, P.C., M.P.
Minister of National Defence

CHAPTER I

International Environment

The Cold War is over. The Warsaw Pact has been disbanded and the Soviet Union no longer exists. In a few short years, we have witnessed a fundamental realignment in the global balance of power, yielding significant advances in arms control, conflict resolution and democratization. We have also seen the outbreak of localized, violent disputes, arms proliferation, as well as the often fruitless struggles of collective security organizations to cope with the challenges of the new era. Progress toward a safer world, most evident in the dramatically reduced threat of global war, is balanced by the persistence of conflict within and between states. It is impossible to predict what will emerge from the current period of transition, but it is clear that we can expect pockets of chaos and instability that will threaten international peace and security. In short, Canada faces an unpredictable and fragmented world, one in which conflict, repression and upheaval exist alongside peace, democracy and relative prosperity.

As a nation that throughout its history has done much within the context of international alliances to defend freedom and democracy, Canada continues to have a vital interest in doing its part to ensure global security, especially since Canada's economic future depends on its ability to trade freely with other nations.

RECENT PROGRESS

Global Relations. The breakup of the Soviet Union significantly reduced the threat of nuclear annihilation that faced Canada and its allies for more than 40 years. The dissolution of the Warsaw Pact and German unification marked an end to the division of Europe into hostile blocs. The Conference on Security and Cooperation in Europe (CSCE), with its broad membership and comprehensive approach to security, has become an important mechanism for upholding the principles — human rights, economic freedom and the peaceful resolution of disputes — enshrined in the November 1990 Charter of Paris. A new transatlantic and pan-Eurasian security framework is beginning to take shape, embodied in the CSCE and two of NATO's creations, the North Atlantic Cooperation Council and Partnership for Peace. Despite some notable exceptions, democracy is taking hold in Central and South America, as well as in parts of Asia, the Middle East and Africa.

Arms Control. Significant progress has been achieved in the elimination, reduction and control of various categories of weapons. The *Treaty on Conventional Forces in Europe* and follow-on agreements provide for stable, predictable and verifiable reductions of equipment and personnel on that continent. The *Open Skies Treaty,* the United Nations arms register, and confidence-building measures carried out through the Conference on Security and Cooperation in Europe have reinforced the tendency toward openness and transparency in military matters. The strategic arms reduction treaties (START I and II) and steps taken by Ukraine, Kazakhstan and Belarus in support of nuclear disarmament and non-proliferation hold the promise of deep reductions in strategic nuclear weapons. Likewise, the *Chemical Weapons Convention,* signed by 158 countries since January 1993, of which 16 have ratified, calls for the destruction of these arsenals, though much work remains before this goal can be achieved.

Other multilateral initiatives are underway to stem the production and proliferation of weapons of mass destruction and their means of delivery, including:

- efforts to secure the indefinite extension of the *Nuclear Non-Proliferation Treaty* in 1995 and conclude a *Comprehensive Test Ban Treaty;*
- stronger International Atomic Energy Agency safeguards;
- work on establishing a verification compliance regime for the 1972 *Biological and Toxic Weapons Convention;*

- the beginning, if a mandate is agreed, of negotiations on a "cut-off" convention on fissile material; and
- the expansion and strengthening of the Missile Technology Control Regime.

These efforts represent an ambitious arms control agenda that will see sustained and complex negotiations in the years ahead.

Regional Conflict Resolution. Notwithstanding frequent outbursts of violence the world over, progress has been made in resolving several protracted regional conflicts. The process of reconciliation in El Salvador culminated in the 1994 general election, mirroring the trend towards democracy and the rule of law across much of Latin America. South Africa held a country-wide election this year, ending apartheid and white minority rule. The Middle East peace process has also yielded progress, most notably Palestinian self-rule in Gaza and Jericho, an Israeli-Jordanian peace treaty, and the outline of an eventual peace agreement between Israel and Syria.

INTERNATIONAL SECURITY CONCERNS

Global Pressures

The world's population is fast approaching 6 billion, with another 90 million added to the total every year. Projections vary, but most observers believe the world will have between 8 and 12 billion people by 2050. If future generations are to enjoy the same opportunities as the current one, agricultural and energy production will have to multiply several times over. This requirement will put enormous pressure on the world's political and financial resources, over and above the severe environmental damage and depletion of natural resources that are likely to result.

UN peacekeeping and humanitarian operations are playing a critical role in responding to the immediate consequences, both direct and indirect, of global population and resource pressures. Armed forces are being called upon increasingly to ensure a safe environment for the protection of refugees, the delivery of food and medical supplies, and the provision of essential services in countries where civil society has collapsed.

At the same time, the complexity, escalating costs, and risks associated with peacekeeping in the 1990s, the financial difficulties facing the United Nations, and declining defence budgets in most industrialized countries mean that the international community cannot intervene every time these pressures reach the breaking point. Clearly, the world's ability to deal with the consequences of overpopulation, environmental degradation and resource depletion is already severely constrained and is likely to become more so in the years ahead.

Refugees. The past decade has seen exponential growth in the number of refugees. According to UN estimates, some 20 million people worldwide have been forced to flee their countries in response to war, famine, deprivation, and ethnic, clan, tribal or religious strife, often of horrific proportions. An equal number of people have been displaced within their own countries. Once uprooted, these populations risk causing further unrest in their new locations. They are often viewed as restive, even subversive, by host governments, particularly if they alter what is perceived as a favourable demographic balance within society. Large numbers of displaced persons put a heavy burden on existing infrastructure, resources and the environment, provoking resentment on the part of the local population.

'Failed States'. The breakdown of authority in certain states is another source of instability. It is characterized by chaos, violence and the inability of political leaders to provide the population with the most basic of services. In recent years, this problem has not been confined to any specific region of the world or even to countries with particularly low standards of living. Examples as diverse as Somalia, the former Yugoslavia, Rwanda and Afghanistan illustrate the extent of the problem. The international community remains heavily engaged in attempts to respond, but success in confronting challenges engendered by scarcity and war is not easily achieved.

Resurgence of Old Hatreds
Among the most difficult and immediate challenges to international security are the civil wars fuelled by ethnic, religious and political extremism that broke out in the Balkans and areas of the former Soviet Union following the collapse of communism. In recent years, rival groups have clashed in a number of these states. Other regions of the world, most notably parts of Africa and Asia, have seen the strength of

fundamentalist groups grow considerably, with civil wars and other violent manifestations showing no signs of abating.

Many of these conflicts have proven relatively immune to regional or multilateral diplomacy and intervention. The task of maintaining ceasefires in the midst of civil wars is especially difficult, given the absence of coherent front lines, lack of discipline among the warring sides, civilian populations subject to horrible depredations and atrocities and, most important, a reluctance by combatants to respect such ceasefires.

Ongoing violence in the former Yugoslavia starkly underlines the dangers associated with attempts by national groups to redraw borders in an effort to create ethnically homogeneous states. The Bosnian civil war may portend similar conflicts elsewhere in the Eurasian landmass. In many regions, a patchwork of minorities live intermingled with no clear lines of demarcation between them. Competing territorial claims could raise tensions and eventually provoke hostilities. Most abhorrent is the practice of "ethnic cleansing", the ugly euphemism for outright massacres or expulsions carried out with the objective of achieving ethnic or religious purity in a given geographic area. Borders redrawn in the wake of ethnic cleansing are highly unstable, as uprooted people often seek the return of lost territory, usually through violent means.

However horrendous the impact for the local populations caught in the middle of civil wars, the absence today of adversarial relations among the world's great powers suggests that these conflicts are more likely to be contained. At the same time, Canada cannot escape the consequences of regional conflict, whether in the form of refugee flows, obstacles to trade, or damage to important principles such as the rule of law, respect for human rights and the peaceful settlement of conflicts. Even where Canada's interests are not directly engaged, the values of Canadian society lead Canadians to expect their government to respond when modern communication technologies make us real-time witnesses to violence, suffering and even genocide in many parts of the world. Thus, Canada continues to have an important stake in a peaceful and stable international system.

Proliferation

The spread of advanced weapon technologies to areas of potential conflict has emerged as another major security challenge of the 1990s.

Whether sophisticated armaments are acquired abroad or produced indigenously, their introduction into volatile regions undermines stability, poses a threat to neighbouring states, defeats arms control initiatives, and complicates military planning and operations, as Canada and other members of the UN Coalition experienced first-hand during the Gulf War.

It will take nearly a decade to implement fully the strategic arms reduction treaties. Denuclearization is a demanding process, involving warhead storage and dismantlement, the removal, warehousing or elimination of dangerous substances, and silo destruction. Moreover, while Belarus, Kazakhstan and Ukraine are implementing agreements governing the return of nuclear weapons to Russia, this consolidation has not yet been completed. Russia has a solid record of central control extending over half a century, but the sheer size of its nuclear stockpile — some 25,000 nuclear charges of all kinds scattered over more than 100 sites — makes this material vulnerable to loss or theft. It is critical that these weapons, and the fissile material from dismantled weapons, be stored under the strictest physical and inventory safeguards.

The arms trade remains lively even if the global market for weapons has shrunk. Significant overcapacity in world defence production exists despite efforts at conversion of military industries. Some states have not instituted the appropriate legislative or administrative mechanisms for controlling arms exports. For many, weapons sales constitute one of the few reliable sources of hard currency. Often, the incentive to sell outweighs concerns about the likely threat to regional or global stability. One consequence is the extensive trade in small arms, including hand-held automatic weapons, hand grenades and land mines. Indeed, men, women and children in 62 countries daily face the threat of being killed or maimed by some 85 million land mines sown at random. Another consequence is the risk that unemployed or under-employed scientists and technicians previously involved in the production of advanced systems will migrate to countries with clandestine weapons programs. Already, organized criminal elements have shown an interest in the lucrative trade in sophisticated weapons and materials.

The transfer of weapons of mass destruction and ballistic missile technologies to so-called "rogue" regimes is of particular concern. These transactions take place, albeit more slowly and with more difficulty, despite the export controls on materials and equipment put in place by countries such as Canada. This then leaves the international community little recourse other than condemnation or punishment after the fact. Similarly, the increasing prevalence of technologies with both civilian and military applications, and the globalization of production and marketing of weapon systems, makes proliferation that much harder to prevent or control, and makes it more likely that the transfer of resources, skills and technology will be irreversible.

Constraints on Policy Making

Advanced industrial states themselves face considerable uncertainty at home, which complicates their ability to cope with global security challenges. Many Western economies are still characterized by relatively high unemployment, volatile currencies, and large accumulated national debts. The trend toward globalization, exemplified by the conclusion of the Uruguay Round of the *General Agreement on Tariffs and Trade*, is balanced by an increasing preoccupation with domestic challenges. At a time of diminishing resources, little money is available to deal with the demands of post-industrial society — the need to repair obsolescent infrastructure, protect and foster a sustainable environment, care for an aging population, improve job training and reform entitlement programs — let alone military priorities in various regions of the world. Canada and most other NATO allies have seen their military budgets decline, acknowledging the fundamental changes on the world scene and the need to reduce overall government expenditures.

Under the best circumstances, predicting international trends is challenging. Given the unsettled nature of global affairs, it is impossible to foresee with any degree of certainty how international affairs will develop in the years to come. In light of the much reduced threat of global war, the world may not be as immediately dangerous today, at least for Canada, yet it is neither more peaceful nor more stable. It would, of course, be wrong to concentrate attention exclusively on extreme cases of disorder in some regions at the expense of real progress elsewhere. Yet, given recent trends, it seems prudent to plan for a world characterized in the long term by instability. Canada's defence policy must reflect the world as it is, rather than the world as we would like it to be. Under these conditions, the most appropriate response is a flexible, realistic and affordable defence policy, one that provides the means to apply military force when Canadians consider it necessary to uphold essential Canadian values and vital security interests, at home and abroad.

CHAPTER II

Domestic Considerations

Defence policy must respond not only to an uncertain and unstable world abroad, but also to challenging circumstances at home. In designing a new defence policy, the Government has sought to remain attentive to the very important domestic influences on Canada's defence posture and, in particular, to current fiscal circumstances.

The Government's broad program for political, social, and economic renewal is focused on preserving the values that make Canada one of the most fortunate countries in the world. At the present time, however, our prosperity — and with it our quality of life — is threatened by the steady growth of public sector debt.

The accumulated debt of the federal and provincial governments currently stands at approximately $750 billion; the federal government's annual debt servicing payments in 1994-95 alone will amount to $44 billion — more than the budget deficit of $39.7 billion and some 27% of the total federal budget.

This situation limits governmental freedom of action in responding to the needs of Canadians and constrains the ability of governments at all levels to deliver essential services. To deal with this problem and avert a crisis of confidence in the Canadian economy, the federal government has been cutting its expenditures. The Economic and Fiscal Update issued in October 1994 confirmed in no uncertain terms the Government's intention to meet the fiscal challenge presented by both the deficit and the debt.

Over the past several years, the need to control the federal deficit has led to significant cuts in most areas of spending, including defence.

Indeed, as the accompanying chart illustrates, the defence funding assumptions contained in the 1994 budget envisaged a level of defence spending in the year 2000 that, in real terms, would be less than 60 percent of that assumed in the 1987 Defence White Paper.

In an environment of fiscal restraint, the Government must continue to constrain all expenditures, including those devoted to defence. The report of Parliament's Special Joint Committee on Canada's Defence Policy took account of this basic reality. It called for a period of relatively stable funding, but at lower levels than those set out in the 1994 budget. Although National Defence and the Canadian Forces have already made a large contribution to the national effort to reduce the deficit, the Government believes that additional cuts are both necessary and possible. The details of the Department's future funding will be set out in the upcoming budget.

Defence Budget Reductions
Since 1987 White Paper

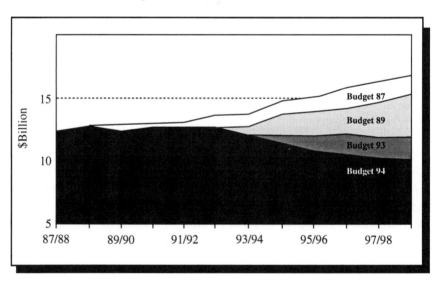

The Department and the Canadian Forces have absorbed past reductions in a variety of ways. Canadian defence commitments have been revised, personnel levels cut back, operations and maintenance budgets shrunk, defence infrastructure reduced, and capital programs cancelled or delayed. As a consequence of the further decline in defence expenditure that forms the fiscal context of this paper, cuts will be deeper, and there will be more reductions, cancellations, and delays. In some areas, the Department of National Defence and the Canadian Forces will do less. The Department and the Forces will also reshape the defence program and operate more efficiently to deliver the elements of the policy outlined in this White Paper.

Although fiscal considerations are a key factor in formulating an appropriate and realistic defence policy, the Department and the Canadian Forces must also take account of a variety of other domestic developments. Canadians have asked for the renewal of responsible government. They want government to show leadership in addressing a demanding political, financial, economic and social agenda. They ask it to be efficient with its use of the taxpayer's dollar: if private industry has had to restructure in light of difficult economic circumstances, government must do the same. Canadians look to government to be effective in developing innovative and constructive measures to address current and future challenges. They demand it be ethical in the style and substance of its decisions, and open in consulting Canadians on important issues.

Beyond meeting these fundamental requirements, all government departments must be mindful of other current issues. These include the need to foster a strong sense of nationhood, to promote industrial growth and international competitiveness, to protect the environment, to provide training for youth and for Canadians affected by economic restructuring, and to ensure that government adapts to demographic changes in the workforce as well as in society as a whole. Notwithstanding the unique vocation of the Department of National Defence and the Canadian Forces, the new defence policy set out in this White Paper takes account of these considerations as well.

CHAPTER III

Combat-Capable Forces

Canada cannot dispense with the maritime, land, and air combat capabilities of modern armed forces. It is true that, at present, there is no immediate direct military threat to Canada and that today's conflicts are far from our shores. Even so, we must maintain a prudent level of military force to deal with challenges to our sovereignty in peacetime, and retain the capability to generate forces capable of contributing to the defence of our country should the need arise. Beyond this basic national requirement, were Canada to abandon the capability to participate effectively in the defence of North America, NATO-Europe allies, and victims of aggression elsewhere, we would stand to lose a significant degree of respect and influence abroad.

Canada's commitment to remain an active participant in multilateral efforts to promote collective security is a reflection of our values and interests.

- Canadians believe that the rule of law must govern relations between states.
- Canadians have deemed their own security indivisible from that of their allies.
- Canadians have a strong sense of responsibility to alleviate suffering and respond, where their efforts can make a difference.

These are the abiding foundations of Canada's commitment to collective security. They have proven their worth in the past and remain equally valid in a global environment that is increasingly interdependent.

Collective Security and the Changing Face of Peacekeeping. If we are to make a significant contribution to collective security, we must recognize that the nature of multilateral operations in support of peace and stability has changed considerably. Indeed, 'peacekeeping' operations have evolved from mainly interpositional and monitoring operations to undertakings that are far more ambitious — and pose far more challenges and risks to our personnel. Canada's traditional goals — the deterrence and reversal of aggression, the peaceful settlement of disputes, and the relief of civilian populations — remain constant. It is the context that has changed. If the Canadian Forces are to play a role in collective security, they must remain a capable fighting force.

Collective Defence. With the transformation of the strategic environment, the role of our collective defence relationships with NATO-Europe and the United States will change. It would be a mistake, however, to discount the merits of these arrangements. From a Canadian perspective, collective defence remains fundamental to our security.

- First, our allies are countries to which we are bound by political values, interests, and traditions that we have an interest in upholding and fostering.
- Second, the practical benefits of collective defence — standardized equipment and procedures, as well as the accumulated experience of joint operations — are of great value to international efforts in support of collective security.
- Third, were a serious military threat to Canada or its allies to emerge, Canada would, once again, seek its security in collective defence arrangements. It is, therefore, important that such arrangements be maintained in peacetime as it would be very difficult to revive them in a crisis.

Managing a Full Spectrum of Conflict. Over the past 80 years, more than 100,000 Canadians have died, fighting alongside our allies for common values. For us now to leave combat roles to others would mean abandoning this commitment to help defend commonly accepted principles of state behaviour. In short, by opting for a constabulary force — that is, one not designed to make a genuine contribution in combat — we would be sending a very clear message about the depth of our commitment to our allies and our values, one that would betray our history and diminish our future. Beyond this, because we cannot expect our political influence in global and regional security arrangements to be significantly out of proportion to our military contributions, we must make the required investment in our armed forces if we are to play any kind of role in shaping our common future.

The Government has concluded that the maintenance of multi-purpose, combat-capable forces is in the national interest. It is only through the maintenance of such forces that Canada will be able to retain the necessary degree of flexibility and freedom of action when it comes to the defence of its interests and the projection of its values abroad. Importantly, the maintenance of core combat capabilities forms the basis for the generation of larger forces should they ever be needed. Indeed, it is the Government's view that from the perspective of promoting our values, protecting our interests, insuring against uncertainty, or even providing value for money, an investment in forces capable only of constabulary operations would be very difficult to justify.

The challenge will be to design a defence program that will deliver capable armed forces within the limits of our resources. A country of Canada's size and means cannot, and should not, attempt to cover the entire military spectrum, but the Canadian Forces must be able to make a genuine contribution to a wide variety of domestic and international objectives.

Flexibility, Capabilities, and Choices. While the maintenance of specialized combat skills and capabilities is essential, the decision to retain combat-capable forces should not be taken to mean that Canada must possess every component of military capability. Indeed, although the Canadian Forces have, over the years, had to divest themselves of several specific capabilities — including aircraft carriers, cruisers, medium-lift helicopters, medium-range patrol aircraft, as well as separate fleets of fighter aircraft for air defence and ground attack roles — they have continued to meet Canada's domestic needs and make effective contributions to international peace and security. We believe that this tendency to specialize in those multi-purpose capabilities we have deemed essential has not undermined our ability to protect our interests or diminished our ability to meet obligations to allies.

Canada needs armed forces that are able to operate with the modern forces maintained by our allies and like-minded nations against a capable opponent — that is, able to fight 'alongside the best, against the best'. To maintain this general capability, we have had to make some difficult choices. We will continue to assess the relative costs and benefits of various capabilities in order to make trade-offs which, while difficult, will be essential if the Forces are to contribute to a broader range of Canadian objectives. It would be misguided to invest in very specific forces and capabilities, whether at the higher end of the scale (aircraft designed for antitank warfare, for example) or at the lower end (forces limited to minimal-risk peacekeeping operations). To opt for either approach would be to forego the capability and flexibility that are inherent in a multi-purpose force. In short, the maintenance of multi-purpose forces represents a pragmatic, sensible approach to defence at a time of fiscal restraint, one that will provide government with a broad range of military options at a price consistent with the Government's other policy and fiscal priorities.

The Government's approach to defence is to maintain the Canadian Forces as a fundamental national resource which makes important contributions to a range of Canadian objectives. The policy and intelligence capabilities of the Department and the Canadian Forces will ensure that the Government has access to independent Canadian advice as the basis for sound decisions. Beyond this, our investment in the Forces' training and equipment will yield a capable fighting force whose skills can be applied not just to a number of specialized tasks, but also to a variety of domestic and international objectives.

The retention of multi-purpose, combat-capable forces represents the only prudent choice for Canada. It is only through the maintenance of the core military capabilities that define such forces that, come what may, Canada will be able to attend to its own security needs — both now and in the future.

CHAPTER IV

Protection of Canada

Taken together, the size of our country and our small population pose unique challenges for defence planners. Our territory spans nearly 10 million square kilometres — fully 7% of the world's landmass. We are bordered by three oceans which touch upon over 240,000 kilometres of coastline. We are charged with the control of our airspace as well as the aerial approaches to Canadian territory. Beyond our coasts, Canada seeks to maintain political sovereignty and economic jurisdiction over 10 million square kilometres of ocean in the Pacific, Atlantic, and Arctic.

Our geography is not merely vast; it is also diverse and extremely demanding. It imposes significant burdens on our military personnel, their training, and their equipment. Canada's territory encompasses mountainous terrain, fjords, vast plains, rainforests, desert conditions, and the unique ecology of the Arctic. Our climate is harsh. Indeed, the economic livelihood of many Canadians is found in remote, difficult environments including three oceans, the North, and distant mines and forests.

Canadians treasure their country, which is rich in both natural beauty and natural resources. They have made it clear to successive governments that they are firmly committed to the protection of both. They are concerned about environmental well-being in general, as well as the management of specific resources, such as the forests and fisheries, which have become urgent issues over the past several years and which will require renewed vigilance and enhanced management.

Providing for the Defence of Canada and Canadian Sovereignty

Sovereignty is a vital attribute of a nation-state. For Canada, sovereignty means ensuring that, within our area of jurisdiction, Canadian law is respected and enforced. The Government is determined to see that this is so.

Some have argued that the recent dramatic changes abroad have eroded the traditional rationale for the role that the Canadian Forces play in the defence of Canada. It would be a grave mistake, however, to dismantle the capacity to defend our country. Canada should never find itself in a position where, as a consequence of past decisions, the defence of our national territory has become the responsibility of others.

Aid of the Civil Power. Throughout Canadian history, provinces have been able to call upon the armed forces to maintain or restore law and order where it is beyond the power of civil authorities to do so. Section 275 of the *National Defence Act* states that the Canadian Forces:

> are liable to be called out for service in aid of the civil power in any case in which a riot or disturbance of the peace, beyond the powers of the civil authorities to suppress ... is, in the opinion of an attorney general, considered as likely to occur.

The role of the Canadian Forces in this context is very precisely defined. When a riot or disturbance of the peace occurs or is likely to occur that is beyond the powers of the civil authorities to control, a provincial attorney general may require the Canadian Forces to be called out in Aid of the Civil Power. In this situation, the Chief of the Defence Staff determines the nature of the response. The Canadian Forces do not replace the civil power; they assist it in the maintenance of law and order.

In recent times, the use of the Canadian Forces in this role has been comparatively infrequent. Nevertheless, the crisis at Oka in 1990 served to remind us that such situations can arise. The Forces played a crucial role in defusing the crisis. They demonstrated that the ability to call upon disciplined, well-trained, and well-commanded military personnel is invaluable in providing government with an effective means to deal with potentially explosive situations.

The Canadian Forces may be called upon to assist civil authorities in situations other than Aid of the Civil Power. The Forces might, for example, be called on to counter acts of terrorism that exceed the capabilities of police forces. In addition to other military resources, the Canadian

Forces maintain a special task force that provides an enhanced capability to respond to any such act immediately and effectively.

Providing Peacetime Surveillance and Control. The provision of surveillance and control is an integral part of the Forces' activities in Canada. Even at a time when there is no direct military threat to Canada, the Forces must maintain and exercise the basic navy, army, and air force skills to ensure effective control over our territory, airspace, and maritime approaches. In and of itself, maintaining the capability to field a presence anywhere where Canada maintains sovereign jurisdiction sends a clear signal that Canadians will not have their sovereignty compromised.

Responsibility for many of the Government's activities in the surveillance and control of Canadian territory, airspace, and maritime areas of jurisdiction lies with civilian agencies such as the Department of Transport. The Canadian Forces, however, make a valuable contribution to this demanding task, which often requires capabilities of greater readiness and reach than those available to civilian agencies. The capability to deploy highly trained Canadian Forces personnel and their specialized equipment anywhere in Canada at short notice also contributes to the attainment of national objectives in such areas as environmental protection, search and rescue, disaster relief, drug interdiction, and fisheries protection.

Securing Our Borders Against Illegal Activities. Canadians face an increasing challenge from those who would exploit the vast size and resources of our country for illegal activities. This applies to the illegal trade in narcotics and other contraband substances, as well as the smuggling of illegal immigrants into Canada. In supporting the activities of other government agencies, the Canadian Forces play a significant role in countering such activities.

During the renewal of the North American Aerospace Defence (NORAD) Agreement in 1991, Canada and the United States agreed to give NORAD a role in counter-narcotic monitoring and surveillance. This is an ancillary mission to which the capabilities of our maritime and land forces have also been applied, and illustrates how existing structures and capabilities can be adapted to address new problems.

Fisheries Protection. Canadians have made clear their wish to protect Canada's fisheries from illegal and highly damaging exploitation. With the dwindling of major fish stocks, the issue has become more urgent.

The Canadian Forces have made an important contribution to fisheries patrols for more than 40 years. The Department of National Defence and the Department of Transport now participate in a comprehensive federal effort, led by the Department of Fisheries and Oceans. The Canadian Forces will devote a significant number of flying hours and ship days to fishery patrols. This arrangement is a good example of interdepartmental cooperation yielding an efficient use of government resources.

One of the most pressing issues in the current East Coast fishery crisis is that of predatory foreign fishing on Canada's continental shelf outside of our 200-mile exclusive fishing zone. Such fishing imperils the future of the fishery and contradicts the spirit of internationally agreed conservation measures. The Government has begun to take action against such activities. While it is the Government's policy to avoid engaging in enforcement action beyond 200 miles unless absolutely necessary to protect a vital natural resource, the Canadian Forces must be capable of taking such action.

Interdepartmental cooperation has been markedly enhanced in response to the recommendations of the Osbaldeston Report and the 1990 report of the Standing Committee on National Defence on maritime sovereignty. Secure communications have been installed, standard operating procedures have been developed, and acquisition policies are addressing the potential benefits of having common and interoperable equipment.

Environmental Surveillance. The Government has identified environmental protection as a major priority. It has emphasized the prevention of pollution and the promotion of "green" practices in its day-to-day operations. The Department of National Defence and the Canadian Forces have been at the forefront of efforts to meet these goals. Indeed, all planning and operations (and this includes allied activity in Canada) are now designed with environmental stewardship firmly in mind.

Beyond this, the Department of National Defence has concluded a memorandum of understanding with the Department of the Environment with respect to the use of the Canadian Forces in environmental surveillance and clean-up. The agreement sets out the role of the Department and the Forces in assisting the Department of the Environment in the event of a serious environmental incident. In addition, as the Forces carry out their routine surveillance missions, they will seek to identify and report potential and actual environmental problems.

Protecting Canadians

Disaster Relief. The Canadian Forces play a key role in responding to natural and man-made disasters. Not only is the Minister of National Defence also the Minister Responsible for Emergency Preparedness, but, as part of a broader initiative to reduce the size of government, the administration of emergency preparedness planning — once carried out by a separate agency — has been absorbed by the Department of National Defence. Memoranda of understanding between the Department and other government agencies govern the coordination of resources in response to emergencies, and the Department will make an immediate and effective contribution to disaster relief.

Search and Rescue. The Department of National Defence and the Canadian Forces make a vital contribution to the maintenance and operation of Canada's search and rescue capability. While elements of this capability are provided by other federal and provincial organizations, the Canadian Forces:

- are responsible for air search and rescue;
- provide significant resources to assist the Coast Guard in marine search and rescue;
- assist local authorities in land search and rescue; and,
- operate three Rescue Coordination Centres which respond to thousands of distress signals every year.

Search and rescue represents a significant challenge for Canadian Forces personnel and their equipment. The distances involved can be enormous and the operating conditions very difficult. Nevertheless, for Canadians, safeguarding human life remains an absolute priority, and the Canadian Forces will continue to play a major role in this vital area.

Objectives

The decline in the direct military threat to Canadian territory has not eliminated an ongoing role for the Canadian Forces at home. We will maintain a level of military capability sufficient to play an appropriate role in the defence of Canada. The Forces will honour the statutory requirement to respond to requests for Aid of the Civil Power. Through the assistance they provide to civil authorities, the Canadian Forces will help protect Canadian sovereignty, and carry out a wide variety of secondary roles.

The Forces will be capable of mounting effective responses to emerging situations in our maritime areas of jurisdiction, our airspace, or within our territory, including the North. Specifically, the Canadian Forces will:

- demonstrate, on a regular basis, the capability to monitor and control activity within Canada's territory, airspace, and maritime areas of jurisdiction;

- assist, on a routine basis, other government departments in achieving various other national goals in such areas as fisheries protection, drug interdiction, and environmental protection;

- be prepared to contribute to humanitarian assistance and disaster relief within 24 hours, and sustain this effort for as long as necessary;

- maintain a national search and rescue capability;

- maintain a capability to assist in mounting, at all times, an immediate and effective response to terrorist incidents; and,

- respond to requests for Aid of the Civil Power and sustain this response for as long as necessary.

CHAPTER V

Canada-United States Defence Cooperation

The United States is Canada's most important ally and the two countries maintain a relationship that is as close, complex, and extensive as any in the world. Canada and the US are partners in the world's largest bilateral trading relationship. The undefended border between them is evidence of the common political, economic, social and cultural values Canada and the US share as advanced industrial democracies. Geography, history, trust and shared beliefs have also made the two countries partners in the defence of North America.

Evolving Security Challenges
Since 1940, when President Roosevelt and Prime Minister Mackenzie King signed the Ogdensburg Agreement, which acknowledged the indivisible nature of continental security and pledged mutual assistance in the event of hostilities, Canada-US defence cooperation has persisted through more than five decades of evolving challenges.

North America's security environment is changing again. Russia retains the bulk of the former Soviet strategic nuclear arsenal, currently numbering some 10,000 warheads. However, under the terms of the strategic arms reduction treaties (START I and II), nuclear weapons are slated for deep reductions, with the strategic warhead total on each side limited to between 3,000 and 3,500. Multiple-warhead intercontinental ballistic missiles, the most destabilizing component of US and Russian nuclear forces, are to be eliminated by 2003. As implementation of START I and II proceeds over the next decade, stability will be further enhanced.

The risk to North America posed by these weapons has diminished with the reduction in tensions, and additional security will be achieved as arms reductions go forward. Potential challenges to continental defence remain, however, especially if one looks beyond the near future. Nuclear weapons continue to occupy a central role in Russian military doctrine. The vast majority of Russia's strategic nuclear arsenal remains in place, with significant financial and environmental obstacles blocking a speedy implementation of the reductions mandated under START I and II. China also maintains strategic nuclear forces able to reach North America, and is continuing to modernize its intercontinental systems.

The proliferation of weapons of mass destruction and their means of delivery is another concern. A number of states have acquired, or are seeking to acquire, nuclear, chemical and biological weapons, as well as ballistic missile delivery capabilities.

Intercontinental threats constitute a longer-term problem. None of the nations with the potential to develop this capability is expected to possess ballistic missiles able to reach North America until well into the next century. Yet nuclear, chemical, biological and theatre missile programs cannot be discounted in planning for future contingencies. One reason is that sophisticated delivery mechanisms are not required in the case of chemical and biological weapons. In addition, weapons of mass destruction already or may soon threaten Canada's friends and allies in Europe and elsewhere, and Canada may want to retain the option of deploying forces to areas where they could face such weaponry.

Bilateral Defence

The institutional basis of Canada-US defence cooperation provides highly valued stability in a volatile and turbulent world. As strategic and fiscal realities evolve, however, so too must our bilateral defence arrangements. Canada will continue to modify its defence relationship with the United States, consistent with the priorities of the new era.

Canada-US defence cooperation is defined by a wide range of bilateral arrangements, including formal government-to-government agreements, interdepartmental memoranda, and service-to-service understandings. These arrangements cover, among other things, joint planning and operations, combined exercises, defence production, logistics, communications, research and development, and intelligence sharing. In addition, there exist numerous bilateral fora involving regular consultations, discussions and meetings.

In examining these arrangements, the Government came to several conclusions. First, Canada-US defence cooperation continues to serve this country's fundamental interests extremely well. Second, the Government wants the Canadian Forces to maintain the ability to work closely with their US counterparts in a variety of situations. Third, even if the Government decided to reduce significantly the level of defence cooperation with the United States, Canada would still be obliged to rely on the US for help in protecting its territory and approaches — and this assistance would then come on strictly American terms, unmitigated by the influence Canada enjoys as a result of its defence partnership with the United States and with our other NATO allies. Finally, while some aspects of the relationship will remain largely unchanged, certain arrangements require updating.

Principal Arrangements

Permanent Joint Board on Defence. Created by the Ogdensburg Agreement of 1940, the Permanent Joint Board on Defence is the senior advisory body on continental security and is composed of two national sections made up of diplomatic and military representatives. Its meetings have served as a window on Canada-US defence relations for more than five decades. The Board has examined virtually every important joint defence measure undertaken since the end of the Second World War, including construction of the Distant Early Warning Line of radars, the creation of the North American Air (later Aerospace) Defence command in 1958, the bi-national operation of the underwater acoustic surveillance system and high-frequency direction finding network, and the decision to proceed with the North American Air Defence Modernization program in 1985.

In recent years, the Board has proven effective as an alternate channel of communication, one through which the resolution of difficult issues has been expedited. In particular, it has helped devise imaginative solutions to the types of problems engendered by the new global security context, such as cost-sharing in an era of declining budgets. The Government believes that the Board will remain a valuable forum where national interests are articulated and where frank exchanges on current issues allow discussion of the full spectrum of security and defence issues facing our two countries.

Military Cooperation Committee. Established in 1945, the Military Cooperation Committee has served as a vehicle for combined military planning for the defence of North America. Its first task was the revision of the wartime Canada-United States Defence Plan. Over the years, this plan has evolved into the Canada-US Basic Security Plan, which provides for the coordinated use of both countries' sea, land and air forces in the event of hostilities. Today, the Military Cooperation Committee acts as a direct link between national military staffs.

As part of the Basic Security Plan, Canada has traditionally assigned forces already tasked for a variety of other missions to the defence of the continent. In the new emerging North American security environment, these forces will now consist of:

- a joint task force headquarters;
- a maritime task group on each coast;
- a brigade group with associated support elements;
- two squadrons of fighter aircraft; and
- a squadron of transport aircraft.

Cooperation on Land. Cooperation between the land forces of Canada and the United States is focused on training. A 1968 Exchange of Notes sets out principles and procedures related to the cross-border movement of troops, enabling land force units from one country to have ready access to training facilities of the other. Additional agreements govern the temporary exchange of small land force units for training purposes, and to oversee bilateral training initiatives and exercises, such as those arranged within the context of the America-Britain-Canada-Australia Armies program.

Cooperation at Sea. The maritime dimension of Canada-US cooperation in the defence of North America involves the surveillance and control of vast ocean areas on both coasts and in the Arctic. This mission is carried out in close partnership with the United States Navy and Coast Guard, and includes planning, operations and logistic support.

Bilateral exercises at sea are held regularly, offering an opportunity to evaluate defence plans, improve operational standards, and enhance the ability of Canadian and US forces to work together. The two countries share surveillance data, as they have done for many years, supported by the joint operation of facilities such as the Canadian Forces Integrated Undersea Surveillance System, which recently opened in Halifax. Exchange of information and services also takes place in support of search-and-rescue and anti-narcotics operations.

Both countries benefit from agreements involving the exchange of fuel and materiel between ships at sea, the shared use of test and evaluation ranges, and support provided during ship visits. Canada's maritime forces have significantly expanded their close cooperation with the United States Navy off North America's Pacific coast. Finally, Canadian and US maritime forces have cooperated in recent years to provide humanitarian relief to areas devastated by natural disasters, as in the aftermath of Hurricane Andrew in 1992.

North American Aerospace Defence Agreement (NORAD). The NORAD agreement formalized over a decade of *ad hoc* Canada-US cooperation on continental air defence which began shortly after the Second World War. Under the agreement, an integrated headquarters assumed operational control over forces made available for air defence. Since then, NORAD has evolved to meet the challenges to North America posed by changing weapons technologies.

In today's changed geostrategic circumstances, Canada will maintain aerospace surveillance, missile warning, and air defence capabilities at a significantly reduced level. The Government believes it is prudent to preserve the ability of Canada and the US to regenerate forces should a strategic threat to the continent arise in the future — in effect, maintain a modicum of equipment, infrastructure and expertise — while reducing operating levels to those required for current peacetime activities.

The North Warning System of radars and forward operating locations will be maintained at a reduced level of readiness. Upon completion, the cost of operating and maintaining the system on an annual basis will be significantly lower. It will retain, however, the capability to conduct higher levels of surveillance and control operations at full readiness should the need arise.

In the coming months, formal negotiations will begin on the renewal of the NORAD agreement, the current extension of which expires in 1996. Canada will seek to preserve the benefits of this longstanding cooperation on aerospace defence matters. The Government will examine closely those areas which may require updating in accordance with evolving challenges to continental security. Canada will work towards an agreement that furthers our national interest and meets our defence needs, now and into the 21st century.

Canada-United States Test and Evaluation Program. In 1983, the Canada-US Test and Evaluation Program was established as an umbrella agreement allowing the US military access to Canadian test facilities. Over the past decade, sonobuoy technology, anti-armour munitions, upgrade packages for the F/A-18 fighter aircraft and, most notably, unarmed cruise missiles have undergone testing in Canada. In February 1993, the program was renegotiated and renewed for a 10-year period. Under the terms of this agreement, Canada has reciprocal access to US testing facilities. In addition, each country has agreed to charge only incremental costs — those related to the conduct of a specific test at the facility, rather than the expenses related to the operation of the entire facility — thereby reducing significantly the cost of Canadian testing, evaluation and certification carried out in the United States.

The Government considers the Test and Evaluation Program an integral component of our bilateral defence relationship. The agreement allows us to test in a cost-efficient manner a variety of key Canadian systems in the United States. In turn, we allow the US to test certain systems deemed essential to continental and global security, subject to approval on a case-by-case basis. The agreement is also very flexible, allowing easy adaptation to changing circumstances. Earlier this year, both Governments announced the end of cruise missile testing in Canadian airspace.

Defence Production/Defence Development Sharing Arrangements. Another aspect of Canada-US defence cooperation consists of an extensive network of defence production, research, and development arrangements. Signed in 1956, the Defence Production Sharing Arrangement has allowed Canadian firms to compete on an equal footing with their American counterparts in the US market. Since 1963, the Defence Development Sharing Arrangement has assisted Canadian firms in developing goods for use by the US military. These arrangements rest on the principle that, given the interdependent nature of North American defence, both countries benefit from the economies of scale arising from specialization.

Canada has long recognized that its own defence market is too small to support a defence industrial base which can meet all the requirements of the Canadian Forces. These arrangements have allowed Canada to take advantage of large-scale US production as well as demand for defence-related goods both in the United States and among our European allies. This is all the more important in an era of diminished resources and increased competition, particularly given that the Uruguay Round of multilateral trade negotiations failed to make much progress in the areas of defence procurement and research. These arrangements also allow Canadian firms to stay in touch with developing technologies and help Canada generate and sustain high-technology jobs in the defence and civilian sectors.

Looking to the Future

Space. In recent years, space has emerged as an increasingly important component of the global security environment. Space already supports the traditional military activities of the maritime, land, and air forces, including command, control and communications, intelligence gathering, surveillance, navigation, mapping, meteorological services and arms control verification. With the advent of missile warfare, the role of space in protecting the modern state has taken on added significance.

Looking ahead, the possibility of developing a space-based surveillance system for North America in the next century will be explored, subject to a variety of military, financial and technological considerations.

Missile Warning and Defence. Canada supports ongoing discussions with the United States, NATO allies, and other partners on the possible expansion beyond North America of the missile warning function currently discharged by NORAD, whose value was demonstrated during the Gulf War.

The Government has followed with interest the evolution of US defence policy and strategy in recent years toward an emphasis on ground- and sea-based theatre missile defence systems. Canada welcomes the decision by the American government to adhere to the strict interpretation of the 1972 *Anti-Ballistic Missile Treaty*. Indeed, we see a strong commitment on the part of the United States to developing a missile defence posture that enhances global stability and is consistent with existing arms control agreements.

For now, Canada is interested in gaining a better understanding of missile defence through research and in consultation with like-minded nations. In the future, Canada's potential role in ballistic missile defence will not be determined in isolation, but in conjunction with the evolution of North American and possible NATO-wide aerospace defence arrangements. Canadian involvement in ballistic missile defence would also have to be cost-effective and affordable, make an unambiguous contribution to Canada's defence needs, and build on missions the Forces already perform, such as surveillance and communications.

Objectives

For more than five decades, Canada and the United States have co-operated in the defence of North America and in support of international peace and stability. The benefits of continuing this relationship are as valid today as ever before. First, Canada gains inestimable training and operational experience applicable not only to North America, but also to UN and other multilateral missions abroad. Second, Canada retains an influential voice in US defence policy formulation in areas where our security interests are directly involved. Third, Canada obtains access to significant defence-related information that would not otherwise be available. Fourth, Canadian companies benefit from access to important technologies and the large US defence market.

As circumstances have evolved over the years, so too have Canada-US defence relations, taking account of new strategic and fiscal realities. The turbulent nature of global affairs and the need to make the most of the limited resources available for defence are leading again to further changes. Modifications to existing bilateral arrangements and the upcoming negotiations on NORAD's renewal are important elements of this process. Meanwhile, Canada will continue to rely on the stability and flexibility its relationship with the United States provides to help meet this country's defence requirements in North America and beyond.

To this end, the Department and the Forces will:

- maintain the ability to operate effectively at sea, on land, and in the air with the military forces of the United States in defending the northern half of the Western hemisphere;

- begin formal negotiations with the United States on the renewal of the NORAD agreement that expires in 1996, ensuring that its provisions reflect North American aerospace defence priorities;

■ as part of a renewed NORAD agreement, cooperate in:

- the surveillance and control of North American airspace;
- the collection, processing and dissemination of missile warning information within North America; and
- the examination of ballistic missile defence options focused on research and building on Canada's existing capabilities in communications and surveillance; and

■ maintain Canada's participation in the Canada-US Test and Evaluation Program, the Defence Production and Development Sharing Arrangements, and other existing bilateral arrangements.

CHAPTER VI

Contributing to International Security

Canadians are internationalist and not isolationist by nature. We uphold a proud heritage of service abroad. We take pride in Lester B. Pearson's Nobel Prize for Peace not simply because it did a great Canadian considerable honour, but because it was a reflection of our evolving international personality. More than 30 years later, Canadians could once again take pride in their contribution to peace as the Nobel Peace Prize was awarded in recognition of the work of peacekeeping personnel. Multilateral security cooperation is not merely a Canadian tradition; it is the expression of Canadian values in the international sphere. We care about the course of events abroad, and we are willing to work with other countries to improve the lot of all manner of peoples.

Canadians are not blind to the lessons of history. Although they recognize that states will want to devote resources to pressing domestic concerns, their experience of two world wars and the Korean conflict has made them wary of the peacetime temptation to believe that their security is assured — particularly when based on wishful predictions about the future. Canada's experience has also underscored the need to develop and maintain effective multilateral institutions that can address security and stability — and that can respond effectively to aggression should other measures fail.

As a reflection of the global nature of Canada's values and interests, the Canadian Forces must contribute to international security. We should continue to play an active military role in the United Nations, the North Atlantic Treaty Organization and the Conference on Security and Cooperation in Europe. We should develop our defence relationships with the

330 Canada's National Defence

nations of the Asia-Pacific region and Latin America, and contribute, where possible, to the security of the Middle East and Africa.

The complex security problems that confront the international community today defy easy solutions. Nevertheless, there is a strong desire to address these problems through multilateral institutions. This derives not only from the state of global political relations, but also from the sense that, at a time when many countries are reducing their military expenditures to devote more resources to domestic issues, multilateral cooperation represents a sound way to pool national resources and use these to the greatest benefit. Thus, now more than ever, multilateralism needs and deserves our support — not only in terms of our words and ideas, but also in terms of tangible Canadian contributions to international security and well-being.

A Canadian Perspective on Multilateral Operations

Over the past few years, the nature of multilateral operations undertaken in support of the United Nations has changed enormously. Where, in the past, these operations were comprised largely of traditional peacekeeping and observer missions, the range of operations has expanded to encompass the complete range of military activity — from preventive deployments to enforcement actions such as the Gulf War. Indeed, the broader nature of these operations has been well-noted in the 1993 report of the UN Secretary-General, *Agenda for Peace.*

As operations in support of UN objectives have evolved, there have been both successes and failures. There have been some very successful operations, such as the mission of the United Nations Transition Assistance Group, which assisted Namibia's transition to independence. The multinational operation in the Gulf in 1990-91, in response to Iraq's invasion of Kuwait, enforced economic sanctions against Iraq and, when this failed to yield Iraqi compliance with UN resolutions, restored Kuwaiti sovereignty in a brief but effective military campaign.

There have been notable disappointments as well. The UN operation in Somalia began as a worthy and ambitious undertaking to restore order, deliver desperately needed humanitarian assistance, and facilitate national reconstruction. As the operation comes to an end, it seems clear that at least two of these three objectives have not been achieved. Similarly, UN operations in the former Yugoslavia have undoubtedly saved lives, but they have also underscored the challenge presented by mission mandates that undergo constant change, and the difficulty of bringing the resources of regional organizations, such as NATO and the European Union, to bear on UN objectives. In yet other cases, such as Rwanda, the UN has been simply unable to act in a timely fashion.

Canada — which has consistently been a strong advocate of multilateralism in general, and the UN in particular — has been an active player in the recent surge of UN operations. Canada will remain a strong advocate of multilateral security institutions. We also believe, however, that the objectives and conduct of multilateral missions in support of peace and stability must reflect a clear sense of perspective. Some of the considerations that need to be taken into account are common to all multilateral operations. Others pertain to the involvement of specific multilateral security organizations — in particular, the UN and NATO.

General Considerations. Canada's extensive experience with multilateral operations has led us to identify certain characteristics in the purpose, design and operational conduct of a mission that enhance its prospects for success. These missions should address genuine threats to international peace and security (as, for example, in the Gulf or the former Yugoslavia) or emerging humanitarian tragedies (such as the situations in Somalia and Rwanda). They must not become ends in themselves; they must be part of a comprehensive strategy to secure long-term, realistic, and achievable solutions (such as the UN's operations in Central America).

The design of all missions should reflect certain key principles:

- There be a clear and enforceable mandate.
- There be an identifiable and commonly accepted reporting authority.
- The national composition of the force be appropriate to the mission, and there be an effective process of consultation among missions partners.
- In missions that involve both military and civilian resources, there be a recognized focus of authority, a clear and efficient division of responsibilities, and agreed operating procedures.
- With the exception of enforcement actions and operations to defend NATO member states, in missions that involve Canadian personnel, Canada's participation be accepted by all parties to the conflict.

Canada's experience — which encompasses UN, NATO, and other multilateral undertakings — also suggests that successful missions are those that respect certain essential operational considerations.

- The size, training and equipment of the force be appropriate to the purpose at hand, and remain so over the life of the mission.
- There be a defined concept of operations, an effective command and control structure, and clear rules of engagement.

The UN and NATO. Canada's experience has also shaped the Government's perspective on the respective roles to be played in multilateral operations by the two most important multilateral security institutions to which Canada belongs — the UN and NATO. Canada's ongoing participation in both organizations reflects the belief that each has a valuable contribution to make in the evolution of international peace and stability. At the same time, each organization has its own strengths, weaknesses, and limits.

Historically, the UN has only rarely been able to achieve the level of consensus required to act militarily. As a consequence, it lacks the staff and the required experience in the planning or generation of multinational forces that would enable it to make use of the military potential of its member states in the most timely and effective manner. Indeed, that the UN even has forces at its disposal is subject to the willingness of individual member states to contribute such forces at the time

The focus of NATO has been narrower: the Alliance is dedicated to the collective defence of its member states. Its restricted membership of 16 like-minded countries has made consensus easier to achieve. As a result, it has much more experience in the design and generation of multinational forces — for defensive purposes — as well as with the planning and execution of joint operations. Moreover, the commitment to participate in the defence of an Alliance country is virtually automatic for all member states.

Canada is strongly in favour of a vigorous and effective United Nations, capable of upholding the political values and procedural means set out in its *Charter,* and believes that situations requiring international military action should be dealt with in accordance with the terms of the *Charter.* The UN's pre-eminent authority to conduct operations requiring the force of arms derives from its membership, which is nearly universal in its scope, and the terms of its *Charter,* which sets the existing ethical and legal context for relations between and, to some extent, within states.

Yet, the UN suffers from serious problems. The organization is plagued by a chronic funding crisis, owing to the failure of member states to honour their financial obligations, and the recent spate of very large, extraordinarily complex, and extremely expensive operations which have put a significant strain on its financial resources. In addition, the Security Council requires reform if it is to serve the international community adequately. Its decision-making needs to be made more transparent. Its resolutions should be more carefully drafted. Non-members of the Council — especially troop contributors — need to be consulted more systematically. In terms of the internal workings, the UN has not been able to discharge effectively its expanded post-Cold War role. Bureaucratic reform, streamlining, and cost-cutting are essential to restore its credibility.

Once the UN has determined its goals, identified the means to achieve them, and set its strategy on a given issue, it should be able to execute its decisions in a timely and effective manner. A standing UN force may provide one option to solve the UN's long-standing problems with respect to the ready availability of forces. The practical issues involved in the establishment of such a force are complex, and Canada intends to see the issue studied thoroughly. In the interim, we will, on a national basis, enhance our ability to contribute to UN operations. Within the limits of our resources, we will strive to respond expeditiously to UN requests for expertise, individual personnel, and entire field units.

Canada will also remain a strong supporter of a reformed NATO. Canada believes that NATO's reservoir of military competence and capabilities should make a greater contribution to UN operations. The Alliance will only do so, however, if its relationship with the global organization is clearly and appropriately defined and widely understood. NATO will make its most valuable contribution to multilateral operations by providing the UN with the vigorous military support that it currently lacks. In carrying out this role, the Alliance should resist the temptation to intrude on the provision of political and strategic direction for the mission; that responsibility must rest with the Security Council.

For its part, the UN needs to recognize that when it calls upon NATO to provide effective military support, the Alliance's proven chain of command and operating procedures should not be constrained by political or military guidance that is unclear, hesitant, or divisive. Such guidance impairs NATO's operational efficiency and effectiveness, does not advance the cause of UN objectives, and ultimately diminishes the credibility of both organizations.

National Considerations. Canada must remain prepared to contribute forces to a wide range of UN and other multilateral operations. Certain international scenarios will result in a prompt Canadian response, such as the need to come to the defence of a NATO state or respond to the emergence of a comparable threat to international peace and security. Although this general commitment is clear, under more normal circumstances Canada can and must be selective if it is going to remain in a position to play a meaningful role. Canada cannot, and need not, participate in every multilateral operation. Our resources are finite. We may not agree with the purpose or organization of a given mission. We may not be convinced of its prospects for success. We may be otherwise engaged. Moreover, Canada is not obliged to take on a major portion of every operation or to contribute forces for longer than seems reasonable. Nevertheless, Canada will maintain its specialization in multilateral operations. We will commit forces to such operations if suitable resources are available, and if our personnel can be appropriately armed and properly trained to carry out the task and make a significant contribution to the success of the mission.

The Range of Choice

Canada's record of commitment to multilateral operations is unsurpassed. While the number of operations in which Canadian Forces personnel have been involved is striking, what is equally important is that these operations have encompassed almost the complete spectrum of military activity. Subject to the principles outlined earlier, the Government is willing to commit maritime, land, and air forces (as well as support elements) to the full range of multilateral operations, including those set out below.

Preventive Deployment of Forces. This entails the deployment of forces between parties to an imminent dispute prior to the outbreak of conflict to defuse tension, enhance confidence, and prevent minor incidents from escalating inadvertently to full-scale hostilities. The Government sees great value in these deployments, as part of a broader diplomatic strategy to resolve a dispute peacefully and prevent the outbreak of hostilities. Indeed, Canada was one of the initial participants in the very first preventive deployment of UN forces, to the Former Yugoslav Republic of Macedonia in 1993, an operation designed to lend a measure of stability to a tense part of the Balkans.

Peacekeeping and Observer Missions. These missions represent the traditional kind of 'peacekeeping', on the Golan Heights, or in Cyprus. They entail the positioning of impartial forces between the parties to a ceasefire, and involve the monitoring of agreements during the course of negotiations intended to lead to a political solution. In recent years, these operations have not enjoyed the same profile as other multilateral operations, including missions in the former Yugoslavia, Somalia, and Cambodia. Nevertheless, where there is a desire to move from a situation of armed conflict to political resolution, traditional peacekeeping missions can make a valuable contribution in assisting the transition. Canada's expertise in this field is unsurpassed, and the Government is committed to the continued participation of the Canadian Forces in such operations.

Enforcing the Will of the International Community and Defending Allies. The most ambitious operations of the past few years have used armed force, under multilateral auspices, to enforce the will of the international community — not only in cases of conflict between states, but within states as well. Recent examples of such operations have included:

- the enforcement of economic sanctions or arms embargoes;
- the use of armed forces to create secure conditions for the delivery of aid;
- the denial of air space through which hostile forces could prosecute a military campaign or attack civilian populations ('no-fly zones');
- the protection of civilian populations and refugees in 'safe areas'; and,
- the provision of deterrence or defence for a UN or NATO member state against armed attack.

The Canadian Forces have been involved in every type of operation listed above, requiring a wide range of military training and capability. Our personnel have helped enforce economic sanctions off Haiti and the former Yugoslavia. They have sought to restore order and ensure the delivery of humanitarian aid in Somalia. As part of UNPROFOR, they have done the same in Croatia, while supplementing this activity by helping to monitor the 'no-fly zone' and participating in the protection of 'safe areas' in Bosnia-Hercegovina. In 1990-91, the Canadian Forces were part of the multinational coalition that reversed Iraq's invasion of Kuwait. Finally, throughout this period, the Canadian Forces have continued to train with NATO allies to preserve the Alliance's capability to defend against armed attack.

Ethnic and religious tensions, the increasing number of 'failed states', and the persistence of inter-state conflicts over borders and resources, strongly suggest that the future nature of multilateral military operations must be multi-dimensional to address a full range of challenges. The goals of these missions — the protection of civilian populations and refugees, national reconstruction, upholding international law, and opposing aggression — are invariably unimpeachable. That does not mean, however, that they will always go smoothly or will not pose significant risks to Canadian Forces personnel — particularly in an environment where the proliferation of advanced weaponry is becoming the rule rather than the exception. Nevertheless, Canada will remain prepared to contribute forces to such operations, whether they are authorized by the UN, or as part of the efforts of regional organizations such as NATO or the CSCE.

Post-Conflict Peacebuilding. The rehabilitation of areas that have been the scene of armed conflict represents an important contribution that the training, skills, and equipment of our armed forces can make to security abroad. Past instances of such contributions include the provision of humanitarian relief supplies and the use of engineers to rebuild infrastructure and remove land mines. Following the Soviet withdrawal from Afghanistan, Canada took the additional step of training refugees to recognize and disarm land mines. These activities can make an invaluable contribution in building a more durable peace, and the Government will explore ways in which the Canadian Forces can contribute further.

Prior to taking office, the Government noted that the relationship between the military and civilian aspects of the new multilateral missions was an area that needed to be explored. The Government will build upon the excellent progress that has already been made. Our accumulated experience with such military-civilian coordination from missions in Ethiopia, Somalia, and Rwanda suggests that armed forces have a critical role to play at the outset of these missions in the establishment of a secure environment and the provision of basic support (such as transport, emergency medical assistance, logistics and communications). Over the long-term, however, reconstructive activities — be they the administration and enforcement of civil law, the provision of medical care, or the distribution of humanitarian aid — are best left to civilian organizations.

Measures to Enhance Stability and Build Confidence. Arms control and measures to build confidence represent an important way to prevent or limit conflict and foster stable relations between states. Over the past two years, for example, implementation of the Treaty on Conventional Forces in Europe destroyed over 7,000 tanks from the countries of the former Warsaw Pact — a total sufficient to equip 32 Soviet-style army divisions.

The ability to inspect and verify compliance remains crucial to the relative success or failure of these arrangements. The Department of National Defence and the Canadian Forces have played their part in past operations of this type and, within the limits of their resources, this will continue.

One of the most interesting and productive means to enhance stability and build confidence has been through multilateral and bilateral contacts between the civilian and military staffs of various countries. Such contacts — which may range from brief visits to full-fledged staff talks and exchanges — serve to build transparency, confidence, and trust through direct personal contact and greater familiarity with differing perceptions of defence issues as well as military culture and doctrine. The Canadian Forces have used such bilateral and multilateral contact programs to discuss a variety of questions, from defence planning to civil-military relations. Exchanges with military forces from Central and Eastern Europe and the Commonwealth of Independent States have shown great promise. The Government will now expand this program of exchanges and extend its scope to include other countries. To this end, we will increase substantially the budget devoted to the Military Training Assistance Program to build up contact programs with Central and Eastern Europe, the Commonwealth of Independent States, Asia, Latin America, and Africa.

Training for Multilateral Missions

The Government believes that combat training — undertaken on a national basis as well as with allies — remains the best foundation for the participation of the Canadian Forces in multilateral missions. In situations short of war, such training equips Canadian Forces personnel with the complete range of skills that may be needed to meet the varied demands of the unexpected situations they will encounter.

Canada will support and contribute to the enhancement of peacekeeping training.

- Recent experiences in UN operations have confirmed the value of cultural sensitivity, international humanitarian law, and dispute resolution training prior to deployment. Such training has always formed part of the preparation for Canadian peacekeepers sent abroad; it will be further enhanced.
- The Government has assisted in the establishment and funding of the Lester B. Pearson Canadian International Peacekeeping Training Centre at Cornwallis, Nova Scotia, under the auspices of the Canadian Institute of Strategic Studies. The Department will sponsor peacekeeping training at the Centre for military personnel from countries participating in NATO's Partnership for Peace and developing countries under the Military Training Assistance Program.

Organizations and Commitments

Strengthening the United Nations. Canada — which has unfailingly lent its political and financial support to the United Nations — remains committed to UN reform. In the security sphere, Canada brings superbly qualified personnel, significant military capabilities, and a great deal of experience to UN operations. Other countries look to Canada for leadership. In addition to its solid record in the financial support of UN operations, Canada has already taken the lead in providing UN headquarters with military expertise to improve its planning and operational capabilities. Canada will continue to advocate that funding arrangements for UN operations be improved. We will also work toward the further enhancement of the UN's command and control system, as well as the development of its administrative and logistics capabilities.

Where the participation of the Canadian Forces in UN peacekeeping operations was once subject to a numerical 'ceiling' or planning figure of 2000 personnel, our recent experiences suggest that we would be better served by a more flexible approach. As a matter of general principle, the Canadian Forces will remain prepared to deploy on UN operations contingency forces of up to a maritime task group, a brigade group plus an infantry battalion group, a wing of fighter aircraft, and a squadron of tactical transport aircraft. Were these forces to be deployed simultaneously, this could conceivably involve in the order of 10,000 military personnel.

Within this upper limit, Canada will increase its commitment of standby forces to the UN from a battalion, an air transport element, and a communications element to the vanguard component of its contingency forces — that is, two ships (one on each coast), one battle group, one infantry battalion group, one squadron of fighter aircraft, a flight of tactical transport aircraft, a communications element, and a headquarters element. If deployed simultaneously, this would represent a commitment of 4,000 personnel, which could then be sustained indefinitely.

The Forces will also remain prepared to deploy, for limited periods, selected specialized elements of the Canadian Forces — medical personnel, transport and signals units, and engineers — in humanitarian relief roles. Other Canadian contributions, such as the provision of observers and technical specialists will be undertaken as feasible.

NATO: Participation and Reform. Canada will remain a full and active member of NATO. The monolithic threat to Western Europe has disappeared and, for now, the principal responsibility for European defence must lie with the Europeans themselves. At the same time, the Government values the transatlantic link that NATO provides, and recognizes that, since 1990, the Alliance has made progress in adapting to a post-Cold War world. Those aspects that reflect a cooperative approach to European security relations, including the creation of the North Atlantic Cooperation Council (NACC), Partnership for Peace, and the development of the Combined Joint Task Force concept, are especially notable.

Canada will press for additional change. The Alliance's fundamental and primary role is to provide for the collective defence of its member states. NATO can, however, make a greater contribution to collective and cooperative security than is currently the case, and the Government will work toward striking an appropriate balance between the Alliance's traditional mission and its newer roles.

Canada will be an active participant in the Alliance's ongoing efforts to reach out to the countries of Central Europe as well as to those of the Commonwealth of Independent States. We give our full support to NATO expansion, but continue to believe that this question must be addressed very carefully — certainly, the process must not exacerbate Russian fears of encirclement or exclusion. Canada will participate in multilateral and bilateral programs that aim to integrate gradually our NACC partners into an effective security order for the Northern Hemisphere.

Finally, Canada will insist that the Alliance become a more efficient organization, in terms of its budgets and operating costs — in the same way that national defence departments in all member states have had to adjust to fiscal restraint. In particular, we will propose that NATO's large and costly bureaucracy be reduced, and that the military budget be spent on activities that are relevant to the new environment.

The Government's perspective on NATO underpins the future of Canada's Alliance commitments. In the event of a crisis or war in Europe, the contingency forces that Canada will maintain for all multilateral operations would immediately be made available to NATO. Should it prove necessary, Canada would mobilize further national resources to provide the additional forces required to fulfil Canada's commitment to the Alliance as set out under Article 5 of the *North Atlantic Treaty.*

Apart from this general commitment to contribute forces to the defence of Alliance territory, Canada will maintain a number of specific peacetime NATO commitments. Set within the context of Canada's earlier slate of Alliance commitments, there are three important changes.

First, Canada will terminate its commitment to maintain a battalion group to serve with Allied Command Europe's Mobile Force (Land) or the NATO Composite Force in the defence of northern Norway. The evolution of European security and of NATO's strategic posture suggests that this battalion group could make a more useful contribution to a NATO force designed to deploy rapidly anywhere within Alliance territory, including Norway. As a result, we would be willing to contribute an infantry battalion group to NATO's Immediate Reaction Force. The battalion group's equipment, which is currently prepositioned in Norway and is particularly well-suited to northern operations, will be returned to Canada to help offset the needs of larger Regular Land Force combat units and the Militia.

Second, Canada will supplement its contribution to NATO's Standing Naval Force Atlantic with the assignment, on an occasional basis, of one ship to NATO's Standing Naval Force Mediterranean. This initiative will further extend the benefits that our naval personnel gain from operating with allied navies, and is in keeping with NATO's broader geographic focus.

Third, Canada has been a major net contributor to the NATO Infrastructure Program. This program once provided a cost-efficient way to pool funds from the Alliance countries to construct infrastructure for collective defence. In light of changes in the European security environment, the full post-war recovery of Western Europe's economy, and the need to address cooperative security needs in Central and Eastern Europe, Canada will scale back its contribution to this program and devote some of these funds to the expansion of our bilateral contact programs with Central and Eastern Europe under the Military Training Assistance Program.

A Continuing Role in the CSCE. Canada has played an active role in the Conference on Security and Cooperation in Europe (CSCE) since its inception in 1973. Our participation has included the signing of the original document (the Helsinki Final Act of 1975), the Stockholm Document on confidence-building measures in 1986, the *Treaty on Conventional Forces in Europe* in 1990, and the Vienna Documents of 1990 and 1992. Canada has also contributed forces to the European Community Monitor Mission in the Balkans (which was called for by the CSCE), and lent operational support to the CSCE mission in NagornyKarabakh.

The CSCE is the only organization addressing regional security concerns in Europe that includes Russia as well as virtually all the countries of Central and Eastern Europe. This gives the organization a particular role in building confidence among its members. It also opens the possibility that the organization, which has played a significant role in forestalling conflict, can also play a role in resolving conflict — a role that could include a range of peacekeeping and related operations. To the extent that the CSCE arrives at a consensus in favour of performing these functions, Canada will be prepared to support such activities within the

342 Canada's National Defence

constraints imposed by budgetary considerations and the availability of suitable resources.

The CSCE lacks an effective decision-making mechanism. Indeed, despite recent measures to upgrade its administrative machinery, it remains more a process than an organization. Yet, through encouraging transparency between its member states and regional organizations (such as NATO and the WEU), as well as the gradual development of a pan-European code of conduct, the CSCE stands to make a valuable contribution to European security over the long term. Canada will remain an active participant in this forum.

Reaching out to Asia-Pacific. Aside from its role in the Korean War, Canada's participation in Asia-Pacific security affairs since the end of the Second World War has been largely limited to the commitment of forces to various peacekeeping and observer missions (including the International Commission for Supervision and Control in Vietnam, and the United Nations Transitional Authority in Cambodia), along with participation in the 'RIMPAC' air and naval exercises with the United States, Japan, Australia, and, on occasion, other Asia-Pacific countries. As our interest in Asia has grown over the past few years, Canada has become more active in a variety of regional security initiatives — particularly through the encouragement of regional security dialogues such as the Asia Regional Forum, the Council for Security Cooperation in Asia Pacific, and the Canadian Consortium on Asia Pacific Security. All of these activities will continue, and, as our economic stake in the region grows, Canada will play a more active role in its security.

To this end, we will expand the current program of bilateral military contacts we maintain with a variety of Asian countries, including Japan, South Korea, and members of the Association of South East Asian Nations (ASEAN). These contacts are currently limited to the presence of defence attaches in selected capitals and the conduct of periodic staff talks and conferences. Our activities in the Asia-Pacific region will be broadened gradually to include a more regular program of visits and exchanges in the area of peacekeeping, including programs at the Lester B. Pearson Canadian International Peacekeeping Training Centre.

A Continuing Role in Other Regions. In addition to its role in the Gulf War, Canada has taken part in more than thirty peacekeeping, observer and humanitarian relief missions in Latin America, the Middle East, and Africa since 1947. Canada's commitment to the stability of these regions through the UN and, where appropriate, regional organizations will continue. The Government will lend greater emphasis to the Latin American dimension of our security policy, both bilaterally and through the Organization of American States. We will assist Latin American countries in such areas as peacekeeping training, confidence-building measures, and the development of civil-military relations. In Africa, Canada will encourage the development of a regional capability to undertake peacekeeping missions, both on a bilateral basis and through programs being undertaken at the Lester B. Pearson Canadian International Peacekeeping Training Centre.

Objectives

The Government is renewing Canada's traditional commitment to participate in the military dimension of international security affairs. Canada will remain an active participant in the UN and NATO, but will push for additional reform within these institutions to make them more relevant, timely, efficient, and effective. Canada will continue to participate in the CSCE, and, within the limits of available resources, more fully develop defence relations with the countries of Central and Eastern Europe, Latin America, the Asia-Pacific region, and Africa.

The dramatic expansion of UN operations — both in terms of number and scope — confronts Canada with some difficult choices. Owing to financial constraints, Canada will have to be selective in its commitments. Canadians will also have to accept that some missions will entail a considerable amount of risk. Nevertheless, by choosing to maintain a multipurpose, combat-capable force, Canada will retain the capability to make a significant and responsible contribution to international peace and stability, within a UN framework, through NATO, or in coalitions of like-minded countries.

To this end, the Canadian Forces will:

■   maintain the capability to assist the Department of Foreign Affairs and International Trade in the protection and evacuation of Canadians from areas threatened by imminent conflict;

■ participate in multilateral operations anywhere in the world under UN auspices, or in the defence of a NATO member state, and, to that end,

- be able to deploy, or redeploy from other multilateral operations, a joint task force headquarters and, as single units or in combination, one or more of the following elements:

  - a naval task group, comprised of up to four combatants (destroyers, frigates or submarines) and a support ship, with appropriate maritime air support,
  - three separate battle groups or a brigade group (comprised of three infantry battalions, an armoured regiment and an artillery regiment, with appropriate combat support and combat service support),
  - a wing of fighter aircraft, with appropriate support, and,
  - one squadron of tactical transport aircraft;

- provide:

  - within three weeks, single elements or the vanguard components of this force and be able to sustain them indefinitely in a low-threat environment, and
  - within three months, the remaining elements of the full contingency force;

- earmark:

  - an infantry battalion group as either a stand-by force for the UN, or to serve with NATO's Immediate Reaction Force; and,

- have plans ready to institute other measures to increase the capabilities of the Canadian Forces to sustain existing commitments or to respond to a major crisis;

■ also maintain the following specific peacetime commitments to NATO:

  - one ship to serve with the Standing Naval Force Atlantic,
  - one ship to serve, on an occasional basis, with the Standing Naval Force Mediterranean,

- aircrews and other personnel to serve in the NATO Airborne Early Warning system,
- approximately 200 personnel to serve in various NATO headquarters,
- participation, at a reduced level, in the NATO infrastructure program, and,
- the opportunity for Allied forces to conduct training in Canada, on a cost-recovery basis;

■ in response to changing geographic priorities, expand bilateral and multilateral contacts and exchanges with selected partners in Central and Eastern Europe, the Asia-Pacific region, Latin America, and Africa, with a particular emphasis on peacekeeping, confidence-building measures, and civil-military relations; and,

■ support the verification of existing arms control agreements and participate in the development of future accords.

CHAPTER VII

Implementing Defence Policy

Canada's military circumstances have changed enormously over the past seven years. Over the same period, the financial condition of the country has worsened considerably. For these reasons "business as usual" is no longer an acceptable approach to defence policy.

The defence policy put forward in this White Paper is hard-nosed and realistic, but also mindful of our global responsibilities. It allows us both to uphold our essential military traditions and renew our commitment to global stability. It clearly represents a major evolution — a step change in Canadian defence policy. It heralds a fundamental transformation of the way in which the Canadian Forces and the Department of National Defence will conduct their operations and do business in the coming years.

In setting this new course, the Government has had to make hard choices. Most areas of defence will be cut — staff, infrastructure, equipment, training, operations — some substantially more than others. The relative weights of the naval, land and air establishments that have prevailed for many years will be adjusted, primarily to allow for the transfer of resources to where they are most needed — mainly to land combat and combat support forces — in response to the added emphasis being placed on multilateral activities, and particularly peace and stability operations.

Maintaining the essential capabilities of the Canadian Forces at a time of fiscal restraint represents a difficult challenge. The defence program has been substantially revised to reflect only the most essential priorities. Everything is being made leaner — everything is undergoing the closest scrutiny. Major cuts in headquarters and support activities will mean more resources devoted to combat forces and less to administrative overhead. This will ensure that the Canadian Forces remain well commanded, properly trained, and adequately equipped for the missions the Government asks them to carry out.

Management, Command and Control

Reductions of National Defence Headquarters and Subordinate Headquarters. While the structural foundations of the Department and the Canadian Forces are basically sound and capable of meeting the challenge, they can be further streamlined. The Department of National Defence and the Canadian Forces will, in particular, continue to improve resource management through initiatives such as Defence 2000 to ensure the best possible use of resources at all levels of the organization. This management policy emphasizes the delegation of decision-making authority, the empowerment of personnel, the elimination of 'red tape' and overlapping functions, and the promotion of innovation. The Department and Forces will, by 1999, reduce by at least one-third the personnel and resources committed to headquarters functions.

Integrated Headquarters. The integrated National Defence Headquarters (NDHQ) has been in existence for more than 20 years. NDHQ fosters a close military-civilian relationship and brings together a wide range of knowledge, skills and perceptions, which all contribute to more focused, coherent, and efficient defence management. At the strategic level, military activity is intertwined with — and inseparable from — social and economic considerations, as well as public and policy imperatives. This was most clearly demonstrated during the Gulf War and the crisis at Oka. International, military, financial, public and Cabinet concerns had to be reconciled promptly, and prudent choices made. A responsive headquarters is also essential if we are to maintain our very active role in peacekeeping and other multilateral operations. Thus the Government can see no compelling reason that would justify reversing the civilian-military integration of National Defence Headquarters.

Command and Control. The Canadian Forces' command and control structure has proven both responsive and adaptable, but takes up too large a proportion of the resources available to defence. In response to the recommendations of the Special Joint Committee on Canada's Defence Policy, a new command and control structure will be put into place by mid-1997. It will be based on sound military command and control principles, and respond to the need to increase the proportion of operational personnel — thus increasing the "tooth-to-tail" ratio. The command of military operations will continue to be exercised by the Chief of the Defence Staff — normally through a designated operational commander — and one layer of headquarters will be eliminated.

Capital Equipment Program. The changed security environment and current fiscal circumstances demand that National Defence radically restructure plans to purchase capital equipment. The emphasis will be on extending the life of equipment wherever cost-effective and prudent. New equipment will be acquired only for purposes considered essential to maintaining core capabilities of the Canadian Forces, and will be suited to the widest range of defence roles. Wherever possible the Canadian Forces will operate fewer types of equipment than is now the case and purchase equipment that is easier to maintain. The Department will also explore innovative ways to acquire and maintain equipment. Planned acquisitions will be cut by at least 15 billion dollars over the next 15 years. As a result, a large number of projects currently in plans will be eliminated, reduced or delayed.

Procurement. The Department of National Defence will adopt better business practices — greater reliance will, for example, be placed on "just-in-time" delivery of common usage items to reduce inventory costs. The Department will increase the procurement of off-the-shelf commercial technology which meets essential military specifications and standards. Full military specifications or uniquely Canadian modifications will be adopted only where these are shown to be absolutely essential. The Department will also enhance its partnership with the private sector. Where business-case evaluations demonstrate potential for increased cost effectiveness, support activities currently conducted "in house" will be transferred completely to Canadian industry or shared with private industry under various partnership arrangements. The Department will continue to seek out new ways to support operational forces. The materiel supply system and its processes will become markedly more efficient through consolidation and the adoption of advanced technology. Further steps will also be taken to modernize and streamline the procurement process in consultation with other concerned departments.

Industrial Impact. In the midst of all these changes it is important to recognize the relationships between Canadian defence policy and Canadian industry. In today's world, multi-purpose, combat capable forces require the support of a technologically sophisticated industrial base to be effective. In addition, in all leading industrial nations there is a close linkage between expenditure on defence R&D and procurement and the growth of many high technological sectors. In Canada, almost 60,000 people are employed in high technology industries like aerospace and electronics, which are linked to defence procurement. These linkages extend far beyond the production of defence equipment to include technological spin-offs into commercial products and access to international markets. The challenge of lower R&D and capital spending and more off-the-shelf purchasing will be to maintain and improve the industrial impact of those expenditures which remain. To this end, National Defence will work with Industry Canada, as well as Public Works and Government Services Canada, towards harmonizing industrial and defence policies to maintain essential defence industrial capability. The Government will seek to foster defence conversion, overall industrial growth, and the international competitiveness of Canadian firms consistent with our international trade agreements.

Infrastructure and Support. Although National Defence has made considerable headway in reducing defence infrastructure and support, further reductions are both possible and necessary. Action is underway to extend significantly the defence infrastructure and support service rationalization mandated in the 1994 federal budget.

Defence Studies. The Government agrees with the finding of the Special Joint Committee that the modest program of assistance to Canadian universities and other institutions involved in defence studies is a highly worthwhile investment. This program will be maintained. A chair of defence management studies will also be established.

Personnel Issues

Personnel Reduction. Personnel cuts will continue. The reductions will be implemented in an orderly, fair and equitable manner. The Government is firmly committed to dealing humanely and reasonably with those of its employees whose jobs are eliminated, and to working with the unions.

Code of Service Discipline. The Code of Service Discipline, set out in the *National Defence Act,* has been in existence for almost 45 years with only limited amendments. There have been significant changes in Canadian social and legal standards during that time. The Government will amend the *National Defence Act* to update its provisions to meet modern military requirements. This will involve, in particular, amendments to the military justice system as it relates to both courts martial and summary trials.

Terms of Service. The Government will place more emphasis on renewable, short-term periods of service for members of the Canadian Forces. The period of service for engagements will depend upon the skills and training required to do the job. Reservists participating in and returning from operational assignments will benefit from the same post-operational care now available to the Regular Force.

Personnel Policy. Military career paths will be restructured to reduce the number of postings and assignments that a permanent member of the Canadian Forces can expect over a lifetime of service. This policy will result in fewer relocations, and thus ease the burden on military personnel and families, and save money for the Government.

The Canadian Forces will reduce military staff in certain occupations and trades as functions are contracted out or reassigned to civilian employees. The new command and control structure will substantially reduce the overall number of senior positions, and the ratio of general officers and senior civilian officials to overall strength, as well as the ratio of officers to non-commissioned members in the Regular Forces and the Reserves, will be significantly decreased.

The percentage of women in the Canadian Forces is among the highest of any military force in the world. Nevertheless, the commitment to making military careers more attractive to women will be reinforced. Although the need for "universality of service" in the military remains paramount, the Department and the Forces will ensure that equitable employment opportunities continue to exist for all Canadians, regardless of gender, race, sexual orientation, or culture, and will strictly enforce the policy of "zero harassment" in the work place.

Proposals for enhancing the federal government policy on reserve leave will be developed. The Government will encourage, and seek out new ways for other levels of government and private companies —

particularly small businesses — to do the same. The Canadian Forces will also emphasize the importance of availability for active duty when recruiting reservists.

Civilian Workforce. The civilian workforce is an integral component of the Defence team. Highly qualified public servants play a wide variety of essential roles within the organization in support of the achievement of the defence mission, from the delivery of skilled services at local levels to the provision of professional administrative, scientific and academic services. While the overall numbers of civilian employees will be further reduced to approximately 20,000 by 1999, our civilian employees will continue to play critical roles in the effective implementation of the new policy.

Total Force

The Canadian Forces are a unified force of maritime, land and air elements. Their structure is based on a Total Force concept that integrates full-and part-time military personnel to provide multi-purpose, combat-capable armed forces. Under the Total Force concept, Regular Forces are maintained to provide the Government with a ready response capability; Reserve Forces are intended as augmentation and sustainment for Regular units, and, in some cases, for tasks that are not performed by Regular Forces — such as mine countermeasure operations. The concept also provides the framework for training and equipping the Reserves.

Progress has been made in the implementation of the Total Force concept, with many reservists now fully ready to undertake Regular Force functions. Indeed, in recent years, several thousand reservists have served in demanding missions at home and abroad. The Total Force approach is right for Canada. The Government recognizes the continuing need for a national mobilization framework; however, changes are needed to reflect Canada's requirement for ready forces if it is to be able to meet domestic needs and contribute to multilateral operations.

Mobilization. The new strategic environment has prompted the Government to reconsider the traditional approach to mobilization planning. Mobilization plans must provide for a graduated and orderly transition from routine peacetime operations to higher levels of involvement, which ultimately could include the total mobilization of the nation. Accordingly, mobilization plans will be revised on the basis of a new, four-stage framework.

- The first stage of a response to any crisis or emergency would involve "force generation"; that is, all measures needed to prepare elements of the Canadian Forces to undertake new operational tasks, and to sustain and support them. These functions will be undertaken within the existing resource framework of the Canadian Forces. They will include the training and preparation of reservists to augment the Regular Force.
- The next stage, "force enhancement", would involve the improvement of the operational capabilities of the existing forces through the allocation of more resources. It would be undertaken without permanent change in the posture or roles of the Canadian Forces, although the formation of temporary units or specialist elements could prove necessary. This level of mobilization is similar to actions taken in response to the 1990 war in the Persian Gulf and all current peace-keeping commitments.
- "Force expansion", the third stage, would involve the enlargement of the Canadian Forces — and perhaps selected elements of the Department of National Defence — to meet a major crisis or emergency. It will involve permanent changes in the roles, structures, and taskings of the Canadian Forces — and could call for the formation of new units, the enhancement of existing facilities, and the procurement of additional equipment. This stage is similar to the structural and role changes undergone by all elements of the Canadian Forces and the Department of National Defence in 1950-1952, when Canada provided armed forces to the United Nations' multinational force in Korea, and to the newly formed NATO in Europe.
- Finally, while a major global war is highly unlikely at this time, it remains prudent to have ready "no-cost" plans for total "national mobilization". This fourth step could touch upon all aspects of Canadian society and would only come into effect with the proclamation by the Governor-in-Council of a "war emergency" under the *Emergencies Act.*

Revised Force Posture. By 1999, the strength of the Regular Forces will be reduced to approximately 60,000 and the Primary Reserve to approximately 23,000. This, together with the new mobilization concept and renewed emphasis on multilateral operations in support of global stability, will dictate a number of force structure adjustments. In light of the need to maintain adequate states of readiness — to respond to UN or other multilateral taskings, for example — the current balance between regulars and reservists in operational units is no longer appropriate. The Government agrees with the Special Joint Committee that the land force must be expanded. A total of approximately 3,000 additional soldiers will be added to the army's field force. The additional resources will be provided through reductions in headquarters, restructuring of the three services, and a reduction in the size of the Reserves.

Reserves. The Reserves are a national institution and provide a vital link between the Canadian Forces and local communities. Their primary role will be the augmentation, sustainment, and support of deployed forces. While the overall number of reservists will be reduced, the quality and overall ability of the Reserves to provide the Total Force with trained personnel for unit augmentation will be significantly improved. A thorough examination of all elements of the Primary and Supplementary Reserves will be conducted with the aim of enhancing their ability to respond to new requirements and the new mobilization approach. The Government recognizes that a greater proportion of the Reserves' resources must go towards improving their operational capability and availability. In particular, the Militia structure requires attention and rejuvenation to ensure that units are more efficient and better able to contribute to the Total Force concept. Consideration will also be given to assigning more service support roles — such as medical, logistics, communications and transport functions — to the Reserves. To the extent that changes may also be required in the Naval, Air and Communications Reserves, the same general pattern will be followed. The Supplementary Reserve, comprised of former military personnel who could augment the Regular Force in an emergency, will be maintained, but will no longer be funded.

Many reserve units, despite long and honourable service, have diminished in size and effectiveness in recent years and their armouries are under-used. The new strategic and fiscal environment will require a streamlining of reserve organizations and rank structures. Every effort will be made to maintain the traditions and effectiveness of reserve regiments. However, local communities must take more responsibility to help sustain Reserve traditions and activities.

Canadian Defence Personnel

		Regular Force	Primary Reserve	Civilians	Total
STRENGTH 1989					
	Total	88,800	26,100	36,600	151,500
STRENGTH 1994					
	Total	74,900	29,400	32,500	136,800
1994 BUDGET: 1998 TARGET					
	Total	66,700	29,400	25,200	121,300
1994 WHITE PAPER: 1999 TARGET					
	Total	60,000	23,000	20,000	103,000
TOTAL REDUCTION					
	1994 to 1999	14,900	6,400	12,500	33,800
	% change	20%	22%	38%	25%
	1989 to 1999	28,800	3,100	16,600	48,500
	% change	32%	12%	45%	32%

The Canadian Rangers reflect an important dimension of Canada's national identity and the Government will enhance their capability to conduct Arctic and coastal land patrols. The Government will also modestly increase the level of support to Cadet organizations to help expand their role in building citizenship and advancing national unity.

Operational Maritime Forces

Since the end of the Cold War, Canada's maritime forces have maintained multi-purpose combat capabilities to carry out a wide variety of domestic and international operations. They have substantially reduced anti-submarine warfare activities connected with the protection of shipping and countering missile-carrying submarines in the North Atlantic, while increasing their participation in UN and multilateral operations.

The navy will be able to form a task group on the West Coast and another on the East Coast from among units of the Atlantic and Pacific fleets. To facilitate this new focus, naval ships are being re-distributed to achieve a better balance between Canada's two open-water oceans. Co-operation and co-ordination between the various government fleets will continue to be improved.

Canada's maritime forces will be adequately equipped to carry out their new array of tasks. There is an urgent need for robust and capable new shipborne helicopters. The *Sea Kings* are rapidly approaching the end of their operational life. Work will, therefore, begin immediately to identify options and plans to put into service new affordable replacement helicopters by the end of the decade.

The Special Joint Committee on Canada's Defence Policy found that submarines can conduct underwater and surface surveillance of large portions of Canada's maritime areas of responsibility, require relatively small crews, can be operated for roughly a third of the cost of a modern frigate, and work well with other elements of the Canadian Forces. It also recommended that, if it should prove possible in the current environment of military downsizing around the world to acquire three to six modern diesel-electric submarines on a basis that was demonstrably cost-effective (i.e., that could be managed within the existing capital budget), then the Government should seriously consider such an initiative. The United Kingdom is seeking to sell four recently constructed conventional submarines of the *Upholder*-class, preferably to a NATO partner. The Government intends to explore this option.

To maintain sufficient capability to sealift troops, equipment and supplies for multilateral operations, the support ship *HMCS Provider* (initially slated to be paid off in 1996) will be retained in service, and plans for the eventual replacement of the existing fleet will be considered. Starting in 1995, the navy will receive the first of 12 modern Maritime Coastal Defence Vessels (to be crewed primarily by reservists), intended to provide a coastal defence and mine countermeasure capability that has been lacking.

Operational Land Forces

The importance of the Canadian Forces' mission to support an allied land campaign in Central Europe has diminished, allowing the withdrawal of our forces from Europe. Multi-purpose combat capabilities are now maintained to carry out a wide variety of domestic and international operations.

Canada's land forces will be adequately equipped to carry out their new array of tasks. The materiel of the three brigade groups will be improved. Current plans call for the acquisition of a variety of modern equipment essential to the maintenance of a multi-purpose combat-capability.

There exists, for example, a recognized operational deficiency in the armoured personnel carrier fleet. Its mobility, protection and defensive firepower must be brought into line with the modern requirements of environments likely to be encountered in today's UN and other multilateral missions. The Canadian Forces will, therefore, acquire new armoured personnel carriers for delivery, commencing in 1997. Modernization of part of the present inventory will add other suitably armoured personnel carriers to the fleet. The relatively new *Bison* APCs will be retained in service.

The fleet of *Cougar* armoured training vehicles that are part of the army's close-combat, direct-fire capability in peace and stability operations will eventually have to be replaced.

Operational Air Forces

The focus of air planning and operations has shifted from missions driven primarily by the former Soviet threat to a more balanced set of national and international priorities. Multi-purpose combat capabilities are now maintained to execute a wide variety of domestic and international operations, as well as to provide support to maritime and land operations.

Canada's air forces will be adequately equipped to carry out their new array of tasks. The *Labrador* search and rescue helicopters will be replaced as soon as possible. While this role may be performed using the same helicopter that we acquire for the maritime role, we also intend to explore other possibilities, including different forms of partnership with the private sector for aircraft maintenance, and potentially, alternative arrangements for financing acquisition of a replacement.

Expenditures on fighter forces and support will be reduced by at least 25% as recommended by the Special Joint Committee on Canada's Defence Policy. To achieve these savings, the Department will retire the CF-5 fleet, cut the cost of fighter-related overhead, reduce the annual authorized flying rate, and cut the number of operational aircraft from 72 to between 48 and 60. The initial training of fighter pilots to operational standards will be modified, with fighter lead-in training formerly done on the CF-5 apportioned between the *Tutor* jet trainer and the CF-18. These changes will serve to prolong the life of the CF-18 fleet and delay the need to buy a replacement aircraft well into the next century.

The multi-purpose capability of the CF-18 will be enhanced through the acquisition of a small number of precision-guided munitions. This will afford the Government a very accurate close air support capability and maximize the usefulness of the aircraft. It will, in particular, provide new options for the use of this sophisticated weapons system in circumstances applicable today with ammunition so accurate as to minimize damage outside the target area.

In the absence of valid offers to buy the VIP A-310 *Airbus,* and in recognition of the future demand for strategic airlift support, it will, as recommended by the Special Joint Committee, be reconfigured for a strategic transport and air cargo role.

Conclusion

Several years after the fall of the Berlin Wall and the collapse of the Soviet empire, Canada finds itself in a world fundamentally transformed, characterized by considerable turbulence and uncertainty. Similarly, at home, Canadians now live and work in a society of more limited resources and new challenges, where many of the old rules and certainties have lost their validity. In these circumstances, ensuring Canada's security and defining an appropriate role for our armed forces is more than ever a challenge for all Canadians.

With this White Paper, the Government has fulfilled its obligation to provide Canadians with an effective, realistic and affordable defence policy. From the outset, our objective was not to discard sound practices in favour of simplistic solutions. Rather, the Government was committed to reviewing carefully every aspect of Canada's defence policy so that it could make reasoned judgements on how best to ensure the nation's security and well-being. At the heart of our approach were extensive and far-reaching public consultations, lasting for most of 1994. The Government believes the defence policy enunciated in this White Paper reflects a Canadian consensus.

The White Paper affirms the need to maintain multi-purpose, combat-capable sea, land and air forces that will protect Canadians and project their interests and values abroad. It also concludes that to maximize the contributions of our armed forces, their traditional roles — protecting Canada, cooperating with the United States in the defence of North America, and participating in peacekeeping and other multilateral operations elsewhere in the world — should evolve in a way that is consistent with today's strategic and fiscal realities.

The Canadian Forces will maintain core capabilities to protect the country's territory and approaches, and to further national objectives. Given that the direct military threat to the continent is greatly diminished at present, Canada will reduce the level of resources devoted to traditional missions in North America. It will, however, remain actively engaged in the United Nations, NATO, and the Conference on Security and Cooperation in Europe. It will become more actively involved in security issues in Latin America and the Asia-Pacific region.

To achieve these goals, the Regular and Reserve Forces will both be reduced and refocused, the command and control system will be reorganized, and affordable equipment will be purchased so our troops have the means to carry out their missions. The Department of National Defence and the Canadian Forces will operate more efficiently, making optimum use of infrastructure and equipment, and ensuring full value is derived from the skills, experience and professionalism of Canada's armed forces and civilian defence employees. The Government will also work towards harmonizing industrial and defence policies to maintain essential defence industrial capabilities.

This policy recognizes that the defence budget will be under continuing pressure as the Government strives to bring the deficit under control. More reductions can and will be accommodated, including the military reductions outlined in this Paper and cuts in the Department's civilian workforce arising from a number of additional facilities closures and consolidations. Further savings will be achieved through the elimination, reduction or delay of major acquisition projects currently included in the capital program. Only a few major re-equipment programs remain affordable, and these will directly support the new defence priorities identified in the White Paper. Taken together, these measures will have substantial implications for the Department and the Forces, their members and employees, as well as for local communities and the private sector across Canada.

This White Paper provides Canada's men and women in uniform and their civilian colleagues the direction they require to carry out their duties on behalf of the nation, whether the world of the future is a peaceful and stable one, or is plagued by increasing violence within and among states. Indeed, whatever the future brings, the new defence policy will enable Canada to respond and adjust as necessary to deal with the range of challenges to our security that could arise, now and into the next century.

Queen's Policy Studies
Recent Publications

The Queen's Policy Studies Series is dedicated to the exploration of major policy issues that confront governments in Canada and other western nations. McGill-Queen's University Press is the exclusive world representative and distributor of books in the series.

School of Policy Studies

Lone-Parent Incomes and Social-Policy Outcomes: Canada in International Perspective, Terrance Hunsley, 1997
Paper ISBN 0-88911-751-9 Cloth ISBN 0-88911-757-8

Social Partnerships for Training: Canada's Experiment with Labour Force Development Boards, Andrew Sharpe and Rodney Haddow (eds.), 1997
Paper ISBN 0-88911-753-5 Cloth ISBN 0-88911-755-1

Reform of Retirement Income Policy: International and Canadian Perspectives, Keith G. Banting and Robin Boadway (eds.), 1996
Paper ISBN 0-88911-739-X Cloth ISBN 0-88911-759-4

Institute of Intergovernmental Relations

Canada: The State of the Federation 1997, Vol. 12, *Non-Constitutional Renewal,* Harvey Lazar (ed.), 1998
Paper ISBN 0-88911-765-9 Cloth ISBN 0-88911-767-5

Canadian Constitutional Dilemmas Revisited, Denis Magnusson (ed.), 1997
Paper ISBN 0-88911-593-1 Cloth ISBN 0-88911-595-8

Canada: The State of the Federation 1996, Patrick C. Fafard and Douglas M. Brown (eds.), 1997
Paper ISBN 0-88911-587-7 Cloth ISBN 0-88911-597-4

Comparing Federal Systems in the 1990s, Ronald Watts, 1997
Paper ISBN 0-88911-589-3 Cloth ISBN 0-88911-763-2

John Deutsch Institute for the Study of Economic Policy

The Nation State in a Global/Information Era: Policy Challenges, Thomas J. Courchene (ed.), Bell Canada Papers no. 5, 1997
Paper ISBN 0-88911-770-5 Cloth ISBN 0-88911-766-7

Reforming the Canadian Financial Sector: Canada in a Global Perspective, Thomas J. Courchene and Edwin H. Neave (eds.), 1997
Paper ISBN 0-88911-688-1 Cloth ISBN 0-88911-768-3

Policy Frameworks for a Knowledge Economy, Thomas J. Courchene (ed.), Bell Canada Papers no. 4, 1996   Paper ISBN 0-88911-686-5

Available from:
University of Toronto Press, 5201 Dufferin St., North York, On M3H 5T8
Tel: 1-800-565-9523 / Fax: 1-800-221-9985